As Nomadism Ends

As Nomadism Ends

The Israeli Bedouin of the Negev

Avinoam Meir

Westview Press
A Member of Perseus Books, L.L.C.

In memory of Giora, my brother

Copyright © 1997 by Westview Press, A Member of Perseus Books, L.L.C.

Published in 1997 in the United States of America by Westview Press, 5500 Central Avenue, Boulder, Colorado 80301-2877, in the United Kingdom by Westview Press, 12 Hid's Copse Road, Cumnor Hill, Oxford OX2 9JJ, and in cooperation with the Negev Center for Regional Development, Ben-Gurion University of the Negev, Beer-Sheva, Israel.

Meir, Avinoam.
    As nomadism ends : the Israeli bedouin of the Negev / by Avinoam Meir.
        p. cm.
    Includes bibliographical references and index.
    ISBN 0-8133-8959-3 (hc) ISBN 0-8133-3556-6 (pbk)
        1. Bedouins—Israel—Negev—Sedentarisation.   2. Negev (Israel)—Ethnic relations. I. Title.
    DS110.N4M38 1997
    305.892'705 6949—DC 20   96-11295
                                                                                    CIP

Typesetting by WordByte, P.O.B. 3102, Beer-Sheva, Israel
The paper used in this publication meets the requirements of the American National Standard for Permanence of Paper for Printed Library Materials Z39.48-1984.

10   9   8   7   6   5   4   3   2   1

Contents

Tables and Figures

Figures

Preface

In the summer of 1971, a young Israeli military reserve officer was assigned for several weeks to southern Sinai. His orders were to conduct routine patrols of Bedouin territory there. During one of the patrols, the squad encountered a jeep with two people aboard—an elderly Bedouin man, escorted by a young one. They were equipped with a jerrycan which carried an official Israeli military emblem. The patrol officer, suspecting that the jerrycan had been stolen from an army base, confiscated it and went away assured that he had taken the most appropriate action. Several days later the officer received a furious telephone call from the Israeli military governor of southern Sinai. It turned out that not only had the two Bedouin been deeply humiliated by the suspicion cast on them, but that the elder man was the Chief Sheikh of southern Sinai. The young officer was accused of causing a great scandal and severely damaging the delicate fabric of relationships with the Sinai Bedouin, established by the military authorities with considerable effort during four years of occupation. In order to pacify the sheikh, the officer was ordered to contact him at once, apologize, and organize a *soulha* (a customary Bedouin ceremony of conciliation).

The *soulha* took place several days later at a neutral location. The Chief Sheikh was apparently conciliated, things returned to normal, but the young and over-enthusiastic officer had learned a vivid lesson in intercultural relationships. That reserve officer, then an undergraduate geography student, is now the author of this book. Perhaps that embarrassing first encounter with Bedouin culture may explain why, about twelve years later, when on the faculty of a university situated in the heart of the Bedouin community in the Negev, I became involved in what turned out to be long-range research on this society in particular and pastoral nomadic societies in general.

My interest in the Negev Bedouin grew out of my broader interest in processes of change. More specifically, it originated in my dissatisfaction with the framework of spatial diffusion dynamics, my previous scientific specialty, which I tried unsuccessfully to apply to Bedouin society. I realized then the complexity and uniqueness of this society and grasped that a far deeper social understanding of pastoral nomadic societies and the Bedouin community was required. This resulted in my growing engagement in field research on various social, economic, and political issues viewed from a geographical perspective that are related to processes of change among the pastoral nomadic Bedouin.

As time went on, and the more I studied and wrote about the Bedouin, the greater my realization grew of the depth of change in this society but also, most important, of the subsequent high level of stress it has generated among these people. Later on it became apparent to me that despite the highly unique Israeli sociopolitical and cultural context of the Negev Bedouin, there are similarities with pastoral nomads undergoing processes of change elsewhere. These similarities stem primarily from a recurrent pattern of considerably narrowed pastoral options of survival left for such societies by state governments. They are related particularly to the ending of pastoral nomadism and the subsequent sociospatial processes. My identification of these similarities was the main impetus for writing this book. In it I have attempted therefore to put together these similar dimensions into a conceptual framework, in light of which I examine processes of sociospatial change within the Negev Bedouin society as nomadism ends.

Some of the processes examined within this framework are based on new perspectives that emerged during work on this book. Others are a product of my previous independent and collaborative published research. Here I owe special and deep gratitude to my dear friend and colleague, geographer-anthropologist Yosef Ben-David, with whom I have been collaborating for almost a decade. His long involvement in research on the Bedouin, his profound and penetrating familiarity with this society, and his readiness to guide me along the intricate pathways of Bedouin society have been indispensable to my own understanding of the issues at stake and to the development of my research in this field. I hope my own ideas and insights on Bedouin and pastoral nomadic issues have been, in their turn, of some use to him.

Many other friends and colleagues have also contributed to my research in this field and to the writing of this book. First and foremost, David Grossman—with whom I collaborated in writing on the Israeli Arabs in general—provided me with many geographical insights in studying the Bedouin and writing several chapters in this book. Gideon Kressel and Emanuel Marx have also enlightened me through their own writings and many discussions from the anthropological perspective. Special thanks are due to Salman Al-A'assem and Aref Abu-Rabia, my Bedouin colleagues, who often illuminated situations and issues that had initially seemed simple to me as an outsider. The various graduate and undergraduate students who participated in my seminars have also conducted research and provided valuable ideas for this book. Yet, responsibility for the interpretations of all these ideas and insights is of course mine.

I owe much to Aharon Kellerman, whose advice and moral support during the writing of the book is greatly appreciated. Yehuda Gradus, Oren Yiftachel, Eli Stern, Shaul Krakover, Harvey Lithwick, Devora Shemer, and Jon Anson—all colleagues in the Department of Geography and Environmental Development and other departments at Ben-Gurion University of the Negev—have always been around when I needed them for advice and assistance. Technical assistance was also always available from Gideon Berman and Danny Aufgang, and my appreciation is due to Pieter Louppen, who patiently and meticulously produced the graphics of this book. Thanks are also due to Chaya Galai for the editorial work. Dov Barnea, Moshe Shochat, and Eli Yifrach from the regional offices of the Ministries of Education and the Interior provided highly valuable data in their respective fields. The financial support provided by the Negev Center for Regional Development and the School of Social Sciences and Humanities at Ben-Gurion University of the Negev is greatly appreciated. I would also like to thank Magness Press, the Institute of British Geographers, the *Journal of Comparative Family Studies,* and *The Gerontologist* for their permission to reproduce copyrighted material.

I would like to pay special tribute to members of the Bedouin community whose hospitality and cooperation during the various fieldwork periods enabled me to conduct my research. I also owe much to the hills around Beer-Sheva which—as I walked home daily from my office on campus—served as a geographical observation post on the Bedouin communities in the Beer-Sheva basin. There too I reflected on what I had accomplished each day in the writing of this book. Finally, I would like to thank my beloved family, my wife Ziona, and my children Maya and Yariv. I apologize to them if, while working on this book during the last two years, I was not always there for them as I should have been.

Avinoam Meir
Department of Geography and
Environmental Development and
The Negev Center for Regional Development
Ben-Gurion University of the Negev

1

Introduction

This book is concerned with processes of change among pastoral nomads as they sedentarize and shift away from the pastoral production process. It takes a subsistence-oriented society, which is highly marginal to the market economy and urban systems—although maintaining some symbiosis with them—and follows its various phases of development and change to the other extreme of these systems. The socioeconomic and geographical range of this continuum is extremely wide, and the effects of the transition upon this society may be highly substantial. Many pastoral nomadic societies have gone through this transformation in recent history. Others, particularly in Africa and the Middle East, are presently in the midst of such a process. In many cases it has been spontaneous, taking place along a time span that has been sufficiently long for these societies to adapt to its consequences.

Yet, the process has not always been voluntary and spontaneous nor has it been always eased by the passage of time. The closer we approach the present, the more evidence is available to suggest that this transition of pastoral nomadic societies is increasingly constrained by the temporal dimension and by the extent of external intervention. Such constraints have often applied considerable pressures to the nomadic pastoralists, hampering their ability to adapt smoothly to these changes. Scientists from a range of social and natural science disciplines have recently begun to investigate how this adaptation can be facilitated and this awakening of scientific interest attests to the degree of stress which pastoral nomads are experiencing worldwide.

The process of sedentarization of pastoral nomads is essentially one of spatial and ecological change. This change is manifested not only in settlement in fixed locations. More significantly, it involves a shift away from a pastoral mode of production towards agropastoralism and farming, often associated with integration into the market economy, and perhaps also subsequently into the urban labor market. Following sedentarization and settlement, however, structural sociospatial changes ensue, and these are the focus of this book. Its objective, therefore, is twofold: first, to analyze these processes as they take place in general among pastoral nomadic societies so that a general conceptual framework is put together; second, to examine the particular case of the Bedouin society of southern Israel in light of this framework so as to provide relevant input.

The Bedouin of the Negev, the semiarid desert of southern Israel, began their trek along the continuum from nomadism to urbanism in the early nineteenth century, and have proceeded at a particularly high pace in the past half century. Studies undertaken in recent years have focused primarily on the Bedouin's traditional pastoral mode of living and on processes of sedentarization and even semiurbanization. The perspective adopted by most studies has been idiosyncratic, with relatively little consideration given to the context of pastoral nomadism in general. Furthermore, most studies have concentrated on sedentarization and the ensuing semiurbanization, resulting from previous political, economic, and geographical processes, as their main objective. Consequently, they have overlooked significant dimensions of contemporary processes that have taken place within this society.

This book explores these processes from a different perspective. Its approach centers on two principal assumptions. The first assumption is based on the notion that processes taking place within a system assume roles of both cause and effect simultaneously. In other words, processes of sedentarization and the shift away from pastoralism are consequences of ecological (i.e., economic, social, or political) processes. Yet, subsequently, the resultant processes of sedentarization and the shift away from pastoralism themselves become generators of change in similar areas within the now denomadizing pastoral society. Hence, the major focus of the present book is the processes that occur as nomadism ends rather than those causing the end of nomadism.

The second assumption on which this book is based relates to the general and specific contexts. The international literature provides abundant evidence of change among pastoral nomads from which some generalized dimensions, relevant for explaining the processes specific to the Bedouin of the Negev, may be extracted. Yet, in most cases, the Third World cultural context within which pastoral nomads are usually embedded does not differ significantly from their own context except insofar as their mode of livelihood is concerned. In contrast, the westernized modern and perhaps post-modern urban-industrial cultural milieu within which the Israeli Negev Bedouin are situated is diametrically different from the cultural context of the Third World. Furthermore, the Bedouin of Israel are an Arab Muslim minority situated within a Jewish state which, until very recently, was embroiled in political conflict with the surrounding Arab world.

Thus, the case of the Negev Bedouin is a unique situation for pastoral nomads, particularly Bedouin in the Middle East. The degree of "subcultureness" and the extent of the cultural, social ,and political gaps between them and the larger Israeli society is considerably more radical than that experienced by their kinsmen in most Middle Eastern countries. Such a gap is likely to generate conflicting forces that can drive change in different directions to those taken by similar societies elsewhere. However, it also provides a wide array of hypotheses to explain processes at work within this particular society. This is the second and major focus of the book: highlighting the uniqueness of the Bedouin society of the Negev within the general scope of the sociospatial processes following on the end of pastoral nomadism.

In order to clarify first the general scope of these processes, an extensive conceptual framework is provided in Chapter 2, which accounts for the possible sociospatial changes following the process of sedentarization. This framework attempts to extract from the vast international literature the relevant general dimensions concerning these processes among pastoral nomads in the Middle East and Africa. The purpose is to tie the major issues of sociospatial change with which this book is concerned into a coherent construct. This framework is anchored in the assumption that the processes of sedentarization and settlement expose pastoral nomads more intensely to avenues that bring them closer to social modernization and economic development. One key process ushers in all the processes with which this book is concerned regardless of whether they originate in external pressure, internal adaptation, and response, or both. This process is the ideological shift of members of the pastoral nomadic society away from tribalism towards individualism. As a result, individuals within the sedentarizing pastoral nomadic society gradually become independent of the particular social bonds that commit them to the traditional social organization. Instead, they are motivated increasingly by their newer, more personal, complex, and varied value-system.

This ideological change entails several sociospatial processes and issues. The major ones with which this book is concerned are successively interrelated and progress from the micro to the macro scale. These are territoriality, demographic change, social wellbeing, and conflict with the state. The issue of territorial behavior is perhaps the earliest manifestation of these processes. The tendency of pastoral nomadic societies toward territorial behavior is, in principle, rather weak. Abandonment of pastoralism and a concomitant shift toward farming, and perhaps even further toward integration in the urban-industrial labor market, carries with it a growing tendency toward territoriality. This tendency filters down from the tribal level to the individual, household level. The implication is that pastoral resources (land and water)—which were previously managed on a tribal basis—become privatized and are managed on a household level. Although this is the major manifestation of territoriality, there are others, for example, sociospatial separation between small subgroups.

The next relevant concern is the issue of demographic patterns, particularly fertility behavior. Pastoral—and now also agricultural and perhaps labor-market—resources become the concern of the individual household or even of the extended family. The rationale underlying fertility behavior may begin to change accordingly. In general, although the direct result may be lower fertility, there is still the possibility of an interim period of increased fertility before lower fertility becomes manifest. Pressures for a higher standard of living and improved literacy and education evolve through exposure to structures of social modernization and economic development. When this happens, the pressure for continued decline of fertility is reinforced.

This process ushers in the issue of social wellbeing, which is related to the changing roles and status of individuals within the family and community. On the one hand, there is a decline in the role of children as producers of resources and an increase in their role as consumers of resources. On the other hand, the status of elderly men declines as they lose their control over family resources. Women are also caught within the dialectics of this process. The critical notion here is that—once the roles and status of these individuals change in the complex course of social transformation—the society begins to lose traditional social institutions and structures, whose communal role was to provide for the wellbeing of its individual members.

With the deterioration of traditional institutions and modes of providing for wellbeing of members of the group, alternative ones are sought. Within the context of the modern state, public social services (education, health, and welfare), may begin to fill the void, transforming gradually the postnomadic society into a public service-dependent society. From the perspective of the state this could be regarded as a step toward its centripetal integration. From the formerly nomadic society's perspective, this may signify the beginning of a political conflict with the state over maintaining its traditional centrifugal tendencies that stem from its nomadic ideology.

This is, of course, only a sketchy description of complex processes. The purpose of Chapter 2 is therefore to discuss each of these four dimensions (i.e., territoriality, demographic transition, social wellbeing, and conflict with the state) in depth within a coherent conceptual construct and thus to serve as a framework for the discussion of processes taking place within the Bedouin society of the Negev.

In modern times the Bedouin society evolved within three different political contexts: the Ottoman Empire (until the end of World War I), the

British Mandate over Palestine (until 1947), and the State of Israel (since 1948). Each of these political contexts had its own impact upon the gradual denomadization of the Bedouin. However, there were also forces beyond the political sphere—primarily economic ones at the local and regional levels—that contributed to the drive toward sedentarization. Yet, in macro-historical terms this process, which commenced in the early nineteenth century, assumed two major stages. Until the formation of the State of Israel in 1948, early stages of transformation of Bedouin society were largely a consequence of Bedouin choice. More advanced stages under the state of Israel were largely compulsive and took place within a relatively shorter time span. Thus, unlike other observers who refer to sedentarization of the Bedouin in the Negev during the 1950s and 1960s as spontaneous, I maintain that genuine spontaneity and voluntariness of this process were manifested only in earlier periods.

From a Bedouin perspective, the change in political contexts reflects not just a change in political regime (in itself significant). It has also entailed a shift in cultural orientation away from the Arab culture of the Middle East toward a more modern Western culture. In addition to this shift across cultural frontier lines, the shift at the local level took place within the context of a settlement frontier. Settlement within the frontier between the desert and the sown in the Negev was not the sole prerogative of the sedentarizing Bedouin. Early attempts in modern times to transform the edge of the Negev desert into a settlement frontier had already begun in the late nineteenth and early twentieth centuries, under the rule of the Ottoman Empire. However, major settlement of outsiders in this region begun only with Jewish Zionist settlement in the 1920s and 1930s and was intensified during the 1940s and 1950s. During this period the region became an arena for competition over land resources and for an encounter between the two cultures. It is here that the major roots of exposure to modernization and development can be found.

Chapter 3 analyzes this initial encounter between the two cultures. It illustrates the change in the nature of the encounter and its impact upon the production of space and the path of development taken by the Bedouin. The main thesis is that the frontier encounter between the Bedouin and the Jewish settlers went through two major stages: a voluntary, symbiotic, and relatively peaceful encounter followed by a compulsive, coercive, conflictive, and relatively violent one. The divide line between these stages is the intervention of state and other core political forces (Jewish and Arab alike) in local affairs. The change in the nature of the frontier encounter is considered the major catalyst of the processes to be analyzed in the chapters that follow.

Yet social and economic changes did not commence only upon this frontier encounter. As noted above, the drive toward sedentarization and toward shifting away from pastoralism began about a century earlier. Therefore, some of the sociospatial consequences of these processes began to manifest themselves earlier too. Chapter 4 discusses the gradual transformation of Bedouin society from a nonterritorial to a territorial one. Obviously, these are ideal types along the nomadism-sedentarism-urbanism continuum (which is itself an ideal construct). Nonetheless, the Bedouin of the nineteenth century Negev desert were beginning to shift away from nomadic pastoralism and thus also from nonterritoriality. More specifically, when the society was still nomadic, social relations shaped spatial ones, and therefore territoriality was not as necessary a strategy for its spatial organization. As the society became sedentarized and shifted gradually away from pastoral to agropastoral engagements, the need for territoriality increased in order to reshape social relations. The process of territoriality is thus highly dependent upon that of sedentarization and settlement but is also related to the growing exposure to modern value systems within the settlement frontier. This process is consistent with the notion concerning the gradual ideological shift from tribalism to individualism.

The shift toward territoriality is manifested in various ways. First, there has been a trickling-down of forms of privatization of tribal pastoral and agricultural resources (pasture, land, and water) from the tribal to the extended and nuclear family levels. The process was initiated voluntarily but later became unavoidable. Second, within the semiurban environment, there has been a process of "privatization" of space per se in the form of spatial segregation between various subgroups. Again, this process has trickled down from the tribal to the extended and nuclear family levels. It is argued that the present phase of settlement in the form of semiurban towns—itself achieved by the state with much difficulty— would not have easily occurred had prior territorialization not taken place. This process is examined within the framework of the nomadism-sedentarism-urbanism continuum. Analysis begins on the eve of sedentarization in the early nineteenth century, continues through embryonic sedentarization during the late Ottoman Empire and then goes on to more advanced stages during the British Mandate, eventually ending with the semiurban stage under the Israeli state.

The gradual shift from tribalism to individualism is reflected even more acutely in the demographic regime of the Bedouin society as its mode of living is transformed. Chapter 5 has four objectives: (1) to describe the process of demographic transition within Bedouin society at the macro level; (2) to analyze the process of change in infant and child mortality; (3) to explore fertility behavior at the micro, household level, and; (4) to discuss the eventuality of an emerging aging process of the Bedouin population. Emphasis is given to the most recent five decades as this is the period of the most significant demographic transformation.

The macro process of demographic transition among the Bedouin of the Negev contains an element that is unique to sedentarizing pastoral nomads. In terms of mortality, the Bedouin rate, at least since the early 1950s, has declined persistently, consistent with the pattern characteristic of western societies. Unlike the latter, however, birth rates increased from a moderate to an extremely high level in the early 1970s, and only then begun to decline. This tendency of the Bedouin to adopt demographic patterns that gradually approach those of more developed Western societies is what sets them off from the pastoral nomadic context of the Third World. The analysis shows the macro processes of sedentarization and semiurbanization to be the overriding explanatory factor in this unique process.

The macro demographic transition process reflects an accumulation of more specific demographic processes. The methodological approach adopted to analyze these and some of the other processes discussed in this book is based on the concept of nomadism-sedentarism-urbanism continuum. This concept assumes that from spatial, economic, social, and often ethnic perspectives, a pastoral nomadic society differs from a sedentarized one. With sedentarization, however, a continuum emerges gradually along which the society may now become stretched and which may eventually reach from nomadism via rural sedentarism to urbanism. This continuum contains socioeconomic and spatial dimensions that can be regarded as stages in development. True, postulating a continuum with entirely distinct stages or phases violates reality as there are no ideal types. Nevertheless, for analytical purposes, it is assumed that these stages can be regarded as distinct throughout the process of change. The method will involve primarily a crosssectional analysis of processes within Bedouin society across the nomadism-sedentarism-urbanism continuum.

At the micro or household level, child mortality—a well-known indicator of change and development—is analyzed first. The analysis will demonstrate the unique pattern of this process not only among the Bedouin but also among sedentarizing pastoralists in general. It thus adds a further dimension to theoretical knowledge on child and infant mortality within societies in transition. This analysis is followed by that of fertility behavior. This is the most significant demographic issue from the perspective of individualization in terms of changing values and behavioral norms. The key to understanding fertility behavior is analysis of changes in fertility rationality as they relate to the notion of ideal family size. There are two major effects: a considerable decline in infant mortality rates, but primarily the diversification of norms due to the processes of individualization of the nuclear family. The latter is itself a consequence of processes that are discussed in previous chapters, including economic development and emergence of western economic rationality. It is argued that the combination of these effects results in an emergence of a latent surplus of children. This in turn leads to changing norms of the desired number of children at the family level and thus to changing fertility behavior. The final issue is that of elders. Its discussion will reveal another indicator of the general demographic change within Bedouin society, namely, an onset of an aging process of this population and a relative and absolute increase of the elderly population.

The geographical and demographic processes outlined above entail social implications that are related to the issue of status and wellbeing of individuals within this society. This is the concern of Chapter 6. The dynamics of mortality—but more significantly of fertility rationality and behavior—bring to the fore the issue of the changing value and status of children within the household economy from producers to consumers of household resources. This process is an outcome of the loss of agro-pastoral opportunities on the one hand and the introduction of modern schooling and education on the other. This generates a dilemma with regard to children's contribution to the family resource production process and therefore their status and wellbeing. The same processes, in conjunction with that of demographic aging, have also raised the issue of the changing status and wellbeing of elderly men and women. In these processes, within the complex course of sociospatial transformation, the special and central economic and sociopolitical roles assigned traditionally to these individuals, which previously guaranteed their status and wellbeing, have changed quite considerably as the Bedouin society has begun to lose its traditional communal social institutions and mechanisms that previously provided for the wellbeing of its members. Special attention is given to the decline of the collective family fund, a traditional mechanism for caring for the elders and for the narrowing of the public phase as regards women's spatial mobility. This process is consistent with the underlying assumption of the concomitant ideological shift from tribalism to individualism.

The emerging void has gradually been filled up by state social services. The purpose of Chapter 7 is to discuss the provision of public education, health, and welfare services to the Bedouin. Each of these services is discussed from its particular perspective. Yet, the central concern is the spatial, functional, and cultural availability, accessibility, and relevance of these services for the changes that has been taking place within the sedentarizing and urbanizing Bedouin society. These concerns will be analyzed through consideration of location, quantity, and quality of service facilities and personnel.

In the field of educational services, emphasis is placed on the very problem of schooling as it interacts with traditional values regarding the role of children within the family. The discussion of health services will focus on the cultural communication barrier that exists between service providers and Bedouin clients—a barrier that is crucial for understanding the wellbeing of the latter in their transition to a new environmental and cultural setting. In both educational and health services, the issue of the status of females as students, as mothers of sick children, or as patients is considered through its interaction with the wellbeing of these sub-groups. Finally, welfare services are represented through a discussion of Bedouin children, elderly men, and women and the manner these services are provided to cater for the decline in the roles of traditional mechanisms for caring for the wellbeing of these individuals.

In outlining these chapters, emphasis was placed on the notion that the sociospatial transformation of the Bedouin is manifested primarily in terms of processes of individualization that gradually detach individuals from tribal institutions and obligations. It was further argued that through the interaction of this process with the other social and economic dynamics, the Bedouin have been introduced into the system of state public service provision. In fact, the Bedouin have become a public service-dependent society and, hence, are manipulable by the government. This introduces a political dimension into the process of change within this society that, in turn, creates a conflict with the state. Such conflict had already been manifest during the Ottoman period and the British Mandate but came to the fore most intensively with the creation of the Israeli state. The purpose of Chapter 8 is to look into this conflict through highlighting the centrifugal-centripetal tension between the Bedouin and the Israeli government.

The centrifugal-centripetal tension stems from the conflicting nomadic and ethnic ideology on the one hand and state ideology on the other. It stems particularly from opposing forces of space production. The centripetal force, through various administrative and "development" measures and policies, contradicts sociopolitical processes within Bedouin society that nurture its traditional centrifugal tendency. One may expect the centripetal force to overcome the centrifugal one, thus affecting the locational structure of the Bedouin. This indeed has taken place at the macro level. However, a closer examination at the micro level may reveal that even at their postnomadic phase the Bedouin's centrifugal tendency has not lost its power. Rather, it becomes reflected at different spatial and functional levels within a landscape of conflict and has been associated with considerable protest against the state. In addition, the internal socio-political dimension of intertribal tension is reflected through competition over the location of scarce public resources in the form of service facilities. All these illustrate how the centripetal-centrifugal tension shapes space production within Bedouin society that to a considerable extent is still capable of withstanding the centripetal power of the state.

Chapter 2 outlines an analytical framework accounting for the sociospatial changes that follow the process of sedentarization of pastoral nomads. It is based on a variety of cases from the Middle East and Africa. This framework serves as a theoretical construct and a basis for the discussion in the subsequent chapters that deal with the particular case of the Negev Bedouin. Chapter 9 closes the circle begun in Chapter 2. It attempts to draw some major implications from the unique case of the Bedouin to those pastoral nomadic societies that have recently entered this framework. These implications can serve as an input to studies that will deal with pastoral nomadic groups that might fall under the rubric in the future. Finally, this chapter addresses major issues arising from the book that are relevant for policies of development of pastoral nomadic societies once nomadism has ended.

2

Sociospatial Change among Pastoral Nomads: A Conceptual Framework

The purpose of this chapter is to provide a conceptual framework that will account for the sociospatial changes among pastoral nomads in the wake of sedentarization. The framework is based on the assumption that pastoral nomads are not entirely detached from social and economic environments that may carry with them seeds of social modernization and economic development. This assumption is, in fact, validated by numerous studies on these peoples conducted in recent decades. However, it is submitted that the processes of sedentarization and settlement expose the pastoral nomads to these social and economic structures at much greater intensity than before.

A process occurs—whether originating in external pressure, internal spontaneous adaptation and response or both—which generates several others. It is these other processes that are at the focus of our concern here. This process may be defined as an ideological shift of members of the pastoral nomadic society from tribalism to individualism. This is, of course, a crude and general representation of what sociologists perceive as a highly complex process. In essence, however, individuals within the sedentarizing pastoral nomadic society gradually extricate themselves from the bonds that commit them to the traditional social organization (e.g., the tribe). They become more highly motivated by their newer, more personal, complex, and varied value-system. This cultural change is taken here as a key to understanding sociospatial change within such societies. As will be explained below, it does not necessarily entail all-encompassing change. Rather, a selective approach to change has been adopted here—one that highlights several key subprocesses that are essential from the perspective of a pastoral nomadic society.

The two concepts—social modernization and individualization— which are central to our discussion are closely related and have been treated in conjunction in the literature on social change. It is difficult to determine the cause and effect relationships between them, since each appears to serve as a precondition for, or characteristic of, the other. However, discussions of the role of individuals within society—at least as pursued by social philosophers—preceded those of social change by sociologists. For this reason and for analytical purposes, they are presented here separately in a logical order that considers individualism first.

Individualism, Change, and Modernization

Individualization, or the process of individualism, is understood best by reference to one of the classic, late nineteenth century sociological distinctions (Toennies 1957)—between *gemeinschaft* (community) and *gesselschaft* (association). The aim of this distinction was to facilitate understanding of social change, usually a trend from the former to the latter type of society. The first type is a traditional rural community, which is characterized by being primitive, rather small, closely-knit, and homogeneous. Relationships within a group of this type are intimate and nonutilitarian, with little expectation of personal gain and repayment. There is a high degree of natural solidarity within the group—with the accent upon community feeling, interpersonal understanding and agreement, and considerably-organized shared experience.

The second, *gesselschaft*, is an urban society which is by nature a larger community. Interpersonal relationships within it are impersonal, utilitarian, and specialized, with little organized shared experience. Competition and struggle at the personal level are common. The accent in this type of society is upon separation of individuals, although there are uniting factors. This explains why this type of society is an association of individuals, in contrast to the community in which, despite divisive factors, unity is the ideal.

Thus, the main difference between the two types can usefully be understood through the dichotomy of sociopetal vs. sociofugal forces (Porteous 1977) relating to community and association, respectively. In many texts, essays and comparative studies on social change (e.g., Vago 1980; Deutsch 1981; Badie 1990), the distinction between the two types of society has been accepted as representative of the differences between, for example, traditional tribal African or Middle Eastern societies as archetypes of the *gemeinschaft*, and the individualistic modern Western societies which represent the *gesselschaft* model.

As is often the case with polar dichotomies (Etzioni-Halevy 1981), the distinction drawn between the societal types of *gemeinschaft* and *gesselschaft* carries considerable limitations. It is questionable whether these are not ideal types rather than true representations of social realities. One is therefore tempted to ask whether all traditional societies are devoid of *gesselschaft* elements, while *gemeinschaft* is absent from modern societies. However, this dichotomy has a methodological value. Despite the conceptual limitations, these concepts provide useful analytical tools for understanding the process of social change (Badie 1990), particularly with regard to transition of a nonmodern society into modern structures.

It is at this juncture that the concepts of individualism and individualization become useful. As in the previous case, it is possible to dichotomize here between communitarianism and individualism—but this is also a polar dichotomy. Therefore, it would be more appropriate to regard it as a continuum. Such a perspective facilitates avoidance of the view of individuals in any societal type as ideal types. Lukes (1973) provides an exhaustive discussion of some of the most basic ideas of individualism, of which the following ones are highly relevant for the present discussion: autonomy, privacy, and self-development.

According to Lukes, autonomy (or self-direction) implies that an individual's thoughts and actions are his own rather than determined by causes or agencies beyond his control. Rationality thus becomes a key issue as he consciously and critically evaluates the pressures and behavioral norms within his group in order to decide whether or not to conform to them. Lukes refers to autonomy as "a value central to the morality of modern Western civilization, and ... absent or understressed in others [(] such as many tribal moralities ... [)]" (Lukes 1973:58).

Emanating from the concept of autonomy is that of privacy. Similarly to the former, it has also been regarded as a modern concept that is largely absent from nonmodern societies. Lukes defines privacy as "an area within which the individual is or should be left alone by others and able to do and think whatever he chooses," "a sphere of thought and action that should be free from 'public' interference" (Lukes 1973:59, 62). The idea of liberalism is closely associated with that of privacy. Drawing extensively from Sir Isaiah Berlin, J.S. Mill, and others, Lukes regards human liberty as comprised of three areas: liberty of conscience, thought, and feeling; liberty of pursuits; and liberty of association among individuals. It is manifested not only in spiritualistic and nonmaterial areas, but also in material matters, such as the institution of private property. Liberty, in its absolute sense, should be guaranteed against authority if the latter attempts to govern through despotism, and against the masses if they attempt to subject the individual to the group.

Finally, the combination of the notions of autonomy and privacy leads to the idea of self-development. The concept of self-development refers to the right of the individual to frame his life plan without being impeded by or impeding others. In its most extreme interpretation, according to

Lukes, it can be located on a continuum ranging from pure egoism to strong communitarianism, that is, the choice of the individual whether to be antisocial, extrasocial or highly social. The combination of the ideas of autonomy and privacy permits him this choice.

In summary, as submitted by Boudon (1990), the very wide autonomy conferred upon individuals by law, custom, and social constraints renders a society individualistic in nature. Many of the ideas of individualism—those highlighted above as well as others—have been articulated within the various theories of, and approaches to the process of modernization.

It appears, thus, that the process of individualization is quite central to modernization and is directly and indirectly related to its many and varied aspects. Eisenstadt (1973) outlines the characteristics of modernization as it gains momentum. Thus, growing differentiation appears to play a major role in the growth of free resources outside the control of fixed ascriptive groups, of types of social organization, of group identification, of institutional roles, and of regulative and allocative mechanisms and organizations. These developments, Eisenstadt argues, have an impact on all spheres of life. Greater specialization allows economic activities—within the context of modernization—to evolve into "commodities" to be marketed or purchased in new types of markets, such as the labor market, in addition to the traditional market for material goods. This enables a change towards a more flexible form of stratification. The latter affords the individual opportunities for upward social mobility through new economic, occupational, and educational channels, rather than through traditional ascriptive status. This social change is also associated with political change in the form of expropriation of power from traditional elites and its dissemination to wider groups in society, thus creating a more differentiated political structure. In sum, there occurs a wide and deep cultural and value-system change.

These elements of the modernization process are closely dependent upon the process of individualization but also strongly affect it. Indeed, in many discussions of modernization one discerns clear traces of the ideas of individualism dwelt upon above. Inkeles (1973), for example, elaborated upon the process of emancipation from traditional cultural values, social networks, and authorities. The individual, he asserted, becomes receptive to new experience and to change—fostering great ambition and lofty aspirations—and above all, rejecting passivity, resignation, and fatalism while taking rational decisions on action (see also Inkeles and Smith 1974). The individualistic ideas of autonomy, privacy, and self-development are clearly reflected in these processes.

Given the central mediatory role of the idea of individualism, what then are the major differences between an "ideal" traditional and an "ideal" modern society? Etzioni-Halevy (1981), following Parsons (1951;

1966) and Smelser (1973) dwells on this question in detail. Traditional societies emphasize immediate gratification—affectivity—which in turn encourages current consumption and discourages exertion and planning. In contrast, in a modern society (especially in the middle class) renunciation of immediate gratification is more common. Furthermore, in a traditional society—where local communities are small and intimate—the emphasis is on diffuse relationships, on collective goals of the family or the community, and on criteria of personal relations (particularism) in allocation of benefits. In a modern society, on the other hand—where small communities are less common, and social structures are more complex—the emphasis is on segmented relationships, on advancement of individual goals, and on objective (universalist) criteria in allocation of benefits. The final major difference refers to social position. In a traditional, nonmodern society these are determined by ascription while, in a modern society, personal achievement plays a major role.

It transpires that economic activity within a traditional society is closely related to the social matrix of kinship and status systems and is therefore controlled by them. In a modern society, this activity becomes separated, fully differentiated, and autonomous from these systems and is therefore more rational. Central to these differences is the role of the family. In a nonmodern society, the family—which is dominant—assumes the economic roles of production and consumption, the social roles of socialization and education and, in some cases, political roles. In a modern society most of these roles are extrafamilial, with resultant decline in dominance of the family, which now retains only the roles of consumption and primary socialization (Etzioni-Halevy 1981).

Since our major concern is social change, the issue now is whether "ideal" social change occurs in the transition from the "ideal" nonmodern to modern societies. This issue is inherent in the wider critique leveled at modernization theory in the social sciences since the 1970s. This critique revolves primarily around the questions of polarization between tradition and modernity, universal convergence of the modernization process towards the Western model, and the failure to take into account the context of dependency in processes of development and change. It follows, particularly in nonWestern societies, that, ideal change from a nonmodern to a modern society is but one among several possible paths, with "ideal" stability as its opposite. Within the range between "complete" change and "complete" stability there are various degrees and diverse forms of penetration of Western influence and retention of prevalent traditional traits. The current view of social change is flexible, taking into account a plethora of options open to nonWestern societies.

The conception of change processes among pastoral nomads fits into this framework. In the introduction to his wellknown volume, *When*

Nomads Settle: Processes of Sedentarization as Adaptation and Response, Philip C. Salzman (1980) challenges the view that a pastoral nomadic society (or in fact any society) has a clear, strongly invariant, and tightly integrated character. Instead, he suggests that it be viewed as fluid, variable, flexible, and adaptable, and introduces the concept of *institutionalized alternatives.* This concept encompasses all areas of activity such as organizational forms, productive activities, value orientation, and forms of property controls. It is the ability of people to choose between these alternatives which lends the society its flexible, adaptable, multiform character. By "institutionalized," Salzman means customary practices that are present, recognized, expected, and accepted. These institutionalized alternatives are concurrently enabling and restrictive—they are available for activation, but this is not mandatory. Their number is limited within any society and their range and pattern varies between societies.

This perspective on society also enables Salzman to challenge the contemporary view of sociocultural change as discrete, absolute, unidirectional, and cumulative, capable of shifting society from one character to another. He suggests, instead, that change can result from shifting between varying combinations of institutionalized alternatives, creating a society that is not entirely different, but reordered. Thus, change is not necessarily associated with considerable discontinuity. On the contrary,

> (t)he differences between the old and new will not be absolute and the shift between ... [them] ... will not be discrete. And cumulative change will only take place if yet a further stage is reached, leaving behind the elements of the first stage. Until this happens the possibility of reversal remains, with the elements from the earlier stage providing a bridge to the previous state and a foundation for re-establishment of the elements previously abandoned (Salzman 1980:7).

Salzman's approach is highly useful for understanding social change. However, it implies that change involves *nothing* that is novel to a society, that *all* alternatives have already been practiced in the collective experience of the society in question, and that *all* the alternatives that may comprise a change process are already institutionalized within what he terms "alternatives in reserve." The notion of entirely new alternatives or practices that may not be part of the sociocultural arsenal of a particular society at a particular time—but are available in that of another society—is disregarded. This does not necessarily weaken the approach, because Salzman himself provides an explanation of the ways in which alternatives are institutionalized. One such way may be the presence of a "deviant minority" which maintains an ideology and an organizational form that are different from those of the majority (Salzman 1980:4). Members of this minority may be considered as the keepers in reserve of these alternatives, which are maintained in a latent form. It is possible, however, to put forward an opposite view—that there may be a similar deviant minority that adopts new alternatives from outside and institutionalizes them into the internal reserve, so that they are present, recognized, expected, and then, perhaps, even widely accepted.

Finally, the emphasis this approach places on the role played by *members* of society in this process facilitates understanding of social change. This notion is of particular value for the discussion of individualism and change. As noted above, the variety of institutionalized alternatives and the possible combinations thereof provide for considerable flexibility and adaptability of the society. The process of change becomes therefore "more under the control of [individual] members of society" (Salzman 1980:6). This control stems presumably from the fact that alternatives accumulate with time, and as a result of previous changes to an assemblage of opened options of an evergrowing choice reserve from which one or several are chosen, usually by a gradually increasing number of members of the society.

It is at this particular juncture that the idea of individualism and the process of modernization discussed above are articulated into the concept of change. It is not the society as an entity, through its "collective rationality" (Livingstone 1985), but rather individuals who make these choices among alternatives and it is individuals' efforts in institutionalizing them which bestow on their society its evolving particular nature. When the number of institutionalized alternatives is constrained—perhaps indicative of a more traditional society—individuals are much less able to express their autonomy, privacy, and self-development values. When the number of alternatives increases, when more of them become newly institutionalized via the activities of the growing avant-garde deviant minority, when growing differentiation takes place, members' ability to express these elements of individualism increases significantly.

Within a traditional pastoral nomadic society, the idea of individualism thus becomes integrated—via the process of sedentarization—into the concept of change (see also Dahl 1991a). Sedentarization, while a highly complex concept, is itself an institutionalized alternative that is subject to selective choice by individual pastoralists. However, once opted for, it opens up a considerably wider range of alternatives than heretofore—some are already institutionalized, others not yet, some manifest, others latent. It provides individual pastoralists with an opportunity for greater exposure to the modern environment with its accent on individualistic ideas. They are increasingly able to decide themselves whether these ideas should become institutionalized, in full or in part, and to which spheres of society they are most appropriate. Complete modernization is not required for adopting some of its elements. Partial modernization can become an institutionalized alternative for pastoral nomads, as is also continuity between their tradition and modernity. Various degrees of institutionalized alternatives are available to this society along a continuum, depending upon the individualistic choice by its members.

Sedentarization and Change among Pastoral Nomads

The view that sedentarization of pastoral nomads is itself an institutionalized alternative enables us to regard this process as highly selective and optional. It transpires from this outlook that the process is not necessarily all-encompassing. Rather, it may occur gradually, creating thus a nomadism-sedentarism continuum—a highly complex concept. Nomadism itself—both as type and as ideology—may imply a continuum from pure to seminomadism (Johnson 1969). In a similar vein, sedentarization of pastoral nomads—again both as type and as ideology—may also be viewed as a complex concept, itself a continuum that may range between partial and complete sedentarism. The latter may introduce further alternatives ranging from rural, via semiurban, to urban forms of settlement. Each of these spatial types may further be regarded as a continuum, offering various economic alternatives for livelihood and these in turn are associated with various social and political alternative forms.

Thus, a hierarchy of institutionalized alternative forms of sedentarization is available to pastoral nomads, and their selection depends upon the complexity of economic, political, and environmental circumstances. As suggested earlier, the essence of sedentarization of pastoral nomads is, in fact, economic change in forms of subsistence and in modes of production. This economic change entails a wide variety of other possible processes of change. However, there is one key process that may usher in most, if not all, of the others. This process is a gradual ideological movement of members of the pastoral nomadic society along the tribalism-individualism continuum. In line with the relativist approach of the previous discussion, the two ends of the continuum should not necessarily be viewed as ideals of absolute change. Rather, the essence of this change is that individuals within the sedentarizing pastoral nomadic society may gradually cast off the bonds that previously committed them—via traditional social and economic organizational forms—to their group. Instead, they are increasingly motivated by their newer and varied value-systems, accessible to them through the alternatives produced by the economic change associated with sedentarization.

The processes that follow major ones of sedentarization and economic change and are associated with that of individualization relate to various spatial-environmental, social, and political spheres. It is submitted that there are four central spheres within the pastoral nomadic domain in which the effects of these major processes are most strongly manifested. These are territoriality, demographic dynamics and behavior, social wellbeing, and political relationships with the state government. Briefly speaking, territoriality—or territorial behavior—is a crucial spatial element that is capable of altering social relationships within the sedentarizing nomadic community and of integrating this society into the rural sector to a point of loss of its previous nomadic cultural and sociopolitical identity. Demographic dynamics and behavior are major manifestations of the social consequences of the changes in modes of production stemming from economic change associated with sedentarization. Social wellbeing of individuals becomes their major concern as the individualization process gains momentum. And relationships with the state authorities become considerably more significant, when and if sedentarization itself intensifies. In the following sections, each of these spheres of change is discussed in more detail. The purpose is to provide a conceptual framework that will serve as an analytical basis for the discussion in the following chapters of these changes within the Bedouin of the Negev.

Territoriality

The idea of territoriality has been recognized as a fundamental spatial behavior concept that shapes the relationships between people and their physical and social environment. There is in general wide agreement that territoriality is common in modern societies, but there is debate as regards nonmodern or premodern traditional societies. The question is why territorial ideas are not practiced by certain societies, and whether, and to what degree they adopt them as common practice (Meir 1995; see also Casimir 1992).

It is generally accepted that the early view of human territoriality as analogous to animal territoriality is a misconception. The present theory (Gold 1982; Castells 1983) is that human territoriality is conditioned culturally and socially; it may be a product of particular social relations but also their determinant. Sack (1986) thus usefully distinguishes between social definition of territoriality and territorial definition of social relations. Casimir (1992) similarly suggests the notions of spatial vs. social boundary defense. Lancaster and Lancaster (1992) have also queried whether social processes can be equated with territoriality. In ideal terms, these types of definition may serve to distinguish a nonmodern from a modern society, but also to elucidate whether and how the former practice within a certain society may be transformed (wholly or partially) into the latter.

Territoriality may thus be viewed as a process that is linked to cultural and cognitive processes (Cashdan 1983), to political and demographic ones (Frantz 1981), or to economic competition over ecological resources (Dyson-Hudson and Smith 1978). These processes involve social relations confined to a certain territory, and their complexity has generated definitions of territoriality which are somewhat contradictory regarding ends and means. For example, Gold defines territoriality as "any form of behavior displayed by individuals and groups to establish, maintain, or defend specific bounded portions of space." (Gold 1982:44). This definition regards territoriality as an end. In contrast, Sack's definition namely, "the attempt by an individual or group to affect, influence or control people, phenomena and relationships by delimiting and asserting control over a geographic area" (Sack 1986:19), perceives territoriality as a means. The latter definition is in accord with the notion that territoriality is an adaptive spatial strategy and behavior and it conforms to a recent definition by Casimir who suggests that

> (h)uman territorial behaviour is a cognitive and behaviourally *flexible* system which aims at optimizing the *individual's* and hence often also a group's access to temporarily or permanently localized resources, which satisfy either basic and universal or culture-specific needs and wants, or both, while simultaneously minimizing the probability of conflicts over them (Casimir 1992:20)(italics added).

It transpires, thus, that adoption of territoriality is a matter of decision by individuals or groups.

Sack (1983; 1986) suggests that three fundamental interdependent tendencies generate complete territoriality: forms of classification by area, forms of communication of such classification so that possession or exclusion become clearly manifested, and forms of enforcing control over access to the area and objects within it. The combination of these basic tendencies yields further sociospatial functions of territoriality: reifying power, displacing attention from relationships between controller and controlled, making relationships impersonal, clearing a space or place for things to exist, containing spatial properties of events, creating an emptiable place for assigning things, objects, or relationships, and engendering more territoriality. These functions of territoriality have been presented in somewhat other terms by Prochansky et al. (1970), Wolfe and Laufer (1974), Altman (1975), and Sommer and Becker (1979). Briefly, territoriality provides domination over an area and control over accessibility to it, a mechanism for protecting privacy, reflection of one's social status, and spatial permanence with psychological benefits. All these functions are combined, according to Edney (1976), to form a spatially predictable organizational structure upon which the individual can safely rely to conduct his routine activities. As Cox (1991) has put it, a specific set of social relations, rather than a merely bounded territorial extent, are being localized for certain reasons.

This interpretation takes us back to the notion of territorial definition of social relationships (common to the modern Western world) as against social definition of territory. The first question is whether the latter strategy is typical of, or suited to, a nonmodern and nonindustrial or pre-agricultural society. Such a society requires neither to define its social relations territorially, nor to communicate the classification of its members through ownership of some space. Membership, usually through kinship relationships, small size of the group, and intimate familiarity within it, is sufficient to award access to the land (Sack 1986). In ideal terms, such a society would be regarded as nonterritorial, a notion also shared by Casimir (1992).

A second question concerns the conditions under which this society begins to adopt territorial practices. It is suggested that these conditions become ripe when a nonagricultural society that is also nonterritorial becomes, for whatever reason, an agricultural one. There is a feedback mechanism inherent in this process that affects both people and land. For people exploiting its resources the quality and value of the region may change, this in turn changing their territorial behavior (Wargo 1988). Thus Dyson-Hudson and Smith (1978) suggest that it is the existence of predictable and dense resources in agricultural environments that raises the need to adopt territorial practices to control access to them. This shift, of course, is a gradual process, but it also gradually introduces forms of classification, communication, and control over access to the area and its resources. One such practice is, for example, subdivision of agricultural land. This is a form of personalizing land and space so that tenure and formal ownership are clearly communicated (Gold 1982).

This does not necessarily imply that tenure and formal ownership are the only methods for personalizing land and space. People develop various ways of establishing emotional bonds and personal identification with places or regions they inhabit, endowing them with unique character (Relph 1976; Entrikin 1991). It has even been suggested recently that these bonds should be regarded as clear indications of territoriality and, hence, that the debate as to whether nonmodern societies are also nonterritorial ones should be reopened (Stea 1994). This, however, does not contradict the dichotomy of nonterritorialism–territorialism. These are indeed ideal types, cited here only for analytical purposes. It would be more appropriate, following Smith (1988) and Casimir (1992), to refer to a continuum of strategies. Indeed, the shift from nonterritoriality to territoriality may be regarded as cumulative (Sack 1986). Accordingly, few uses of territoriality are practiced by premodern societies and the number of uses increases to a complete gamut within modern urban societies. When scanning the spatial behavior of a particular society as it develops, one can thus identify a continuum within it ranging from minimal to maximal territoriality.

So far we have dealt with the issue of transition to territoriality within nonmodern societies in general. There has been a recent spate of straightforward discussions of territoriality among pastoral nomadic societies. It may be attributed to the revival of attempts to understand the relationships between pastoral nomads and their environmental resources. New data about these relationships have enabled various writers to challenge the past conceptions of these societies as completely territorial.

The notion that pastoral nomadic societies are in principle nonterritorial was dwelt upon by Rapoport (1978). Culturally, they are characterized by nonformal social controls, nonverbal behavior, nonwritten laws and symbols, together with egalitarian ideology. From a group organization perspective the role of these characteristics is to avoid or resolve conflicts and these are indeed considerably less common than among sedentaries. The mechanism adopted by pastoral nomads to achieve this "nonconflict" structure is distinction between desired and undesired encounters, between members and nonmembers of the group and avoidance (through mobility) of undesired encounters. Due to this mobility, social relations are shorter in duration and less permanent. It establishes group identity for group members and also provides the group with spatial flexibility and avoidance of territorial rigidity. The spatial flexibility is so dearly guarded by pastoral nomads that one might rightfully consider it as a kind of resource (Casimir 1992; Behnke and Scoones 1993). Thus, mobility may be perceived as generated by sociopolitical concerns as much as by ecological ones. Consequently, boundaries are defined socially rather than spatially—which implies that the tendency of pastoral nomads towards territoriality is weak.

It has been noted that the small group, rather than the large one, is the most desired phase among pastoral nomads (Tapper 1979). This leads us to the issue of privacy and consideration of the notion of privacy in such a society can help clarify the issue of nonterritoriality among pastoral nomads. In principle, the structure of social relations and their intimacy and closeness within the small mobile group renders them highly predictable. There is little need, therefore, to resort to formal and external controls that may be manifested in territorial elements such as classification, communication, and enforcement (Rapoport 1978). Havakuk (1986) dwells upon the notion of privacy within traditional Middle Eastern pastoral nomadic Bedouin societies. Privacy in its Western sense was an unfamiliar concept among the nomadic Bedouin, as the individual had virtually no independent role or status and was cast within the framework of a group. He was strongly tied to his family by a heavy load of duties and responsibilities, his identity derived mainly from his group identity, and his survival within the desert environment as an independent individual was almost impossible. His private life and affairs were reduced to the most intimate aspects of his personal and nuclear family encounters. This issue is closely related to that of the concealment of personal identity which Levi (1987) has referred to in his discussion of the Sinai Bedouin.

This practice had an impact upon the spatial structure of the dwelling unit and the community. At the household level, the female quarter within the tent actually performed the function of a family bedroom in which all family members lived under very crowded conditions with very little privacy. Personal territoriality, under these conditions, was irrelevant. The same logic applies at the subtribal camp level: the individual household was part of the group of agnate families with nonformal social control and with a heavy load of duties and responsibilities that ensured reciprocity in terms of economic, social, and political defense and well-being. Here, too, the concept of minimal privacy generated minimal territoriality. Dozens of tents were laid out with one common principle: household tents were erected with almost no physical separation in order to provide mutual defense for the entire group from outside attacks (Havakuk 1986). The household unit had thus no existence as an independent territorial unit (see also Dahl 1991a).

Given these notions within the group level, the notion of weak tendency towards territoriality at the intergroup level may now become more comprehensible. Several examples from the Middle East may serve as illustration. The first example is based upon the Lancasters' (1986; 1990) discussion of the Rwala Bedouin in north-western Arabia. The Rwala—who originally had an ideology of equality and autonomy—became camel-pastoral nomads due to certain political circumstances. In order to cope with a physically, economically, and politically uncertain habitat in the Arabian desert, they had to combine nomadism—as a new mode of living—with their ideology. In such circumstances, having a fixed territory was a disadvantageous survival strategy. In order to clarify past misconceptions that the Bedouin had a distinct territory with overt territorial behavior, the Lancasters distinguish between the concepts of *dira* and territory. The Bedouin did not regard *dira* as a fixed geographical location. Rather, it was a moving territory, a concept also elaborated upon elsewhere by Mirga (1992). This moving territory could in principle be delineated spatially around any moving individual male.

In light of their egalitarian ideology that scarce and valuable grazing and water resources were God-given and thus free to all, competition was almost nonexistent. On the contrary, the Rwala were obliged to adopt cooperative management of the land for the benefit of all members.

Regulation of mutual access to these resources became necessary, however—achieved through various mechanisms which required a large
amount of information but involved also substantial uncertainty. *Khuwa,*
namely brotherhood, links were therefore established between families or
groups, usually, but not necessarily, along genealogical lines. These links
served as resource and information pools and were a structural-political
prerequisite for survival within an uncertain environment. The unpredictable nature of this environment required many *khuwa* bonds with
many groups to allow each group spatiotemporal flexibility of grazing
opportunities. A group territory was thus flexible. It was not exclusive,
owned, sellable or economically valuable (see also Lancaster and Lancaster 1992; and Chatty et al. 1991).

Another case study which sheds further light on the issue of territory
is Fabietti's (1986a; 1986b) discussion of the Shamar Bedouin in the province of Ha'il in northern Arabia. This case study is also cast within the
sociopolitical context, and the notion of a flexible territory is reiterated:
the Bedouin did not conceive of their *dira* as something immutable or permanent. Fabietti describes the Bedouin's image of the territory as a given
area, usually with undefined borders. This area contains resources ex-
ploitable by its occupants, but others were also permitted to use them.
This use, however, was selective, depending upon the type of resource.
Pasture could be exploited by other groups rather freely but access to
water wells owned by an individual tribal group *(fukhud)* required permission conditional upon appropriate maintenance. The notion of *dira*
implied thus only effective control over water and pasture resources. The
area itself was not the tribal territory; rather the *dira* assumed an exclusive
political and contextual meaning as a territory in relation to other
Bedouin groups.

The Tawara Bedouin of southern Sinai (Perevolotsky 1987) provide a
final example of what is considered in this study as a minimal territorial
tendency of pastoral nomads. Perevolotsky recognizes the significance of
the sociopolitical perspective, that is, a deeply rooted ideology of "reci-
procal altruism" in which long-term bonds were formed between individuals or small groups, resulting in a tradition of cooperation. However, to
this ethos he adds the ecological perspective of cost-benefit analysis of
territoriality. Recognizing the benefits of sharing dense but unpredictable
and randomly distributed resources, the Tawara resorted to cooperation
and pasture-sharing as a rational spatial strategy. They were well aware
that the patchy rainfall pattern in semiarid and arid environments creates
patchy and random distribution of areas of pasture. Under such conditions, it was not beneficial to rely on a fixed territory and they thus
adopted a strategy of open grazing territories. Perevolotsky argues, therefore, that the costs of "rigid territorialism" (lost access to others' pasture

and water resources in times of need, wastage of one's own pasture due to inability to exploit it to the full, and a high potential cost of defense of these resources) outweighed the benefits of territoriality accruing from exclusive usage of pasture.

The discussion of territoriality has focused so far on the intragroup and intergroup levels. It reveals that social and political relations determine the extent of territory—which takes on a spatiotemporal flexible nature. Territoriality per se does not shape social relations within this society. If there has been some tendency towards territoriality, it occurred primarily at the tribal or confederative levels. Marx (1974; 1978), similarly to Fabietti (1986) and the Lancasters (1986), argued that in the Middle East the tribe was the largest political organization, while the confederation was merely a territorial one. The prime duty of a Bedouin tribe towards the confederation was the preservation of its territorial integrity against encroachment by extraconfederative forces. Anywhere within the common confederated territory, however, free access to all pasture lands and natural water resources was practiced by all tribes. This was achieved through an extensive network of personal links that was almost coextensive with the spatial expansion of the confederation. In the past this confederative territory, however, was neither formalized nor manifested in clear communicative and formal devices as would have been the case under complete, ideal territoriality. It is only in this sense and at this level that one can refer to quasiterritoriality among the Middle Eastern Bedouin in their pastoral nomadic phase.

In sum, the above discussion suggests that the pastoral nomadic Bedouin of the Middle East had a weak tendency toward territoriality during their nomadic phase. This notion is supported in general by studies of pastoral nomads in Africa (Swift 1988) and elsewhere (Casimir 1992). However, we are primarily concerned here with the shift away from the pattern of minimal territoriality towards territoriality. It is submitted that this shift may commence due to two sets of circumstances. The primary process, as suggested earlier, is economic, namely the transition—for whatever reason—of pastoral nomads into an agricultural mode of subsistence. It should be clarified that the transition between ideal types is presented here for analytical purposes only. Pastoralism seldom exists exclusively as a mode of living and usually involves some farming or other supplementary activities. The line separating pastoral nomadism and agricultural sedentarism is often very thin (Dahl 1991a; Harbeson 1991). The shift referred to should rather be perceived as a shift in the relative weights assigned to either one of these activities. The secondary set of circumstances—which is more politically oriented—relates to the tendency adopted by large tribal or confederative groups to formalize their territory.

Fabietti's (1986) discussion of the Shamar Bedouin in Saudi Arabia sheds light on the former process. In the 1960s, the Saudi government launched an agricultural development project and proposed distributing tribal land for this purpose on the basis of tribal membership criteria. It refused, however, to recognize the traditional power of control exercised by the Bedouin communities of the region over their resources. As time passed the Shamar Bedouin—who had initially displayed ideological resistance to this approach—began to shift away from their traditional ideologies toward more practical ones. Individuals were allowed by the state to own the distributed parcels of land, a move which triggered the evolution of a land market. A process of territorial privatization thus began in which the right to private property replaced the traditional tribal collective rights of access to the land and its resources. Concurrently, profitability of agricultural activities increased as the need to rely upon traditional forms of pastoral production declined. Also, a monetarization process begun, particularly as the Bedouin economy became functionally integrated into the regional town of Ha'il.

Bedouin who became involved in these activities began to foster the independence of individual domestic units from their descent tribal groups. Consequently, tribal cohesion and solidarity deteriorated considerably. Fabietti (1986) concludes that expropriation of traditional rights from the tribe generated a process of intratribal social differentiation. Social relations were now based less upon tribal or descent group affiliation and more upon individual wealth and private property. In other words, the Shamar Bedouin began to cross the dividing line from social definition of territory into territorial definition of social relations. This type of processes has been replicated to a large extent in many other similar circumstances in the Middle East and East Africa (e.g., Harbeson 1991).

While this example refers to a shift toward territoriality primarily in terms of land tenure, Rapoport (1978) dwells on the social and psychological impacts of the sedentarization and settlement processes. In a rather conceptual discussion, he suggests that sedentarization of pastoral nomads—especially within a constrained choice context—can become a destructive process, which may lead to radical changes in personal and group value systems. It may entail several effects: drastically reduced mobility, increased population density and size, and increased sociocultural heterogeneity. These imply that the length and permanence of social interactions, particularly unwanted ones, also increase. Under these circumstances, the sedentarizing pastoral nomads may begin to lose their social identity which was previously maintained through communal mobility. Also forfeited are the traditional pastoral nomadic mechanisms of sociospatiofugal tendency and options for distinguishing between group members and nonmembers, which were indispensable for conflict resolution.

These changes are likely to destroy the traditional social mechanisms for spatial order. Social boundaries are gradually replaced by spatial and geographical ones. Land tenure and overt defense of resources become common values and a basis for sociospatial differentiation and hierarchization at the macro and micro levels. These processes require the adoption of new means and rules of space management. Rapoport discussed the role of fences and walls and the division of the housing unit into subunits as examples of protecting space and privacy as resources. At a higher level of aggregation, nonwritten residential rules (regarding, for example, intergroup mixture), as well as other spatial-environmental rules (such as spatial movement and trespassing), may become common. Both the physical means and nonwritten rules resemble those which the sociobehavioral and geographical literature (e.g., Porteous 1977; Ley 1983), has described for modern urban societies.

The secondary process which can trigger territoriality among individual members is the formalization of tribal or confederative territory. A process of this type is discussed by Lewis (1987) with regard to the Bani Sakhr Bedouin of Jordan. This process began in the late nineteenth century at the tribal level, but filtered down the organizational structure toward subtribes and individual tribesmen during the 1930s, concurrently with the introduction of farming. Lewis, however, does not specify the process of tribal boundary demarcation. This is documented by Stewart (1986) in the context of the boundary between the Ahaywat and the Tiyahah Bedouin of central Sinai in the mid-nineteenth century. Stewart's assumption is that, in bringing the notion of formal boundaries into practice, the Bedouin were undoubtedly influenced by the growing activities of the Egyptian and Ottoman states in the area in the second half of the nineteenth century. Nevertheless, outsiders were barred from resources within the tribal territory by force of an agreed, defined, documented, and clearly demarcated boundary.

The notion that territorial tendencies at lower ranks are related to formalization of tribal or confederative territories can also be inferred from Hobbs' (1989) account of the Khushmaan Bedouin of the Ma'aza tribe in eastern Egypt. Despite tribal ideology—which allows no individual rights over places and resources—individual households developed deep emotional bonds to small specific areal units and their resources. These assumed symbolic and behavioral meanings for them. With the formalization of tribal territory, which commenced in the early nineteenth century and was recognized by Egyptian governments, individual households begun to express their exclusive tendencies towards these places and resources more openly and explicitly, if not formally.

It transpires from this that territorial tendencies may exist in a latent form among pastoral nomads, being put into practice only when the ideological conditions are ripe. This example may be seen as an illustration of the notion discussed above that institutionalized alternatives are kept in reserve and are activated only when circumstances make them desirable. In essence, pastoral nomadic societies are located at the minimal territoriality end of the continuum and begin to move away from it primarily when major economic and political processes begin to affect the society and environment. At this stage, however, territorial capacities imply that the relationships that exist now between the number of persons that can be supported directly by agricultural or other resources may be different from the type of relationships that existed previously between the number of animals and pasture resources that was crucial for the survival of the pastoralists (Dyson-Hudson and Dyson-Hudson 1980). This leads us to the relation between the demographic issue and the process of sedentarization.

Demographic Dynamics and Behavior

In contrast to the issue of territoriality, that of demographic dynamics and behavior among pastoral nomads during transition has received relatively little attention. This may perhaps be attributable in the main to difficulties in identifying and defining the various groups along the nomadism-sedentarism continuum, enumerating them or obtaining accurate vital statistics concerning them. Yet the issue is of considerable significance, particularly given that sedentarization and a shift in the balance between pastoral and nonpastoral modes of production has become a dominant reality for many pastoral nomadic societies. As indicated above, this shift implies major changes in ecological relations of food production that are associated with changes in economic and social structure. These processes have important consequences in terms of demographic regime and dynamics, but primarily in terms of individual demographic behavior. It is the latter issue that is of particular importance and it will be discussed after the more general discussion of demographic processes during transition away from pastoralism.

In discussing demographic dynamics we assume that a particular mode of production is associated with a certain set of social relations and in turn produces a particular demographic regime in terms of fertility and mortality. Thus, as a society makes the transition between modes of production, the system of social relations changes so as to produce a suitable demographic regime (Woods 1982). It is possible to regard traditional pastoral nomadism and sedentary farming as distinct modes of production, even though a certain proportion of the subsistence resources in each mode is gained from the other. Obviously, the same reservations concerning the difference between ideal types and a more realistic continuums apply here as before.

Several writers (Swidler 1972; Tapper 1979; Livingstone 1985; El-Sammani 1989) have suggested that there is a close association between animal and human demographics within a pastoral nomadic society. Pastoralists maintain an optimal size range of herds/flocks, requiring a certain size of labor force. This, in turn, has an impact upon the drive to maintain optimal demographic size and structure of the pastoral group. The implication is that some balance is sought between human fertility and mortality. These are subject to restraints and self-regulating mechanisms which, as explained by O.D.I. (1976a, 1976b), are regulatable through social codes and behavioral norms or nonregulatable due to environmental or physiological causes. It follows, however, that age-specific mortality rates among pastoral nomads are comparatively higher than among sedentaries. By and large mortality cannot be controlled, given the poor medical technology and services available to these peoples. There is evidence, however, that fertility can actually be controlled through socially accepted behavioral norms, together with irregulatable factors (Spencer 1972; Legesse 1973; Irons 1975). The balance thus achieved between mortality and fertility yields considerably low natural increase rates.

Certain key social elements of pastoral nomadic societies have already been outlined in the previous discussion of territoriality. These include basic and expanded kinship group structure along lineage lines; the further organization of these into larger corporate units; the hierarchical and gerontocratic nature of society; its collectivist and egalitarian ethos, and the submergence of the individual within the group's identity and interests. The shift away from pastoralism into a sedentary farming mode of production entails changes in this social formation. Some of the major changes have been discussed above directly or indirectly. To put it simply, the economic changes, which may be manifested in livestock and land commercialization, division of labor, and monetarization of the economic system, may also be followed by two major types of social change. The first is a weakening of the traditional lineage, kin group, or tribal identity which becomes associated with the general sedentary sector. The second, the emergence of a class system, social polarization, and inequality due to the territorialization process, and the growing link to the land and to the labor market, entail also a general exposure to a new set of social values (Frantz 1975; Cole 1981; Galaty 1981).

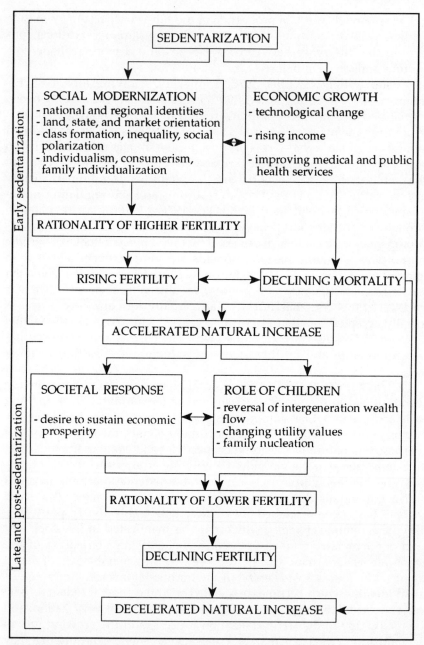

FIGURE 2.1 A general model of population dynamics of sedentarizing and urbanizing pastoral nomads (*Source*: Adapted from Meir 1986a).

As suggested by Meir (1986a), these changes toward a more modern social structure are consistent with those outlined by social demographers as capable of generating a major shift in demographic regime or, more conventionally, a demographic transition process. However, a rather unique process of increasing fertility may take place through relaxation of traditional social control on over-population. The process of increasing fertility rather than the usual one of fertility decline, thus adds a further dimension to the conventional understanding of demographic transition processes. As for mortality, it declines, although not consistently, due to an improvement in standard of living, as manifested through technological change, increase in income, and growing exposure to public health services. Hence, on balance, the natural increase rate rises.

As the shift away from pastoralism gains momentum, the ex-pastoral nomadic society becomes an integral part of the rural agricultural sector. Its fertility patterns may begin to revert into the more usual one, namely a tendency to decline. When this is coupled with the already declining mortality rate, a new demographic regime emerges, characterized by a declining natural increase rate. This process, together with the macro-level economic and social processes that generate it, is summarized in Figure 2.1.

The discussion of this process referred to the societal level of pastoral nomads as they make the shift away from their mode of production. The change in demographic regime, however, is made possible primarily through the process of individualization that, as suggested earlier, is one of the major social consequences of sedentarization. The process of territorialization discussed above is one such manifestation. The process of individualization, in terms of making reproductive decisions, may be another. It is related to the issue of fertility behavior of individual pastoral nomadic nuclear families as decision-makers.

The general issue of fertility behavior has been treated by social scientists from both the economic and sociological perspectives. Recently, Peres and Brosh (1991) made the case for a spectrum of explanations of fertility decision-making and behavior, ranging from the rational-individualistic (the economists' approach) to differential attitudes toward societal norms (representing the sociological approach). The economic approach (Schultz 1973; Schultz 1974; Becker 1981) regards fertility behavior as a product of rational decision. The couple attempts thus to maximize an economic pay-off function for the household. This function is framed within resource constraints, and is subject to direct and indirect costs and alternative uses of resources. The sociological perspective suggests that commitment to norms and values, that are rooted in the prevailing economic, demographic, and ecological conditions, is the direct determinant of fertility decisions and behavior (Peres and Brosh 1991).

Norms and values receive particular emphasis in anthropological studies of traditional societies such as pastoral nomads. To employ the terminology of Nag (1975) and Howell (1980), there is a general tendency in these societies, as we have already seen above, to maximize the welfare of the group rather than that of the individual household and hence also the welfare of the group in terms of the balance between resources and population. Social control, therefore, leaves the individual very few behavioral options. It follows that a group rationality exists which determines individual fertility behavior.

The tension between group rationality and individual rationality begins to emerge in the course of cultural evolution and social change. Following Robinson and Harbeson (1980), it is suggested that traditional societies become increasingly complex, with differentiated values and behavioral options available for individuals. Within the wide nexus of economic and social behavioral alternatives, some already institutionalized and others new, there exist certain behavioral options in terms of fertility decision-making. In this process, it is likely that individual rationality may become more dominant in relation to that of group rationality. This leads to an increase in the variability of fertility behavior within such transitional groups (Peres and Brosh 1991).

These general processes will now be discussed within three cultural-ecological phases: pastoral nomadism, early sedentarization, and late sedentarization. These phases are used as analytical frameworks, as in reality such ideal types rarely exist. In his discussion of fertility rationality within Third World societies, Caldwell (1982) proposes a dividing line between two types of society: one with an economic rationality of high-level fertility, and the other with an economic rationality of low-level fertility. Traditional rural Third World societies fall within the first type. Caldwell, however, overlooked the existence of pastoral nomadic societies. Many observers note the significant proportions of these peoples within the rural population in many of these countries (e.g., Livingstone 1985). Many others argue that these peoples have been increasingly marginalized from mainstream economic growth and development processes to the extent where they may be denoted Fourth World societies (e.g., Stea and Wisner 1984; Swift et al. 1990; Harbeson 1991). On this basis, it is suggested here that pastoral nomads be perceived as a possible subtype within the rural Third World.

If we accept this subdivision, each subtype-the pastoral nomadic and the rural agricultural sedentary-may have distinct fertility rationalities and behavioral patterns. This distinction yields differential levels within Caldwell's high fertility category. Ample evidence for such bi-level high fertility from Asia and Africa suggests consistently that fertility levels of pastoral nomads are lower than those of their sedentary neighbors or their nomadic kin who have already settled (Barth 1964; Henin 1968; Paydarfar 1974; Ganon 1975; O.D.I. 1976a, 1976b; Swift 1977b; Tapper 1979; Brainard 1981; Roth 1985; Roth and Ray 1985; Sindiga 1987; Meir 1987a).

The pastoral nomadic phase is governed by a social structure in which nuclear families are strongly influenced by group norms. These families adopt a rationality of lower fertility within the "high fertility range" due to the continual pressure to hold the group's size and demographic structure in balance with the optimal size of the herd or flock. It follows that the pastoral nomadic group's rationality and norms have an impact on the individual household in terms of demand for children and fertility decisions. These can be implemented by socially-regulatable norms, which are practiced through behavioral methods such as bride price, delayed marriage, delayed co-residence after marriage, and abstinence (Douglas 1966; Spencer 1972; Legesse 1973; Irons 1975; and Sindiga 1987). Obviously, such norms are "supplemented" by environmental factors of disease, food shortages and other health hazards, all of which synergistically act to suppress fertility (O.D.I. 1976a, 1976b).

As the shift away from pastoral nomadism toward early sedentary forms commences, two processes that are relevant for fertility behavior may take place. These are related to environmental and social resource management. First, from an environmental perspective, as farming activities become more dominant, territorial and land capacities now reflect the number of persons that can be supported by crops rather than the number of animals supported by pasture. In pastoral nomadism, livestock ecology generates longer food chains (land-animal-man) and thus lower labor requirements. Upon rural-agricultural sedentarization, however, food chains become shorter and therefore, labor requirements are higher. The nuclear family may thus indeed become more self-dependent as higher food energy levels become available. But concurrently, greater family labor resources are now required. Secondly, from a social perspective, having more children may become a source of social prestige, replacing the livestock wealth criterion that prevailed at the pastoral nomadic phase (Douglas 1966; Sindiga 1987).

It follows from these processes that demand for children begins to exceed supply, leading to a rationality of higher fertility within the "high fertility range" than in a pastoral nomadic society (see also Frank 1981). In Easterlin's view (1978), this leads to relaxation of existing social norms of fertility control. Such rationality is also facilitated by the fact that the environmental health factors that previously tended to suppress fertility are now likely to disappear through better access to education and health services (Bongaarts, et al. 1984). Thus, the influence of group fertility

norms upon the individual household which typified the pastoral nomadic phase begins to wane.

It is only upon intensified sedentarization and, perhaps, a shift toward
the urbanism complex (see Salzman 1980; Galaty et al. 1981; Galaty and
Salzman 1981), that the ex-nomadic nuclear families can cross the major
divide between high and declining fertility. A key process is an emergence of a fertility rationality that is a combined consequence of two subprocesses. First, the changing utility role of children within the family
becomes a major driving force. This is attributed to the loss of pastoral
and agricultural opportunities, increasing role of formal education and
schooling (Ibrahim and Cole 1978; Denga 1983; Tan and Haines 1984;
Dahl 1991a), and the effects of the now more capitalistic mode of production, in which the family labor force is controlled by external agents
within the labor market. At this juncture, the utility role of children
within the nuclear family is gradually changing from that of resource-
producers to resource-consumers.

The second process is a change in the relationships between the nuclear family and its socially relevant group (extended family, tribe, etc.).
The social processes that accompany the new ecological context are complex and have been discussed in various studies (e.g., Petit 1962; Frantz
1975; Kressel 1976; Cole 1981; Galaty 1981). The shift away from the collectivist ethos toward one of individuation of rights over resources, and
the disintegration of large kinship-based corporate units, now gain momentum. There also occur a rise in the degree of economic independence
of the individual household within a monetized system, an increase in
materialism and conspicuous consumerism as a wealth status symbol,
and growing exposure to the "Westernization effect" and to Western educational values and systems. These tend to free the younger members
from tribal or group authority and particularly from that of elders. These
processes lead to greater family nucleation, individualization, and personal independence in decision-making than during early sedentarism
and pastoral nomadism.

Following Caldwell (1982), the gradual crossing of this major divide
implies that the direction of the flow of wealth within the nucleated and
individualizing family, that previously occurred from children to parents,
now begins to change as parents need to "invest" more in their children
than they did in the past. As individuals now have the option of investing
in the quality of their children rather than their quantity, the large family
is seen to constitute a threat to higher standards of living that may have
already been achieved (Davis 1963; Becker 1981). Under such circumstances, it is quite possible that supply of children may exceed demand,
and a "surplus" of children may emerge. This surplus may lead to a

change in fertility rationality toward the smaller family and hence to lower fertility.

In conclusion, individual households may go through a considerable change as the pastoral nomadic society shifts toward rural sedentary farming and urban labor market modes of production. This notion is consistent with Tabbarah's (1971; 1976) "demographic development model," which refers to the ideal family size and the relationships between supply and demand for children during a process of development. Obviously, the process is gradual within a pastoral nomadic society, as in any other society, and various groups vary in their tendency to abandon the pastoral mode of production and means of doing so. Consequently, there emerges within this transitional society a continuum of fertility rationalities, behavioral norms and patterns, and a variability which may narrow in time toward the low fertility edge.

The crux of this discussion is that the ideal of the smaller family and thus lower fertility, which may become indispensable at later stages of sedentarization, is not necessarily new. It is an institutionalized alternative that was already selected in the pastoral nomadic ecological setting. However, at that phase it was a group norm aimed at maximization of the group's wellbeing, to which individuals had to conform. This norm may be recruited now from the reservoir by individual households who have cast off previous group norms and values, and who may adopt it voluntarily for their own wellbeing irrespective of that of their group. This implies, however, that concern for the wellbeing of individuals is also becoming individualized. This notion carries the discussion into the next issue, that of social wellbeing during the sociospatial process of change that is associated with sedentarization.

Social Well-Being

The above discussion has revealed that the process of sedentarization and the altering socioeconomic ecological setting are accompanied by changes in the relationships between the individual pastoralist and his group. These changes may entail modifications in the mutual responsibility between the individual and the group. Individuals and households assume now greater responsibility for their own future than for that of their group. The main implication of this shift is that the status of individuals within society may be altered, with subsequent possible changes in their wellbeing. The change in status may cause them to resort to external social resources to gain those basic needs which previously were met internally by traditional social institutions. Potentially all members may be exposed to the consequences of these processes. We are concerned here in particular with two groups of individuals, whose roles, status and wellbeing are most likely to change considerably. These are the children and elderly men who assume unique status within any traditional Third World rural society and among pastoral nomads in particular. Although there is lack of consensus about women, their roles are also discussed.

In the previous section we referred to the changing role of children from producers to consumers of resources as the main cause of the changing fertility rationality. Further elaboration of this issue can facilitate understanding of the nature of the change in their status and its implications. The relationships between children and resources within a pastoral nomadic society can be seen primarily through their role as a labor force. The nature of the pastoral production process requires the participation of all members of the extended family. Therefore, children begin to contribute to this process in its widest sense from an early age, as early as five. There is often a division of roles, whereby the load and responsibility of labor increases with age. Gender also plays a role in the division of labor, boys being more involved in herding and related activities, while girls take part more in domestic tasks (Swift 1984; Dahl 1991a; Samantar 1991).

Parents must invest a considerable amount of time in their children if the latter are to become competent and responsible herders and fully accepted members of the group. This process entails not only the transmittal of cultural and spiritual knowledge, but primarily preparation of the children for assumption of the highly important pastoral roles. These require many geographical, environmental, biological, economic, social, and political "databases" (King 1972; Ezeomah 1979; Ezeomah 1985; Sifuma 1984; Meir 1985; Dahl 1991a). The immense reservoir of knowledge and understanding that is involved in the pastoral production process in fact makes the acquisition of these "databases" by pastoral nomadic children an informal educational process that may be equated with the formal process in modern societies. It reflects the high status of children as potential producers of resources and income for the family and the group that otherwise would have to be derived from external sources.

In fact the relationships between children and production of resources constitutes only one among several dimensions of their status. Another, still an economic dimension, is their role in adulthood as supporters of and providers for their elder parents. At a certain age the latter retire from the cycle of active participation in the pastoral production process and become dependent upon their children. This is a form of old-age security that is common within Third World traditional societies (Willis 1980; Knodel et al. 1992). Another dimension of the status of children is a sociopolitical one. Many pastoral nomadic societies, particularly in East

Africa, have an age-set organization in which teenagers become warriors. Participation of children, particularly first-born males, in these age-set activities is critical to their future status as fully accepted adults within the group (Heron 1983; Ponsi 1988).

It follows that children within pastoral nomadic societies pursue roles that are of particular importance in terms of the wellbeing of the group, whether it is the extended family or wider social circles. Their status therefore is an ascribed one, derived from that of the group to which they belong. Hence, the group has a responsibility towards ensuring the wellbeing of children. Yet, in some respects, particularly those that should be of interest to the group, children are inferior to adults. For example, Swift et al. (1990) notes the relatively low nutritional status of pastoral nomadic children exactly at the stage of their life when they participate heavily in the pastoral production process. This, however, is compensated for at later stages of life when their participation is less intensive. Nevertheless, the risks posed of nutritional stress to the health of nomadic children are quite evident.

Elders, or senior men, are located at the other edge of the social and age structure. The issue of status of children among pastoral nomads has been discussed quite extensively by many writers. The status of elders received relatively little attention and even scantier note has been taken of its implications for change. This is attributable perhaps to the fact that researchers have not considered the possibility of change in elders' solid status as a viable possibility. Indeed, such change has not been common among pastoral nomadic societies, or at least not sufficiently evident. Yet, under some circumstances, such change may become apparent, and hence a brief discussion of elderly status within pastoral nomadic societies is in order.

Pastoral nomadic societies, similar to many traditional Third World rural societies, assume a clear gerontocratic nature (Abu-Zeid 1959; Petit 1962), which means that elders have a supreme formal status. They actually control all affairs that are associated with the pastoral production process (e.g., Biruk et al. 1986). Usually they do not participate physically in the labor process but rather act as managers of the livestock capital, whereas labor itself is performed by younger members of the group. All decisions that are related to the production process are in their hands, from direction of movement between grazing areas, through regulation of the division of labor and family herds into specialized units, to building-up client-patron relationships with other families (Hashi and Mohamud 1991). The decision-making processes require the same "databases" that, as described above, are transmitted to the younger generation within the informal educational process. The acquisition, control, and utilization of such information bestows on them supreme status not only as heads of their group, but also as professional educators in the complex craftsman-ship of pastoral production.

Elders, in fact, may be considered the carriers and reproducers of the entire pastoral nomadic culture in terms of subsistence and survival, spir-itual matters, and social values. They reproduce the historical heritage of the group, and their experience is a highly respected and utilized asset. In the absence of other sources of learning they serve as behavioral guides for members of the group vis-à-vis both the economic production process and social reproduction in terms of social relationships within the group. Their central position within the group also assigns them a similar posi-tion externally for purposes of representation and negotiation with other pastoral and nonpastoral individuals, groups and agencies. In fact, it is possible to explain the collective life within traditional pastoral nomadic societies primarily through the central and elevated status of elder per-sons.

It follows from this brief discussion that in traditional pastoral no-madic societies, care and provision for and the wellbeing of elder persons are built into the social system through various social institutions. One such institution is their focal social status itself. Another institution, as noted above, is the support of their adult children which includes eco-nomic support as well as traditional types of medical care. The same gen-eral conclusion is relevant to the wellbeing of young children. The in-formal educational process, as well as caring for other basic needs, are provided for internally by the traditional social institutions the role of which is to guarantee the status of children.

There is lack of consensus among observers with regard to the status and wellbeing of pastoral nomadic women. In fact, the entire discussion of this issue has only in recent years begun to gain momentum, particu-larly through pastoral development programmes (e.g., Jowkar and Horo-witz 1991; Jowkar and Horowitz 1992). It is generally agreed among observers that the power and status of a pastoral nomadic woman in the Middle East are anchored in her own personal ascriptive qualities. For example, her age, number of male children she has borne, her intelligence and wit, skills in producing handicrafts—all these are manifested in the number of visitors calling upon her, how they treat her, and the amount and kind of gifts they give her (Kressel 1992b) which indicate her social position within the group.

The issues upon which observers are divided relate to women's in-volvement in the pastoral production process and in public social life. With regard to the pastoral production process, the prevailing view has been that women are involved primarily with animal husbandry and primary animal health care and not directly in animal production activi-ties proper (Oxby 1989). The latter activities, which are the most significant in this process, are men's roles. However, recent research (Dahl 1987; Bruggeman 1994) suggests that in most pastoral societies management of milk resources, including milking proper, are in most cases assigned to women, particularly when livestock is kept close to the campsite. Even in remote pasture sites, young girls may join men and help them with significant tasks such as watering, milking and herding animals. Thus, women's involvement in this process provides them with some control over animals and their products, although they may not often own them outright. This control, together with their expertise in husbandry, awards them some degree of power within the family social unit. Bruggeman (1994) suggests that such qualifications must be taken into consideration in pastoral development programmes to avoid economic and social disempowerment of women.

The second issue is that of women's involvement in public life. Cunnison (1966), Marx (1967), Nelson (1973) and Levi (1987), referring particularly to Middle Eastern pastoral nomadic societies, suggest a division between the female's world, which is the private and domestic sphere of the tent, and the male's world, which is the public and political sphere of the camp. From this separation it follows that no formal part of political activities is assigned to women, which logically leads to the notion of their inferior social and legal status. In adopting this idea of separation between the two worlds, one should then accept the above view that women are only lightly involved in pastoral production activities. Yet, as shown by Bruggeman (1994), most often this is not the case. Indeed, researchers also differ over this division between the two worlds and over women's role in domestic and public decision making, particularly relative to the male household head. Thus, while Asad (1970) argues that the final decisions on all household matters among the Qababish Bedouin of Libya are made by male household heads, Barth (1964) maintains that among the Baseri of south Persia this process is carried out jointly by the couple. Even Nelson (1973) argues that confinement to the domestic sphere does not necessarily deprive pastoral women of all political power or render them socially weak. Women have a variety of control mechanisms to pursue their agenda, for example by allying with other women and power-playing different men off against each other. They have some informal power even over the issue of divorce which they cannot initiate on their own. Perhaps a major reason for this lack of consensus among researchers is related to insufficient regard for informal political transactions between spouses within the family relative to formal political ones at the tribal and inter-family arenas (Marx 1986; Lewando-Hundt 1984). From such consideration it transpires that women have more power at their disposal, and a higher social status than hitherto suggested by many observers.

The process of sedentarization, and the shift away from pastoral production as the primary source of livelihood, may change the status of children. It is not suggested here that the position of children within society deteriorates, but, as argued above, that the cultural value and social norm of multiplicity of children may change. Nuclear as well as extended families may begin to take a different view of the value of children. Consequently, their status within society may change. Several of the underlying mechanisms for these changes have already been discussed in previous sections (see also Edgerton 1971; Goldschmidt 1980). The primary process, however, is related to a shift from the informal to the formal educational process. This shift may not necessarily be associated only with sedentarization. Various studies suggest it may take place even within some small nomadic circles, particularly wealthy families (Gorham 1978; Gorham 1980), and in some circumstances, as in Iran (Varlet and Massoumiam 1975; Sandford 1977) within wide sections of pastoral nomadic groups. However, there is no doubt that the process of sedentarization provides an important opportunity for introduction of previously nomadic children into the formal educational process, through its provision by various governmental and other agencies in fixed locations.

Provision of public educational services to pastoral nomads has encountered many difficulties, some of them logistic, almost everywhere. The main difficulties, however, stem from negative parental attitudes to the ideas of formal education and schooling for their children. These ideas are generally regarded as potentially capable of changing the value of children to the pastoral production process in particular and to the society at large in general. These attitudes are related to several issues: loss of child labor in terms of shadow prices; loss of children's competence in herding and other pastoral-related and domestic duties; loss of control over confinement of girls to the domestic sphere and their exposure to undesired pre-marital affairs; emergence of a gap between children and parents due to acquisition of literacy and different types of knowledge than required by pastoral nomadic culture; alienation of children from their family and society due, on the one hand, to their severance from pastoral labor and age-set duties, and exposure to external educators and curricula on the other hand; and, finally, the direct cost of schooling (Meir 1985; Swift et al. 1990). The negative attitude toward formal education is, therefore, reflected in markedly low schooling and literacy rates for both nomadic boys and girls as reported from various countries in Africa and the Middle East (Ezeomah 1979; Gorham 1980; Bahhady 1981; Nkinyangi 1981; U.N. 1984; Adaw 1986).

Perceived from a different angle, it is the negative attitude of pastoral nomadic parents toward schooling and formal education that explains the potential for changing the value and status of children. These ideas become more viable options upon sedentarization. Indeed, most governments have found it easier and more convenient to deliver sedentary-type educational services to the ex-nomadic population than mobile services to nomads. This approach has, in many cases, become a planning ideology, in which governments regard provision of public services as the main rationale for sedentarization of pastoral nomadic peoples (Meir 1990).

However, it appears that in recent decades the ideas of formal education and schooling have begun to penetrate deeper into nomadic societies proper, and that the direction of causality may now have begun to change. In other words, while in the past sedentarization was the main exposure outlet for formal education, at present there seems to be a growing demand for education from within the nomadic peoples themselves, impelling them further to shift away from the traditional mode of living. While this process may occur as a consequence of the general introduction of modern formal education into rural areas in the Third World, it is particularly evident under stressful ecological conditions such as long droughts. Thus Dahl (1991a, b) suggests that, because the social rewards of pastoralism are still reserved for the owners of herds (that is, the elders), many young members now find the herding activity less attractive than education, which may open avenues for government employment or other jobs. Younger pastoralists are no longer willing to postpone their economic independence and inheritance of social status from their parents into the distant future. Even parents, as argued by Mace (1989), are beginning to prefer investment in children's education and schooling over their participation in the pastoral production process.

The process of changing preferences is thus indicative of change in the value and therefore the status of children within the sedentarizing pastoral nomadic society. As children increasingly abandon the pastoral production process and are drawn into the formal educational process, their traditional status as a group and communal resource begins to forfeit it significance. Hence, members of pastoral groups are starting to question the very future of pastoralism. However, their exposure to the concept of formal education and schooling may lead them to weigh the very idea of their relationship with the group, in terms of both social obligations and economic and social rewards, against the rewards that may accrue from education. In other words, pastoral nomads begin to adopt individual modes of social and economic behavior that will provide them with access to avenues of social advancement that are independent of the traditional ascriptive paths.

The change in the status of young as well as adult children has some bearing upon the status of elders. This is mediated through the decline in fertility that may ensue from the declining value of children (see, e.g., Knodel et al. 1992). The issue has received little attention in studies of social change among pastoral nomads, was dealt with primarily within the context of disastrous situations (e.g., de Bruijn 1995), and we can therefore only hypothesize about it here. As the traditional economic and social value of children changes, elders may lose the absolute control over affairs that are associated with the pastoral production process. Their role as managers of the livestock capital may diminish further and the latter may begin to lose its dominance within the economy. The rich "databases" they acquired and transferred to the younger generation within the informal educational process may begin to lose their relevance, thus undermining their role as professional educators in the craftsmanship of pastoral production. Their experience with respect to economic production, social reproduction, and representation and negotiation with other pastoral and nonpastoral groups and agencies may become obsolete. This explanation, that rests upon the consequences of education, need not be the sole possible one. Processes already described above, such as land privatization and the ensuing nucleation of the family as an economic production unit, and shifting toward agricultural commercialization upon sedentarization, may also contribute to this process.

In general terms, the elders' role as the carriers and reproducers of the entire pastoral nomadic culture and, in fact, their supreme status within their society, may begin to deteriorate. This process entails individualization of elders within a society that previously regarded them as a central communal and group asset. It may be considered highly significant from a social stability perspective. The magnitude of social change that is associated with it can only be appreciated in light of the supreme position that elders enjoyed previously. It is, therefore, reasonable also to assume that traditional social institutions for care and provision for elders, that were previously built into the social system, may also begin to disintegrate. Thus, the deterioration in the social and economic status of elders may affect their social and economic wellbeing.

Sedentarization may also change the roles of women within the pastoral nomadic society. While in certain respects this may imply an improvement in their social status and wellbeing, in many others their social and economic status has deteriorated. These changes are connected to internal and external processes. Internally, one of the traditional status determinants of women was related to the value of children within the pastoral nomadic society. As the economic and sociopolitical value of children may decline upon sedentarization, the status of women as childbearers may also deteriorate. Yet, Kressel (1992a) suggests that this role of married women becomes more manifest as they lose previous status indicators, such as access to pastoral resources, upon sedentarization. For example, Beck (1978) has indicated that the decline of the pastoral economy due to sedentarization and the integration between the pastoral labor force and the wage labor market, as men seek jobs outside the tribal realm, deprive women of the pastoral resources which previously gave them some power.

Moreover, due to these changes, men rely less on women's traditional domestic roles, including satisfying their sexual needs (Kressel 1992b). In addition, this integration of male labor in the wage economy provides men with formal and informal educational opportunities which bring them closer to the mass culture, while women remain confined to the traditional sphere. They are therefore forced into greater involvement in domestic activities and responsibilities while cut off from those activities which previously carried more economic weight and therefore social responsibility and power. They are thus detached further from the public sphere. Consequently, sedentarization entails further seclusion and concealment of married and unmarried women especially in towns, in order to ensure the preservation of family honor and continuity of traditional gender roles (Kressel 1992b). Yet, one must not ignore the possibility that upon sedentarization, formal and informal educational opportunities may become available to women as well, especially young women (Nelson 1973). These may open new opportunities for improvement in their social wellbeing, as education provides them with information which is becoming an important resource, perhaps replacing the lost traditional resources.

The above discussion has reviewed the changes in roles, status and wellbeing of elders, children and women upon sedentarization. Due to lack of research, the description of the possible change in the status and wellbeing of elders is, of course, only speculative. However, accepting it as a working hypothesis yields an important general conclusion that is relevant also to the changing status of young and adult children and women. The process of social and economic individualization of elders and children within the post-nomadic society may lead to their detachment from traditional social institutions and resources that previously provided for their wellbeing. Such is also the case with women, although processes of individualization following sedentarization, as might be implied from the above discussion, appear to affect them negligibly, if any, until very late after sedentarization has begun, while elders and children are affected considerably earlier. Concurrently, this process carries the potential that individuals may become dependent upon social resources that are external to the traditional society. These resources are now public goods, e.g., educational, health, welfare and other public services provided by governments and other public agencies. Therefore, they also become dependent upon external decision-makers who control the provision of these public goods in terms of availability, accessibility, and cultural relevance. The wellbeing of individuals may now be affected by such external dependence upon central authorities. The issue of evolving relationships with the authorities is now of growing importance for the ex-nomadic population which previously had little contacts with a state government and its authorities. This issue is discussed in the next and final section of this chapter.

Pastoral Nomads and the State

The relationships between pastoral nomads and modern states have been dealt with directly and indirectly in numerous studies published in recent decades. While this issue is multi-faceted, one conclusion drawn from the wealth of studies is that in many countries in Asia, the Near East and Africa these relationships have become increasingly complex during this century. This is especially evident as nation-states gain power, a process that in general begun earlier in Asian and Near Eastern countries than in Africa. The increasing complexity contrasts strikingly with the relatively simple pattern of relationships in the days when nation-states were politically weak. This section suggests a particular pattern of relationships that has evolved between pastoral nomadic societies and the state, reflecting the conflicting political tendencies of the parties involved.

Until the turn of this century in the Near East, and until the second half of the century in Africa, nation-states could impose little control over their peripheries. Hence, the peripheral spatial position within remote desert environments was advantageous to pastoral nomads, and from their perspective yielded a quite simple pattern of relationships. In the Middle East in particular, they were capable of determining the terms of their relationships with agriculturalists and therefore with the state, and consequently posed a threat to its political stability. This often took the form of encroachment upon agricultural lands. Moreover, through their strong tribal organizational structure, they were able to accumulate supplementary income as administrative agents for the state.

However, the spread of modern means of transportation and military technologies facilitated improved state control of desert peripheries. Consequently, pastoral nomads have been reduced to a subservient position (Kressel 1993). Thus, in the course of this century, the balance of power has tipped in favor of the state, which has begun to encroach upon the power of pastoral nomads. The latter have been gradually driven into a socioeconomic marginal position whereby spatial peripheriality has been transformed from a benefit to a disadvantage.

This process, in which pastoral nomads have been forced to give up their power and freedom in their traditional territories, is also responsible for the increased complexity of their relationships with the state. Many writers and commentators would share the view that at present "(p)as-toralists are constrained as much by governments as by grass: they are not free wanderers, not independent transhumants, but minorities regarded as untidy nuisances by administrators who have consistently attempted to make them settle" (Davies 1977:21). It follows, as suggested by Swift (1977a), that pastoral nomads have apparently lost all their power and ability to determine their future. This view may reflect reality to a considerable degree. Bradburd (1995) even puts this process within a wider context of the development of the state which, by definition, requires everywhere the suppression of independent local political power of any kind, not only as regards pastoral nomads. Yet, it might also be argued that within such a seemingly simple structure of relationships there remain mechanisms whereby pastoral nomads are still capable of manifesting their power. Governments indeed impose various constraints over the location, migration, and resource utilization of pastoral nomads, attempting thus to control and settle them (Havakuk 1986). However, pastoralists have been attempting actively and passively to escape this control and thus to express their power spatially and functionally.

It transpires that opposing forces and tendencies are immanently built into the system of relationships between pastoral nomads and the state (see also Gilles and Gefu 1990). These stem from the conflicting ideologies of the parties, which generate tension between opposing spatial locational dynamics (Meir 1988). On the one hand, there is the centrifugal force that drives the conduct of pastoral nomads. On the other hand, there is the centripetal force which motivates the pursuits of the state. In the past the pendulum was mostly tilted towards the pastoral nomadic side, at other times towards the state, with few intermediate situations. Pastoral nomads could always retreat into the desert where state control was weak. At present the situation is far more complex, as the ability of pastoral nomads to exploit the advantages of peripheriality has diminished considerably. Yet, even under present political circumstances of modern powerful states, this tension between forces still prevails, and is likely to exist at the nomadic phase of pastoral societies. However, as will be argued below, it may endure even upon sedentarization. It is at this phase that the relationships with the state become most complex.

The notion of tension between centripetal and centrifugal forces, which was originally suggested by Hartshorne (1950), refers in fact to the tension between integrative and disintegrative forces operating simultaneously within the state. Centrifugal forces weaken the cohesion of a state, and may include physical as well as cultural elements. In the modern state, cultural elements such as language, religion, level of education, standard of living, and economic, social and political attitudes of various segments of society outweigh the physical elements of territorial size, spatial shape and geographical barriers as disintegrative forces. In contrast, the centripetal force tends to increase cohesion. This force is the state's raison d'être. It is supposed to become universally accepted and shared by all members of the community who should recognize the need to become what Bergman (1975) suggested as a political community.

This conceptualization of the centrifugal-centripetal tension was singular, spatial, and static. It has more recently been suggested that this theory could be improved if states were not considered separately but rather within the world system, so that the interstate effect is taken into consideration as a centrifugal force. It could also benefit from considering the issue of vertical social and not only spatial integration to minimize the effects of centrifugal forces (Taylor 1985). However, most important for our present discussion is the issue of spatial dynamics. That is, the very location of certain social and ethnic groups may have an impact upon the tension and balance between centrifugal and centripetal forces. Many states in the Near East and Africa still contain a significant proportion of pastoral nomadic populations within their rural sector. In these states the locational issue could become an important one within the tension framework. For these societies, being spatially dynamic and mobile is their raison d'être, manifested in a carefully calculated strategy to avoid drought and maintain environmental resources often disregarding state boundaries. This is a centrifugal ideology which stands in sharp conflict with that of the state.

The ideological centrality of mobility, i.e., nomadism, that contributes to the centrifugal tendency of pastoral nomads, is supported also by the social elements of tribalism and ethnicism. The issue of tribalism, dwelt upon earlier in this chapter, was considered by Pounds (1972) as the most disruptive of all centrifugal forces. The explanation is rooted in the stronger identification of tribesmen with their tribe or clan as political entities and their loyalty to it rather than to the state.

Yet, pastoral nomadic groups should not necessarily be taken to be socially monolithic. First, realignments between groups for the establishment of new corporate units may take place to guarantee access to grazing and water resources as need arises. Secondly, there is often annexation of external, nonnomadic groups, usually of sedentary origins, such as the Bella slaves of the Tuareg pastoralists in Mali or fellaheen in the Middle East. These groups, whose annexation may have been either voluntary or forced, have nevertheless become dependent upon and socially segregated from the host pastoralists, generating social stratification along ethnic lines (e.g., Randall 1984). This form of social stratification is manifested in social and spatial separatism, and compounds that generated within these societies along tribal dimensions. It constitutes a strong centrifugal element. As argued above, it serves not only to utilize grazing resources more efficiently but also to preserve the cohesion of tribal units and, through spatial fission, to avoid or resolve inter-group conflicts (Rapoport 1978; Kressel 1976).

Thus, the strong centrifugal force within pastoral nomadic societies, which is an outcome of the combination of nomadism, tribalism, and ethnicism, determines their locational dynamics, with an extensive spatial dispersion and migration pattern. It outweighs the periodic and seasonal symbiotic tendency of pastoralists to gravitate toward sedentary centers, which may increase undesired contacts with state authorities.

This pattern, however, is a source of conflict with the centripetal tendency of the state. The conflict revolves around several issues. The first of these relates to resource management. Harbeson (1991) explains why pastoralism, as a form of resource utilization, is being misunderstood by governments. First, the common holding of pastoral resources (land and often water) is held responsible for Hardin's process of "tragedy of the commons" which many pastoral societies are undergoing. Second, pastoralists are assumed irresponsive to market incentives and thus ineffective managers of their environment by permitting excessive overstocking which allegedly degrades their rangelands. Third, the nature, rationale and extent of mobility of pastoralists is taken by governments as a manifestation of a romantic lifestyle that is now anachronistic (See also Behnke and Scoones 1993).

Both Harbeson and Behnke and Scoones, as well as others (e.g., Sandford 1983) show that for each of these theories there is strong refuting evidence. Various writers (e.g., Aronson 1981; Johnson 1993) show, therefore, how pastoral resources, such as lands held collectively by pastoral groups, are often subject to nationalization by the state. In this process, pastoral resources are dealt with according to national perceptions of utility determined by national needs and are treated with according to cost-benefit considerations to optimize their utility to the state rather than to the pastoral nomads. By adopting this attitude, governments refrain from assisting the pastoralists in solving their problems within the pastoral nomadic framework, causing their economic marginalization within a spatial periphery.

Another issue that carries seeds of conflict is provision of public services. This issue was discussed above, where it was argued that educational services may have a disruptive effect upon the pastoral production process. The tension between pastoralists and state authorities in this arena is similar to that existing in pastoral resource management. Governments incline to regard services as public goods that are to be managed under cost-benefit considerations, and tend therefore to maximize the utility of provision from their perspective. Pastoralists, however, have in recent decades begun to appreciate the idea of formal education. Yet, it is the *form* of provision of public services, rather than the provision itself, which they resist, regarding such services as spatially, functionally, and culturally inappropriate (Meir 1985). The most conflictual problem in this issue is the sedentary nature of these services, since governments aim at providing them in fixed locations (Gorham 1978). Another problem is related to the tribal or ethnic background and origins of the staff, and stems from inter-group mistrust and therefore reluctance to use services (Imperato 1975; Nestel 1985). Finally, there is the question of faith in the substance of the particular service, whether curricula in the case of educational services or medicines and forms of treatment in the case of human health and animal veterinary services (Swift et al. 1990).

The final issue relevant to the centrifugal-centripetal tension is sedentarization of pastoral nomads. Not all sedentarization processes have been initiated by governments. Salzman (1980) outlines four causal models of sedentarization of which only one, which he terms "political and military defeat and degradation," falls within this category. Yet, this category may be further divided into processes of voluntary sedentarization (which differ from a spontaneous process), in which the pastoralists cooperated with the government, and processes which involved a substantial element of coercion. The latter subtype, forced sedentarization, may be considered the highest form of imposition of state power over pastoral nomads. Nonetheless, this issue is closely associated with the previous issues. From the perspective of governments, efficient national utilization of resources within traditional pastoral territories, and provision of services to pastoralists, can be maximized only when the latter give up their nomadic way of life and become involved in agricultural production in fixed locations. In fact, it has often been suggested that governments use the argument of improved services to nomads, secured food supply, and greater earning opportunities from commercialized farming and other nonpastoral sources (e.g., I.L.O. 1967; Humphrey 1978; Dahl 1991a) as the main justifications for their attempts to settle nomads.

At this point it is worth noting that even within the framework of pastoralism under the modern powerful state, pastoralists have been able to maintain their centrifugal tendency quite significantly. First, there is ample evidence from the Near East and Africa suggesting that some governments have recently begun to rethink the notion of sedentarization as the sole solution to pastoralists' problems. Various development projects have been designed and implemented to allow for continuing nomadic pastoralism or some versions thereof, including identification of traditional pastoral social institutions that can be recruited in order to implement these projects efficiently (Livingstone 1985; Swift 1988; Stone 1991). Second, government provision of public services did not always take exclusive sedentary form. Mobile veterinary, health, and educational services for pastoral nomads have long been operated by various governments (Meir 1985; Swift et al. 1990), and the idea of service centers within traditional pastoral territories has also been recently suggested (F.A.O. 1991). This indicates that pastoralists, by expressing their desire to continue their nomadic lifestyle, have succeeded in resisting the centripetal tendency of the state and maintaining their locational dynamics.

It is within the context of government-initiated sedentarization, however, that the centrifugal-centripetal tension may be maximized. The main reason is that government's perception of pastoralists as irrational economic actors may often be carried over to their sedentary activities, as happened for example in Ethiopia (Samantar 1991; Harbeson 1991). However, usually governments do not realize that when they make the transition to sedentarization and farming, pastoralists carry with them many of the cultural traits that stem from their pastoral nomadic ideology (Frantz 1975; Cole 1981). Central to these are the notions of mobility, self-reliance, and independence which, as elaborated by Dahl (1991a), are of great worth to these peoples and still affect the rationalization of their behavior as settlers. Hence, they often tend to engage in certain additional activities such as trade and transportation (Chatty 1972/3), let alone small-scale sedentary pastoralism and maintenance of strong relationships with relatives still practicing pastoralism. The latter strategies, as explained by Marx (1980; 1981a; 1984), are adopted by the settling nomads to reduce uncertainty involved in integration into the external, national economy.

While these pastoral values may fade away with time, they continue to feed the centrifugal tendency of the settlers at early and even advanced stages of sedentarization. This tendency may persist in encapsulated form even though the settling pastoralists appear to be succumbing to the state. The ex-nomads may still maintain their ability to activate this institutionalized alternative as a means of preserving their values, which may take several forms. First, the settling pastoralists may desire a settlement scheme that is in spatial harmony with the traditional social and ethnic structure. Their objective is to avoid or minimize possible inter-group conflicts due to increased population density in the settled environment (Rapoport 1978; Harbeson 1991). Second, they may wish to maintain some form and magnitude of livestock production to minimize economic uncertainty in the new geographical and functional setting. This may lead to a third problem, that of the need to be able to exploit their traditional pastoral resources of land and water, including the traditional arrangements of rights of access. Fourth, they may demand that public services be delivered in a manner that meets their social and cultural needs. This issue refers both to location of service facilities and to the cultural relevance of their substance (such as school curricula), in order to maximize the wellbeing of the settling nomads. Finally, if all these fail, they may apply strong pressures for return to nomadism, as indeed has been the case in several countries (La Bianca 1990).

Governments' compliance with pastoral nomads' views of these issues may facilitate their attempts to nationally integrate these societies. Such compliance suggests, however, that the settling pastoral nomads are potentially capable of spatially and functionally activating their centrifugal tendency. This dialectical pattern of relationships between the ex-nomads and the state is substantially more complicated than that which prevailed in periods when pastoral nomads were in stronger control of their pastoral territories and resources. However, this complex relationship also suggests that in many countries in Asia, the Near East, and Africa, settled pastoralists, as well as their nomadic kinsmen, are now potentially more capable of de-marginalizing themselves into more harmonious social, economic, and political integration within the modern state.

Conclusions

This chapter has suggested that the ideological shift of pastoral nomads along the tribalism-individualism continuum during sedentarization implies that they may gradually free themselves from the bonds that commit them to their group and become motivated by newer and varied value-systems. This process ushers in several others in which the effects of sedentarization are most centrally manifested. Territoriality becomes a common spatial behavior, and by generating social stratification it alters social relationships within the community from social definition of territory into territorial definition of social relations. This process changes the relationships between population and resources, and there emerges a continuum of fertility rationalities and patterns, with a strong tendency towards declining family size. Individual households become thus liberated from group fertility norms and adopt this new ideal for their own wellbeing. As the individualization process gains momentum, the social wellbeing of individuals, rather than that of the group, becomes their major concern. The change in the value and status of children, elders and women may lead to external dependence for wellbeing upon state authorities via the provision of public services. The issue of relationships with state authorities becomes now significant and more complex for the ex-nomadic population which previously had little contacts with them. A unique dialectical process of locational and functional dynamics now evolves. The settled ex-nomadic society continues to manifest its traditional centrifugal tendency, despite the seemingly powerful imposition of the centripetal force by the modern state.

There is an apparent paradox within this process. Arguably, during sedentarization, pastoral nomads become individualistically motivated by new value-systems that dissociate them from their traditional group. Yet they continue to manifest their traditional centrifugal tendency. This paradox may be resolved by recalling that social change means shifting between varying sets of institutionalized alternatives to create a reordered society. Change is not necessarily associated with discontinuity but rather with recruitment of some institutionalized alternatives from the cultural reservoir. As such an alternative, the centrifugal tendency of pastoral nomads has been internalized by members of the group. It may itself contain individualistic elements that may make it easier to carry it over into sedentarism. Therefore, it must not come into conflict with adoption of additional social values of personal upward status mobility. Furthermore, the latter process, which may contribute to disintegration of the group, may not be absolute. In addition to kinship relationships, sedentarized nomads may retain certain other group-forming elements which derive from the new agenda which confronts them upon sedentarization under the modern state. Individualization processes, as part of modernization, may not necessarily negate their traditional centrifugal tendency. On the contrary, within the context of the modern state, they may reinforce this tendency albeit now in an encapsulated manner.

3

Bedouin Encounters with Agents of Change

Change, as argued in the previous chapter, implies shifting between various sets of institutionalized alternatives which are recruited from the internal cultural reservoir. It also involves, however, selective addition of new external alternatives which are utilized as needs arise. This entails introducing external change agents, the encounter with which may shape both the process of adopting alternatives and the process of change. In the case of pastoral nomads in arid and semiarid areas, this encounter takes place within the context of a settlement frontier, i.e., the area that separates the desert and the sown (Reifenberg 1950).

A frontier region does not become occupied, settled, or developed by state authorities and institutions. This requires individuals or groups that depart from their social and spatial origins and penetrate the unfamiliar region. In certain contexts they act on behalf of state or other nonstate organizations or communities. In others they act on their own initiative, which may later become integrated within national or wide communal goals. The microscale local activities of these individuals or groups may influence the transformation of the region from a nonintegral, unsettled, and undeveloped frontier into an integral part, to varying degrees, of the state and society. During this process their encounter with the local indigenous society—which takes place on a local and daily routine basis—may be a major factor for change, though not the exclusive one.

During the nineteenth century encounters of the Negev Bedouin with change agents were quite limited. Two major groups of outsiders interacted with them. First, officials of the Ottoman Empire (until 1917) and the British Mandate (1917–1948) were involved in Bedouin affairs in the Negev either through routine governance or through certain development activities (Marx 1974; Grossman 1994a). This involvement was conducted virtually by remote control and primarily through tribal sheikhs as intermediaries. In addition, the nineteenth century has been described as the era of rediscovery of the Holy Land. Many individual travelers and explorers toured the country, including the Negev, and semiofficial British exploration missions also paid short visits (Ben-Arieh 1970). These outsiders could be regarded as the earliest representatives of the modernizing Western world. However, there was little long term interaction between them and the mass of Bedouin tribesmen, and their impact in terms of change was almost negligible.

The second group of outsiders were merchants from Gaza and other towns, as well as villagers and town-dwellers from the southern Coastal Plain and southern Hebron Mountains. The Bedouin maintained various social and economic contacts with them, consistent with the usual symbiotic relationships of pastoral nomads with their human environment. A subgroup of these were fellaheen (peasants) who migrated into the northern Negev from the beginning of the nineteenth century on. The latter two groups of merchants and fellaheen, as will be seen in the next chapter, had a considerable impact on Bedouin society, particularly in terms of economic development. Yet, the Middle East-North African realm (MENA) (Kressel 1992a) remained the main cultural source of their contribution to the process of change within Bedouin society.

The intensive encounter of the Bedouin with the outside world commenced, therefore, only when Jewish settlers began to settle the Negev in the decades preceding Israel's statehood. Jewish settlement in the Negev frontier before 1948 can be divided into three stages (Kark 1974; Kellerman 1993b). In the first stage (1880–1917), under the Ottoman rule, the goal was to formulate ideas and plans with regard to the viability of settlement in the southern coastal plain of Palestine. Only one Jewish settlement was established in this period in the northern Negev. In the second stage (1917–1939), under the British Mandate, the focus was on further experimentation and on land purchases and only one settlement was added. The third stage, the pre-state period (1939–1947), signaled the beginning of more systematic and intensive Jewish settlement in the Negev.

The present chapter describes the encounter between the Negev Bedouin and these settlers as agents of change and offers insights into the context within which the major processes of change took place later. The process of Jewish settlement in the Negev continued more intensively after 1948, extending the critical initial encounter and the state of frontiership of this area well into the late 1950s. Hence, the discussion of this issue covers both the prestate and poststatehood decades.

The Bedouin-Jewish Encounter: The 1940s

The Political and Social Contexts

The frontier encounter between the Bedouin and Jewish settlers in the Negev has both political and organizational dimensions. The former is also ecologically-oriented. Historians of Palestine as well as of the Middle East are well aware of the concept of "the struggle between the desert and the sown" (Reifenberg 1950). The settled frontier in these areas advanced and retreated in accordance with the balance of power between central governments and the pastoral nomadic Bedouin. The latter's encroachment upon settled territories in Palestine was ecologically rather than politically motivated. Their main motivation was to gain better means of subsistence beyond the border of the settled-unsettled zone. It was political only in the sense that the consequent struggle took place within a territory that was dominated by the Ottoman Empire.

From the second half of the nineteenth century, while still under the Ottoman Empire, and even more so under the British Mandate after the First World War, the Bedouin began to realize their inferiority in terms of arms and transportation in comparison to Western technology. This technological inferiority compelled them to cease their attempts to encroach upon settled territories (Kressel 1993). Indeed, it was one of the incentives for the transition to seminomadism, combining pastoral economy with dry-farming agriculture. Therefore, as far as the Negev Bedouin were concerned, Shafir's (1989) generalization that the Arabs in Palestine were a sedentary agrarian and not a tribal population must be relaxed. Agrarianism and territoriality among the Negev Bedouin at the onset of the Jewish settlement were only beginning to emerge, as will be seen in the next chapter. Although the importance of tribalism was already beginning to decline, it was still significant among the Bedouin in those years (Ashkenazi 1957).

The Zionist (and later Israeli)-Arab conflict over controlling land and territory in Palestine is another aspect of the political dimension, perhaps more important in retrospect. In a process initiated in the 1920s, the British Mandate government begun to semilegalize Bedouin land ownership in the Negev—thus upgrading land values in the real estate market and making land transactions a potentially substantial source of income for them (Ben-David 1989; Kressel et al. 1991). Since virtually any offer of land transaction was accepted by Jewish organizations, many Bedouin, particularly sheikhs, sold patches of land, beginning with marginal low quality land and later even selling premium land (see Porat and Shavit 1982; Porat 1991). These land transactions—in the Negev and elsewhere in Palestine—were violently denounced by Arab leaders in Palestine and the Middle East. Nevertheless, they facilitated the subsequent establishment of a Jewish settlement frontier in the Negev (Kimmerling 1982; Kellerman 1993a) and its inclusion within the future state of Israel.

The political context of land transactions thus put Bedouin land-sellers under considerable pressure. Bedouin who were involved in land transactions had to confront three pressure groups: the British Mandate government, which tried to ban such deals; the Palestinian Arab national movement and local Negev Bedouin activists, who denounced land sellers and threatened their lives; and Jewish buyers, whose land acquisitions made the sellers wealthy (Bar-Zvi 1977; Porat 1985). Eventually, in many cases, the high prices offered by Jewish buyers (at times more than double their real value) outweighed the other pressures but forced the Bedouin into a double standard: selling land discreetly but voicing overt loud opposition (Weitz 1965). Kark (1974) has noted that neither side found it necessary to resort to legal registration of land transactions. The Bedouin in particular argued that there was no government in the desert (Amitai 1983; Meitiv 1986). They were thus expressing their loyalty to their traditional political centrifugal attitude vis-à-vis central governments.

The second relevant context of the encounter between the Bedouin and Jewish settlers in the Negev relates to the organizational framework of these societies. Although a population census was taken in 1946, the Bedouin population could only be estimated roughly as between 57,000 and 95,000 (Muhsam 1966). They were divided into five clans loosely organized in about 100 tribes, mostly located in the northern Negev (Ashkenazi 1957). Many of these tribes were historical and territorial rivals (Bailey 1980). Throughout the prestate period, the seminomadic Bedouin were a small minority of the Arab population in Palestine (about 5 percent) and very loosely integrated into the Arab core institutions. In contrast, Jewish settlement of the frontier through land acquisition became possible only through utilization of a unique organizational framework (Kark 1974). The financial resources of world Jewry were harnessed to promote the collectivist social ideology in kibbutz-type settlements in the Negev frontier, as in other frontiers in Palestine. These settlements were supported by the organizational apparatus and institutional infrastructure at the core of the Jewish settlement (Yishuv) in Eretz-Israel (Palestine).

It is within these contexts that the Negev Bedouin encountered Jewish settlers as the earliest permanent representatives of Western culture. While in other frontier regions of Eretz-Israel there had been some Jewish population prior to the major Jewish settlement waves, only a few Jews lived in the Negev frontier before the 1940s. For the seminomadic pastoral Bedouin there, whose territories, life, and Middle Eastern culture had previously suffered minimal interference, the encounter with Jewish settlers was therefore virtually their first encounter with Western culture, carrying heavy potentials of tension and conflict.

Data on the nature of this frontier encounter in the Negev were gathered from several sources: personal interviews with Bedouin elders and Jews who participated actively in the encounter in an official or private capacity; archives in kibbutzim; and national and institutional archives (Zivan 1990; Meir and Zivan forthcoming).

The Encounter: Ideology, Practice and Consequences

Jewish settlement in the Negev during the 1940s (see Fig. 3.1) was launched with three agricultural "observation outposts" (1943), continued with the "eleven settlements" (1946) and culminated in an additional seven "stronghold settlements" and several others (1947) on the eve of the War of Independence (Kark 1974; Kellerman 1993b). All these settlements, mostly kibbutzim—with a total population of about 3000 by 1948—were established under the auspices of core Jewish settlement organizations on prepurchased land. Their establishment contravened the British Mandate 1939 White Paper policy and regulations with regard to Jewish settlement in Palestine (Porat 1985; Danin 1988; Weitz 1965). Within this context, settlement in the remote and poorly accessible Negev desert environment, amidst an alien Bedouin population, involved a considerable degree of uncertainty in terms of ecology and security.

The encounter between the Bedouin and the settlers was conducted primarily between representatives of Jewish settlements and Bedouin sheikhs or other Bedouin individuals. The representative of the individual kibbutz was usually the *mukhtar,* a preselected person who was the local "chief" for Bedouin affairs and handled all contacts with them, including the diffusion of tensions (Danin 1977). Occasionally Jewish field-guards also assumed these tasks.

Jewish settlers were split over two central issues concerning their settlement within Bedouin territory: their attitude toward the Bedouin and whether to practice Bedouinization in cultural-behavioral terms. Two opposite approaches emerged with regard to relationships with the Bedouin. The militants advocated an "iron hand" approach toward the Bedouin to ensure immediate security. At the other extreme was the peace-seeking approach that advocated mutual respect for life styles and interests (Amitai 1983; Keren 1987). Each *mukhtar's* stand vis-à-vis these approaches determined his own kibbutz's communal attitude toward the Bedouin.

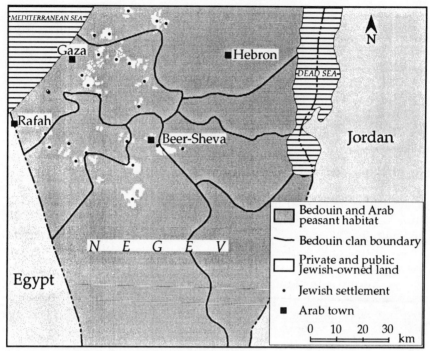

FIGURE 3.1 The Negev frontier in the 1940s *(Source:* Adapted from El-Aref 1937 and Kark 1974).

In general, the peace-seeking approach was predominant, primarily due to the socialist ideology of kibbutzim, particularly with regard to its "international comradeship" element (see also Kellerman 1993a) and its resulting need to establish neighborly relation. This attitude was also inspired by institutional guidance from core Jewish settlement organizations. Consequently—as was often the case in Jewish settlement frontiers elsewhere (Nimrod 1994)—the kibbutz settlers found it instrumental to establish local liaison committees to handle bilateral neighborhood affairs with the Bedouin, in addition to those matters handled by the *mukhtars.* This attitude proved mutually useful and highly beneficial for both sides, especially in the early years of frontier settlement.

In general, this attitude was counterbalanced by Bedouin traditional hospitality toward outsiders. However, the Bedouin were not unanimous in their acceptance of the settlers. Some groups and individuals rejected the penetration of outsiders, especially Jews, into their territory and became quite hostile. Water pipelines to kibbutzim were therefore repeatedly sabotaged by some Bedouin; occasionally local roads were sabotaged or blocked to hamper Jewish transportation or to extort thru-passage charges; and even some minor bloodshed occurred. This experience caused some regression from the peace-seeking attitude and an occasional resort to forceful measures, as advocated by the militants. Yet, throughout most of the prestate years, this approach was confined to forceful reaffirmation of the need for Jewish-Bedouin mutual respect.

The Jewish settlers were split also over the issue of Bedouinization. The question that concerned settlers was not the need for complete Bedouinization, but whether adoption of certain Bedouin cultural traits was necessary in order to foster social relationships with them. It is noteworthy that in those years Jewish core leaders and local settlers were influenced by British-style romanticization of Bedouin culture in the Middle East, similarly to Jewish settlers elsewhere in Palestine with regard to Arab villagers (Selwyn 1995). David Ben-Gurion, then national leader, even naively envisioned the creation of Bedouinized Jewish groups which would combine modern and traditional Bedouin cultural skills in order to transform the Negev desert into a settled region (Ben-Gurion 1954). Local settlers were thus advised to adopt Bedouin behavioral norms in order to counter Bedouin demographic and cultural dominance (Weitz 1960).

Kibbutzim varied in the extent to which this advocated behavior was actually pursued. The further south the kibbutz—deep within Bedouin territory and more isolated from the core and from other Jewish settlements—the more inclined it was to adopt Bedouin cultural traits. Yet, even among those who tended toward Bedouinization, it was practiced mostly by *mukhtars* and field-guards. It took several forms: erection of Bedouin-style hospitality tents *(shig)* or huts *(madafe)* at kibbutz gates; adoption of Bedouin clothing artifacts; carrying symbolic Bedouin weapons; raising thoroughbred Bedouin racing horses and camels; participation in horse and camel races or in wrestling matches; modest dress for women outside kibbutz quarters; relating Bedouin legends and quoting Bedouin proverbs; and willingness to accept the Bedouin traditional legal and judicial system for local conflict resolution. The latter two sociocultural traits were in particular considered by the Bedouin as the highest form of Bedouinization. Those few *mukhtars* and field-guards who reached this level were even awarded Bedouin names, and accepted as honorable Bedouin, and some were even selected as arbitrators in Bedouin internal conflicts (Efrat 1992; Meitiv 1977; Meitiv 1986; and Bar-Zvi 1971).

This limited-degree Bedouinization, and the more general peace-seeking attitude toward the Bedouin, were essential for gaining their confidence and establishing an atmosphere conducive to peaceful coexistence. To a considerable degree this conduct shaped the mutual relationships of the Bedouin and the Jewish settlers during the 1940s, particularly at the microlevel, generating thus benefits to both the Bedouin population and to Jewish settlements.

Although the Bedouin were largely detached from their Arab core in Palestine in those years, they were not cut off from information with regard to Jewish settlement projects and their economic impact elsewhere in the country. Thus, despite widespread Arab hostility to Jewish settlement in the Negev, the Bedouin generally favored the new Jewish settlements in their territories in anticipation of development impact—particularly in irrigation and farming technology—as well as in hope of diversification of their income sources. Indeed, the frontier encounter benefited the Bedouin considerably. Firstly, there were immediate benefits from land transactions, patronage fees paid in some circumstances by the settlers to sheikhs, and wages paid to individual Bedouin hired as guards of the cultivated fields of Jewish settlements.

But beyond these, there were certain more basic benefits. The most important of these was water supply. Although irrigated farming had commenced among the Bedouin during the 1940s, their own water sources could barely supply their joint farming, domestic, and animal needs. Most of their agriculture was therefore of the dry-farming type. Moreover, the water resources developed by the settlers and their core institutions were insufficient to support Bedouin irrigated farming, and were irrelevant for their dry-farming techniques. However, the Bedouin still benefited from water supply in several ways. At the local level, a special pump and outlet tap were made available gratis to Bedouin whenever a well was dug by a Jewish settlement. Although the Bedouin were familiar with the art of digging wells and practiced it extensively, they emulated local Jewish initiative and dug their own private wells in the vicinity of those of the settlers, using the same underground source. On a larger scale, the Bedouin also attempted, with the aid of settlers, to imitate the project of damming winter flash flood water (Bar-Zvi 1971). At the regional level, the major pipeline that conveyed water from northern sources to the local kibbutzim was also made available to sheikhs and to Bedouin families living along its route, as well as to the few regional British Mandate police stations staffed by Bedouin. Some of the sheikhs even sold these water allocations to their tribesmen, benefiting thus twice, after collecting their pipeline-passage fee and the fees for guard duties.

The second way in which the Bedouin benefited from Jewish settlement was the evolution of a local smallscale labor-market. Various employment opportunities became available to the Bedouin with gradual growth and development of the new settlements. These included, as indicated above, a few jobs for field-guards, but primarily labor for projects such as the abovementioned dam, a kaolin quarry operated by one of the kibbutzim in the Negev Highlands, the regional water pipeline project, crop harvesting as share-croppers, camel-plowing of cultivated fields, and transportation by camels to and from the dam or the mine. Due to the Bedouin traditional distaste for manual labor, however, their participation in these labor-market opportunities was only temporary, and they did not become a major source of income.

Some technical services in the new settlements—such as carpentry, locksmithing and other machinery facilities—also became available to Bedouin. They were also allowed to graze their livestock in stubble fields in the dry season. Another economic benefit to individual Bedouin was the purchase of goods on their behalf in city markets in the north by *mukhtars* and settlers. Some *mukhtars* even acted on behalf of the Bedouin in their attempts to receive seedlings of trees from the Forestry Department in order to plant them as a future source of construction material for dwellings and other purposes. On occasion, *mukhtars* provided a coverup, hampering governmental attempts to curtail the traditional Bedouin engagement in smuggling activities.

An additional area in which the Bedouin were aided by the settlers was provision of medical services. In the late 1930s the Jewish land purchasing organization already stationed a Jewish physician in Beer-Sheva, specifically in order to establish social relationships with the Bedouin (Gal-Pe'er 1979, 1985). Consequently, virtually every Jewish settler was subsequently regarded by the Bedouin as a healer. Some of the *mukhtars* were also active in this sphere and their kibbutzim became local small-scale centers for medical services for the Bedouin, including some primary outreach services, and guidance in elementary sanitation. Given Bedouin remoteness from medical services in central locations, lack of other local facilities, and their extremely high mortality rates (see Chapter 5), this primary smallscale medical aid proved highly significant.

Jewish settlements also derived benefits from the encounter with the Bedouin, first and foremost in the security sphere. The settlements were always located on legally purchased land, but nonetheless their security was a major concern for both national leaders (Yaari 1943; Knaani 1981) and the settlers themselves. The Jewish settlers were strangers to the indigenous Bedouin and were often perceived as a nuisance. Therefore, as a demographic and ethnic minority it was incumbent on them first to seek sheikhs' patronage in order to gain some degree of initial security. This was done, as indicated above, through payment of a monthly patronage fee to the local sheikh, above and beyond the price paid for land purchased from him earlier (Bar-Zvi 1971). In some cases the settlers paid an additional monthly sum in wages for tribesmen hired as field-guards on the advice of the local sheikh and for local Bedouin police officers (already in the pay of the British Mandate authorities for service in the desert police stations), or in fees for guarding water pipelines after the sheikhs had been paid for construction permits within their territories.

However, sheikhs' patronage alone could not guarantee complete security. Although the sheikh was considered a formal patron, the loose sociopolitical tribal structure hampered his control of individual tribesmen. Traditionally, the Bedouin considered stealing and looting from settled farmers an integral part of their survival strategy. Therefore, many of the fields cultivated by the Jewish settlements—often located quite far from the settlements—were under this threat. Protection of machinery and crops by a single Bedouin field-guard was thus rather problematic, and it was necessary for additional Jewish guards to accompany the Bedouin guards or, on occasion, to guard against them.

An additional security problem related to Bedouin pastoral nomadic concepts of territoriality. As shown in the previous chapter (and discussed in detail in the next chapter), these concepts differed drastically from those of the settlers, who were of Western origin. Thus, even though the land had been sold to the settlers, the Bedouin still demanded their rights of access to their traditional pastures and water resources, in line with their resource-sharing ideology. This explains why Bedouin flocks often trespassed on kibbutz fields, generating frequent clashes and even some minor bloodshed on both sides. This problem was particularly acute in the case of the more nomadic Bedouin from northern Sinai whose seasonal grazing migration into the Negev was carried out in line with intertribal agreements and who were hard put to comply with the new reality of settlement by outsiders.

One of the security areas in which Jewish settlers were assisted considerably by individual Bedouin was quasimilitary local intelligence. This activity became institutionalized particularly after the construction of the regional water pipeline from the north in 1946 (Danin 1977). The gathering of local information, which was initiated at the national level, was assigned, among others, to *mukhtars* and Jewish field-guards, whose social networks were highly instrumental. This facilitated collection of information systematically from paid Bedouin informants and field-guards, and even from some Bedouin policemen. For the Jewish settlers, this information was highly valuable even during the relatively peaceful years before 1948. For the individual Bedouin involved, selling information became an important economic resource.

Securing environmental resources for initial development was the second area in which encounter with the Bedouin was useful to the Jewish settlers. Obviously, the most important economic advantage was land transactions. The social networks of *mukhtars* and Jewish field-guards became instrumental in these activities as well, particularly in obtaining possession of land purchased from Bedouin One of the problems that faced Jewish authorities and settlers was how to maintain their rights over acquired but uncultivated land. This was necessary in order to prevent its becoming *mawat* (wasteland) due to lack of use, a situation that, under the Ottoman law, constituted legal grounds for its return to the original owner after three years. Here, too, many Bedouin became instrumental. Apart from their assistance in extracting legally purchased land from the previous owners, Bedouin also leased and cultivated land plots from Jewish organizations. In his account of early settlement attempts in the Negev, Bar-Zvi has indicated that these lease payments were channeled into a local fund aimed at promoting contacts and maintaining social relationships with the Bedouin (Bar-Zvi 1971).

Securing water resources was the next immediate environmental concern, and there was no doubt among the settlers that Bedouin aid in this regard would be crucial to success (Meitiv 1958). Indeed, due to the traditional Bedouin custom of sharing water with neighbors, local wells were made available to the settlers, despite their low discharge, in anticipation of future reciprocity (Keren n.d.). In 1946 the Bedouin also allowed the construction of the major water pipeline from the northern core region through their tribal territories (Gavri 1985).

The Bedouin were helpful to Jewish settlements in several other economic ways. First, they possessed a considerable store of knowledge of harvesting local runoff and subsurface water and of dry-farming, albeit at a primitive level, and, obviously of flock grazing. Porat's detailed discussion of this issue (Porat 1992) reveals that—contrary to prevailing myths—these skills were of considerable benefit to the settlers. In addition, some kibbutzim bought sheep dung from Bedouin for fertilization, others bought barley from them for marketing in core region markets, and still others bought poultry for canning in a local small factory. Extraction of kaolin from the mine in the Negev Highlands was made possible with Bedouin assistance and labor (Efrat 1982; Bar-Zvi 1976). Although the main regular supplies to Jewish settlements came from core markets, local markets in the few Bedouin villages and the town of Beer-Sheva, as well as individual Bedouin neighbors, supplemented various daily needs in goods and services (such as postal services and public transportation).

In summary, despite the long-range objective of the settlers to guarantee Jewish domination over a territory which would be included in the future state of Israel, the prestate encounter between the Bedouin and the settlers as agents of change took place with relatively little institutional involvement from above. The Bedouin themselves were not politically involved in the national conflict over this objective. Hence, neither side exerted any significant pressure on the other. On the contrary, development of peaceful neighborhood relations was in their mutual interest, being beneficial to the Bedouin and serving the initial consolidation and growth of the Jewish settlements. This early encounter—which could have proved calamitous for both sides due to its unique contexts—turned out to be relatively positive and nonconflictual. It developed spontaneously and voluntarily into open, interactive, and symbiotic relations between the Bedouin and the Jewish settlements.

The Encounter in the 1950s

The Context

A major turning point in the relationships between the Bedouin and the Jewish settlers in the Negev was reached with Israel's War of Independence (November 1947 – March 1949). Locally, the change related to the battles which ensued when the Egyptian army invaded the Negev and was repelled by the Israeli Defense Forces (IDF). These hostilities shifted the focus of Jewish-Bedouin relations in the Negev from a regional and local sociocultural encounter to a national Israeli-Arab political conflict. The inhabitants (Bedouin and Jews alike) lost their ability to mutually shape their relationships at the local level. This was now determined by events at the state and national levels.

As had been the case in the prestate period, during the Egyptian military invasion of the Negev the Bedouin were not monolithic in their attitude toward the Jewish settlements. There was minimal direct involvement of the Bedouin in attacks on Jewish settlements by the Egyptian army. However, some individual Bedouin and groups took action in this regard. This included attacks on patrol units along the regional water pipeline, mining of transportation routes, preventing access to local water wells, or attacks on settlers outside the settlements. Many of these acts were committed in order to repudiate previous cooperation with the settlers in intelligence, land transactions, and other activities. Yet, other Bedouin continued to cooperate with the Jewish settlements during the war in intelligence work or by providing basic supplies.

However, the Bedouin suffered as a result of the political changes in the Negev after the war. On the one hand, their sources of subsistence shrank considerably. The Egyptian army also expelled many Bedouin who were suspected as having cooperated previously with the Jewish settlers or who had refused to support the invasion of the Negev. On the other hand, as the war went on, the initial policy of the newly-born State of Israel to avoid inflicting damage on the Bedouin, underwent a change. Morris (1987) has shown the split between those civil and military officials who supported expulsion of all Bedouin from the Negev and those who advocated allowing the loyal ones at least to stay. Eventually, about

17,000 Bedouin were expelled by the IDF forces during and after the war (Morris 1993). Many others, however—loyal to their traditional pastoral nomadic territorial ideology and anticipating that their traditional territorial rights would not be violated by the political change—chose to leave the Negev temporarily (Amitai 1983). Their number can be estimated at about 30,000 at least. Whether voluntarily or otherwise, all the Bedouin who left the Negev ended up in the Egyptian Sinai or in Jordan. By the early 1950s, only about 11,000, belonging to eighteen tribes or fractions thereof, remained in the Negev.

Some of the tribes that remained in the Negev signed agreements with the IDF to guarantee fair treatment by the authorities and respect for their land rights in exchange for their loyalty and cooperation. However, for the first time they had to deal with the Israeli state authorities rather than with the settlers. The British Mandate authorities had scarcely interfered previously with their affairs (Marx 1974), let alone with their encounter with the settlers. Now, however, the state political apparatus intervened very intensively in the delicate fabric of relations.

Soon after the war the military authorities took immediate action with regard to the Bedouin, as they did with Arabs elsewhere in Israel. First, the attempts of those tribes that left the Negev during the war to return to their territories, elaborated upon in detail by Morris (1993), were foiled by the IDF. This led to considerable bloodshed and casualties on both sides, particularly during the early 1950s. Second, a military administration was appointed over the remaining Bedouin. This entailed separation of many from their traditional territories and pastoral and agricultural resources and their relocation into a closed zone, a process that took several years. This 1,000 sq. km. enclosure (the *sayig*) was located east of Beer-Sheva and away from the borders (Weitz 1965; see Fig. 3.2). As will be seen in the next chapter, relocation into the *sayig* caused a considerable increase in population density there. This relocation process created a long-standing land dispute between the Bedouin and the state that has not been settled yet completely.

State attitude toward the Bedouin during the 1950s was influenced by several factors. The most significant of these were the military and international ones, the details of which were discussed by Milshtein (1985) and Lustick (1985). The Negev frontier was highly permeable during the early 1950s to Bedouin infiltrators who either collaborated with Arab armies in intelligence, sabotage, and terror or sought access to their previous territories (Morris 1993; see also Meir, Tsoar and Khawaldi 1992). Consequently, the state adopted a rigid attitude toward the Bedouin at large and particularly those whose traditional territories were located close to the new borders. This included additional expulsion or relocation of those who managed to return to the Negev and some others as well.

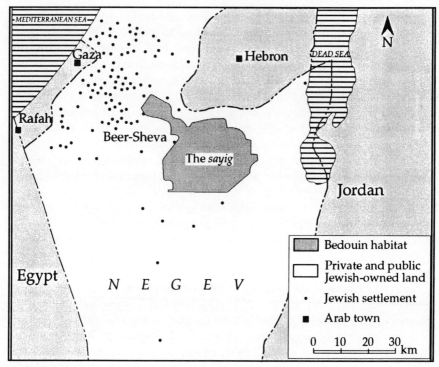

FIGURE 3.2   The Negev frontier in the 1950s (*Source:* Zivan 1990).

Second, settlement blocks were established near the borders during the 1950s to act as a buffer and to absorb the mass immigration of Jews from Europe and North Africa to Israel. Consequently, dozens of new Jewish agricultural settlements and development towns were established in the Negev, especially in its northern part (see Fig. 3.2). Many of these were located on land of absentee or relocated Bedouin (Artzieli 1978). Third, the development of the regional labor market and economy by the Israeli state was geared primarily towards absorbing the new Jewish immigrants. As many of the Bedouin became landless and devoid of sufficient economic resources (Marx 1974), these developments imposed a further constraint on their already meager subsistence level within the *sayig*.

These contexts may be framed within the more general one (see Chapter 2) of the control of Bedouin pastoral nomads and their relationships with central governments in the Middle East (see also Kazaz 1972; Bailey 1971; Chatty 1980). This particular context added a further element of tension to the intricate system of relationships between the Bedouin and the Jewish population in the Negev. During the 1950s, despite these problems which were condensed spatiotemporally into a small area within a short period, Bedouin welfare was not a top priority on the government agenda. The latter was preoccupied with more pressing problems and therefore, according to Weitz (1965), adopted an attitude of "no long-range policy" regarding the Bedouin, which remained in effect at least until the mid-1960s.

Yet, the problems of regional security, land ownership, local governance, and provision of social and economic services required heavy government involvement in Bedouin affairs to an extent hitherto unknown to them. Economically, until 1956 Bedouin were denied access to their traditional marketplace in Beer-Sheva (see Ben-David and Kressel 1995). Also, although some work-permits were granted to them by the military administration, their free integration into the labor market did not become possible until the late 1950s (Ben-David 1986). As their traditional pastoral and dry-farming economy within the *sayig* became highly constrained, many Bedouin intensified their involvement in smuggling goods and narcotics across the borders.

Administratively, in 1954 most of the Bedouin were awarded Israeli citizenship, and the idea was even broached (but soon abandoned) of exploring the possibility of converting them to Judaism (Geva 1994). However, some Bedouin tribes persisted in their violent resistance to Israeli sovereignty and in their attempts to maintain territorial and tribal coherence across borders. This was particularly the case with those groups in the Negev Highlands and Western Negev who still lived outside the *sayig*. Consequently, some were driven away into the Sinai and others into Jordan (Wallach 1985), while still others were relocated into the *sayig*. From then on—except for several dozens of families—the Negev Highlands remained virtually empty of Bedouin.

The circumstances of the encounter between the Bedouin and the Jewish settlers in the Negev in the 1950s had thus changed radically. Politically, the focus of relationships between the Bedouin and the Jewish population now shifted to the military administration and state bureaucracy (see also Horowitz and Lisack 1977). This reduced considerably the relative importance of existing direct neighboring contacts. Spatially, maintenance of these contacts was possible now only for a small number of the relocated Bedouin, due to severe movement restrictions imposed by the military administration and to the distance from their previous neighbors (see Fig. 3.2). Finally, from a demographic perspective, the Bedouin, previously a large majority, now became a small minority. By the end of that decade they constituted no more than 11 percent of the Negev population, compared to at least 95 percent in the previous decade.

The Jewish-Bedouin Encounter

The nature of the relationships between the Bedouin and the Jewish population—previously characterized by broad mutuality—now became largely unidirectional and considerably narrower in scope. Backed now heavily by state authorities and core institutions, the majority, i.e., settlers now had no need to resort to local aid from the Bedouin, particularly as the reduced Bedouin population was left with virtually little to offer. Given the major ecological and political change in the structure of their economy, they became almost totally dependent upon the state and its bureaucracy for their survival. Furthermore, the new types of Jewish settlements, such as semicommunal moshavim or development towns established during the 1950s, were largely irrelevant in terms of the social encounter, due to their different social organization and the immigrant composition of their population.

Kibbutzim were no longer the sole settlement types in the region, but remained virtually the only ones relevant for the Bedouin in terms of direct social encounter. However, only few kibbutzim were spatially available to them. Indeed, many of the dimensions of the previous encounter had disappeared. Bedouinization attempts were no longer relevant. Collecting intelligence was now the responsibility of state security authorities, as was provision of public services such as health and water supply. Due to employment regulations the Bedouin could no longer expect gainful employment in kibbutzim. In short, the range of benefits to the Bedouin from their encounter with Jewish settlers during the 1950 contracted considerably.

Informal discussions within kibbutzim (e.g., Shoshani 1954) revealed their awareness that the position of *mukhtar* would soon disappear. Moreover—in contrast to the previous decade—most of the activities of settlers in their relationships with the Bedouin were no longer institutionalized at the entire kibbutz community level. The more socialist-oriented kibbutzim were more inclined toward communally-institutionalized assistance to the Bedouin, and it so happened that these few bordered on the *sayig*. However, they did not participate in the early phase of the frontier encounter as they were mostly established after 1948. The focus of the new phase of encounter thus shifted down to initiatives of isolated individual members, or former field guards and *mukhtars*, whose status vis-à-vis the present state bureaucracy had now diminished considerably.

The initiatives taken by these individuals were all geared toward assisting the Bedouin in their attempts to survive the hard years of the military administration. Given the various administrative and military constraints imposed on the Bedouin, the ability of kibbutzim to provide direct economic aid to them was quite limited. They concentrated, therefore, on other kinds of local support, e.g., a small informal elementary school for Bedouin children established near one of the kibbutzim, or the effort of a governmental agricultural extension expert, a former *mukhtar*, who helped introduce new strains of wheat into Bedouin dry-farming economy, thus making it more dominant and profitable. Other individual settlers helped Bedouin families by buying goods for them in Beer-Sheva which was administratively largely inaccessible to the Bedouin in those years.

Judged in contextual terms, such support was sporadic and narrow compared with the 1940s. The kibbutzim were left with the possibility of giving moral support to the Bedouin. This indeed became a major activity, particularly lobbying for the Bedouin which became an important political resource for them. The most urgent issue during the early 1950s was how to foil government attempts to relocate Bedouin tribes, particularly those that had been cooperative and friendly during the 1940s. In a few cases such intervention attempts were successful, but in many others the kibbutzim were helpless in the face of the bureaucracy and military authorities. Another area of assistance was lobbying for or actually obtaining transport and work permits outside the *sayig* for individual Bedouin. In general, the more socialist-oriented kibbutzim were very active politically in trying to end the military administration (Amitai 1988), but this was not canceled until 1965.

Another important area of lobbying related to the land ownership dispute. As the next chapter shows in more detail, Bedouin concepts of formal land ownership began to develop only during the British Mandate, and most of them had no formal deeds. Consequently, in those years the state neither recognized their territorial rights nor attempted to solve this problem. Kibbutz lobbying in this regard emanated, presumably, from their embarrassment at taking possession of land of absentee or relocated Bedouin which had been transferred to them by the government. Therefore, they openly criticized the "no-policy" policy. Some of them became members of a public council during 1956–1961, established in an attempt to win the Bedouin formal land ownership. These lobbying attempts, however, achieved little success in the face of the rigid government attitude toward the Bedouin.

Some kibbutzim formulated local agreements with Bedouin neighbors concerning usage of local resources (see, for example Naor 1986). Together with the lobbying activities, these initiatives were aimed at preserving the friendly atmosphere and fostering lasting neighborly relationships with the Bedouin. The state, however, wanted to impose order upon the Bedouin, and perceived the activities of the kibbutzim as an obstacle. Consequently a conflict emerged between Jewish settlers and the military and state authorities. In some cases, kibbutz members were appointed government or military administration officials, and were caught in the midst of this conflict. The kibbutz settlers were thus torn between their ideological commitment to the Bedouin and their civil duty to support the state.

This dilemma, which had been very minor during the 1940s, now generated considerable tension between the Bedouin and the settlers. The relationships were further complicated by the security issue. As part of the policy of rural frontier settlement in Israel (see Efrat 1981), the quasi-military mission of securing the borders against infiltrators was assigned to the kibbutzim—in close cooperation with, and under the full supervision of the military authorities (Meitiv 1969). As indicated above, many of the infiltrators were Bedouin who had previously lived in the Negev. They were economically motivated by the desire to exploit their previous pastoral and dry-farming lands, or politically and militarily motivated by the desire to take revenge through sabotage and terror or serving the Egyptian and Jordanian intelligence agencies (Dayan 1976). Many also participated in smuggling goods and narcotics from Egypt to Jordan, crossing the Negev and trespassing on Jewish settlements, especially those close to the borders or located in the more remote areas of the Negev Highlands. Altogether, these hostilities imposed a heavy security burden upon Jewish settlements. But beyond that, they further complicated their relationships with their neighboring Bedouin, many of whom provided refuge for infiltrators or cooperated with their kin across the borders.

These ties were further complicated by the issue of Bedouin land ownership and usage of pastoral resources. The Bedouin attempted repeatedly to graze their livestock on their traditional lands, some of which had now been transferred into the possession of Jewish settlements. What seemed natural and right to them, under their traditional law and custom, was regarded as trespassing under Israeli law by the settlements. It took a whole decade for the Bedouin to adapt to the new reality, but in the meantime it became a source of friction and tension with the settlers, causing numerous local clashes and even casualties on both sides. Consequently, kibbutzim were often heavily and bitterly criticized by the Bedouin. Those directly involved in these affairs made every attempt to pacify the Bedouin either through compensation for casualties or leasing stubble fields to them for grazing purposes and allowing them to use water from local irrigation pipelines (Gavri 1985).

The military and security tension with the Bedouin reached its peak in 1959, when an Israeli army officer was murdered by Bedouin near the Egyptian border. Consequently, severe punitive measures were taken against Bedouin still living in this area, including forceful expulsion to

Sinai or relocation into the *sayig*. After that, no major incidents of a military or security nature were recorded. Following these measures, and particularly after the Six-Day War of 1967, the frontier character of the Negev virtually ceased to exist and a new phase of Bedouin development began. Early signs of this phase emerged by the mid-1950s when the state began to realize the need to reconsider its approach to the Bedouin. The reconsideration process was manifested, as indicated above, in the awarding of citizenship to the Bedouin (a process still not entirely completed), and easing of the restrictions on movement and employment. It continued with the lifting of the military administration in 1965. Its culmination was the plan—which was initiated in the early 1960s, began to be implemented only in 1966, and is still uncompleted—to relocate the Bedouin in towns and thus to further integrate them into the civilian and economic systems.

Conclusions

The nature of the frontier encounter between the Bedouin and Jewish population changed considerably between the 1940s and 1950s. From a voluntary and relatively peaceful area, the frontier was transformed into an alienated, coercive, and at times even violent one. The politicization of space in the Negev by core institutions and state policy seems to have signified the turning point. Evidence gathered by Meir and Zivan (forthcoming) from other frontiers, such as the United States and Australia, suggests the same idea of a double-phase process of frontier encounter and its transformation due to politicization of space by the settlers' core institutions (see, e.g., Spicer 1961; Wishart 1976; Cronan 1983; Clement 1987; Golley 1993). In the Negev the relationships between each group in the frontier and its core during the 1940s was relatively weak. During the 1950s, however, the power of the Jewish core—now transformed into a state apparatus—increased considerably while that of the Bedouin diminished drastically. Jewish settlers were now backed by a strong but centralist core, which supported them but rendered them highly dependent. However, an even heavier dependency constraint was imposed on the Bedouin. Thus, by assuming the centralist role, this core heavily constrained the ability of both the Bedouin and the Jewish local population to maintain their previous links and to shape their future relationships.

This chapter described the encounter between the indigenous pastoral nomadic Negev Bedouin and the Jewish population as agents of change. It also exposed the political context within which major processes of change within Bedouin society took place in later years. For the Bedouin, this was the first intensive encounter with Western culture, perhaps unparalleled in its nature and intensity elsewhere in the Middle East. As far as the Bedouin are concerned, the ensuing processes of change took place under previously unknown circumstances of external political pressure and administrative intervention within a constrained spatiotemporal framework. The intensity of the change thus derives not only from the cultural gap but also from the transformation of Bedouin society from an Arab majority into an Arab ethnic minority within the State of Israel and the transformation of the previously pastoral nomadic semiarid Negev environment into a settled space.

Under such conditions, change was likely to be quite intensive, as the traditional alternative institutions which the Bedouin could draw from their cultural reservoir had to compete with external institutions. The latter are shaped by the positive and negative consequences of the encounter with the external modern Jewish population. It is within these contexts and circumstances that the processes of sociospatial change within the Bedouin society, outlined conceptually in the previous chapter with regard to pastoral nomadic peoples in general, will be analyzed in the following chapters.

4

Territorialization

The Jewish population of the Negev and the State of Israel have been highly significant agents of change for Bedouin society since the 1940s and the 1950s. In some crucial respects, however—primarily territorialization and sedentarization—change, in fact, began earlier. As suggested in Chapter 2, territorialization of a pastoral nomadic society is an outcome of sedentarization. However, these spatial processes are closely interrelated and the former may intensify as the latter progresses. Territorialization of the pastoral nomadic society is considered here as the most fundamental structural subprocess resulting from—but simultaneously reflected in—the major process of individualization. The significance of adopting territorial behavior—which is a fundamental spatial behavior element—is that it is capable of altering social relationships within the sedentarizing pastoral nomadic society. The integration of this society, through this process, within the settled rural and urban society, is facilitated to the point where the previous pastoral nomadic cultural and social identity diminishes and even disappears. This generates other processes of social and spatial change.

This chapter examines the evolution and maturation of territoriality within the pastoral nomadic Bedouin society. The discussion of this issue is presented jointly with examination of the process of sedentarization. It begins with the early shift of this society toward territoriality during its transition to sedentary agriculture in the nineteenth and early twentieth centuries—a process that is referred to in this discussion as the rural phase of territoriality. The discussion is based on information drawn and interpreted in terms of territoriality (Meir 1995) from sources which have dealt with sedentarization. Later phases of the process—which emerged during the transformation of the Negev frontier into a settled space—took place partly under the British Mandate but particularly in the State of Israel. The nature of sedentarization has changed considerably, developing a semiurban character, and territorialization has therefore assumed additional meanings and dimensions.

Emergence of Territoriality—The Rural Phase

The Ottoman and British Mandate Periods

This phase of the process may be considered as originating within the local cultural reservoir of institutionalized alternatives. Yet, there were also external influences to which the Bedouin adapted voluntarily. Under the Ottoman Empire and the British Mandate, these influences were primarily geopolitical and economic in nature. However, there was also a remarkable social dimension to this process. At later periods—mainly under the state of Israel—these influences, particularly the economic one, yielded to the dominant external coercive state political influence.

Geopolitical and Economic Dimensions

Until about the mid-nineteenth century the Negev Bedouin could be regarded primarily as pastoral nomads who were, socially and culturally, an integral part of Middle Eastern Bedouin society. Their origins can indeed be traced to the Arabian Peninsula, from which they migrated to Palestine over the centuries, directly or through the Sinai Peninsula (Marx 1974; Bailey 1980). It is assumed, therefore, that they were practicing spatial strategies consistent with those of pastoral nomadic Bedouin groups elsewhere in the region (see Chapter 2). That is, they were characterized by a rather weak tendency toward territoriality. The embryonic stages of their shift toward sedentarism presumably began during the first half of the nineteenth century at the earliest. However—due primarily to international geopolitical processes—from then on they gradually formed a distinct group with different processes of development and change.

Archaeological evidence (Rosen 1987; Ben-David and Orion 1990; Finkelstein and Perevolotsky 1990) suggests that, in previous centuries certain elements of primitive agriculture were already practiced by the nomadic pastoralists of the Negev. Yet, farming land did not provide a fixed or solid basis for Bedouin subsistence. It had no market value and competition for its possession was almost nonexistent. In fact, Barslevski (1946), Kressel et al. (1991) and Bailey (1980) indicate that it was a free commodity to the extent that land gifts were quite common. Livestock was the dominant mode of production, and accordingly, the Bedouin assigned value only to grazing and water resources within their area of habitat, with free access based on the principles described above. As far as territoriality is concerned, they were informally obliged only to their clan territory, and even this obligation emerged rather late. During their pastoral nomadic phase, the Bedouin did not regard this territory as an area common to all member tribes. Transition toward territoriality began, thus, only with the transformation of Bedouin pastoral nomadic subsistence to a seminomadic system of more balanced pastoral production and farming, and particularly with the growth of the latter. This gradual process commenced in the first half of the nineteenth century and culminated in the first half of the twentieth century. In the 1930s the Negev—particularly its northern parts—was described by Al-Aref (1937a; 1937b) as primarily an agricultural district.

The Bedouin were capable of initiating this shift toward greater emphasis on farming because it was an institutionalized alternative in their cultural reservoir, although practiced previously only to a minor degree. This, as Ben-David (1989) suggests, caused at least some of the Bedouin to adopt an active approach, probably because of their realization of the instability in the Ottoman Empire in general and Palestine in particular (Bailey 1980). This instability begun with the short term conquest of Palestine by Napoleon in 1799 and continued with the Egyptian conquest by Ibrahim Pesha (1832–1840), with restoration of the Ottoman rule between and after these periods.

The shift toward greater emphasis on the agricultural mode of production began, however, even prior to these geopolitical events. It is quite possible that consecutive droughts at the end of the eighteenth and early nineteenth centuries also contributed to this process (Grossman 1994b). This combination of political and ecological processes generated a situation in which, already in the first half of the century, the Bedouin pastoral nomads began to perceive land as a multi-purpose resource. Its growing value for more intensive and profitable agriculture gradually emerged.

The early process of territorialization of Bedouin society began at about this stage. The case of the Azazme Bedouin of the Negev Highlands (see Figure 4.1) illustrates its development and provides a useful basis for understanding the evolution of the notion of territoriality among Negev Bedouin in general. The discussion of the early process is based on research by Bar-Zvi and Ben-David (1978) and Ben-David and Orion (1990), who studied the transformation of this group from a pastoral nomadic to a seminomadic pastoral-agricultural mode of production during the nineteenth century. These studies provide useful information that is interpreted here in terms of the shift toward territoriality.

The Azazme migrated to the Negev from Sinai early in the nineteenth century. They were attracted to the region by the same reason that caused pastoral nomads elsewhere to migrate to the frontier of the settled regions—the growing political instability and the resulting subsistence opportunities and prospects. Although relatively isolated in the Negev Highlands, they soon developed some sense of territoriality. This was

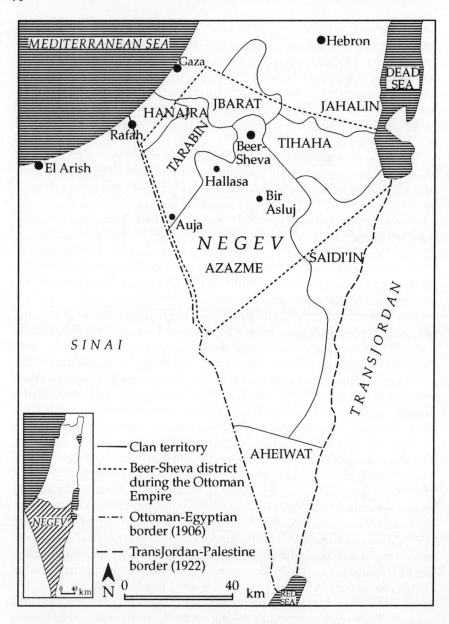

FIGURE 4.1 Clan, administrative, and international borders in the Negev in the early twentieth century (*Source:* Adapted from Bar-Zvi and Ben-David 1978).

triggered perhaps through contacts with Bedouin of the northern Negev who, in turn, may have grown familiar with territoriality concepts through contacts with their neighboring settled areas. The notion of *dira* (habitat) thus began to develop from the flexible traditional type to greater rigidity. For the Azazme, the *dira* included now its pastoral and farming lands, and became an area that belonged exclusively to a household unit. The inclusion of cultivated areas, by necessity, made the *dira* a spatially-fixed entity. Moreover, for the first time the household dira began to be delineated by boundaries. It could no longer be described in terms of a moving territory.

The new meaning of the *dira* emerged in four stages. The first stage was the search by an Azazme household for a grazing area in the Negev Highlands near a water source. The possession of these resources—at times acquired by force—was then declared publicly by this household. The spatial extent of the *dira* was determined by daily summer grazing distances from the water source. At that stage, water and pasture were still tribally-communal with free general access. This pattern was consistent with traditional pastoral nomadic concepts of resource-sharing and a weak tendency toward territoriality. However, some distinction in form of ownership begun to emerge. Wells that supplied water permanently became the possession of the tribe and took its name. Seasonal wells became family-owned and were named after it.

The pastoral *dira* then became a spatial basis for local expansion and development, which constituted the second stage. Land suitable for dry-farming was divided among expanded families along local morphological features, primarily local water divides. The household *dira* thus emerged in parallel to others up along the drainage basin and included the valley and its surrounding hills. A combination of pastoral and farming rationalities guided this division. The objective was to exploit water potential all over the local drainage basin in order to overcome the problem of patchy and random precipitation, typical of such arid environments. This method also ensured simultaneously hill-slope grazing and runoff water supply for down-hill and valley farming lands. Possession of farming land—which became analogous to private though informal ownership—emerged thus as a means of distinguishing the *dira* from the communal tribal territory. Each *dira* was named after its social unit, whether a household, a *hamula* (a group of agnatic families), or *rubah* (a group of *hamulas*). One of the early practices, which shaped its nature as a nontribal territory, was the immediate privatization of a newly-developed water source (whether a well or cistern) by the household, alongside tribal-owned water sources.

A more formal parcellation of cultivable land was the third stage. Dry-farming in this particular area was quite risky from an ecological perspective. On the basis of present data and on the assumption that there has been no significant climatic change since the early nineteenth century (Tsoar 1995), the annual amount of precipitation in the Negev Highlands must have been below 100mm compared to above 200mm in the northern Negev. Despite the risks involved, the idea of utilizing land for dry-farming rather than for predominantly pastoral uses began to gradually penetrate the consciousness of the Azazme Bedouin. This caused an increase in demand and competition for this resource. Consequently, further coordination between *hamula* or *rubah* elders and heads was now required for the process of land division, associated with more formal means of delineation and demarcation of flat land parceled plots. One of the early forms of distinguishing plots was use of stone piles *(r'joum)*, and others were adopted later. The Bedouin began thus to adopt forms of spatial classification and communication of land tenure.

The formation of the *dira* in its new meaning reached its final stage with the gradual intensification of the use of facilities catering for more sedentary-oriented dry-farming. These facilities *(mantara, zaliba, mutmara,* etc.)—already previously part of the reservoir of technological alternatives—were needed for storing crops and fodder, dry dairy products, and household chattels. However, perhaps one of the most significant indications of the changing nature of the *dira* was the emergence of "formal" cemeteries *(makbara)* in fixed locations, which in time became foci of pilgrimage. The significance of this phenomenon lay in the assignment of spiritual and ritual meanings and emotional valuation to sacred places and objects within the *dira*.

It will be recalled from our conceptual discussion in Chapter 2 that Sack (1986) suggested reasons for a society becoming territorial. Specifically, the predefined territory is needed as a container or mold for the spatial properties of events; it is a spatial object to which other attributes are assigned and which assumes place-clearing and maintaining functions for things and objects to exist. The main implication of the processes described for the Azazme Bedouin is that as it evolved into a spatially-fixed and delineated territory, the *dira* also gradually took on these properties.

In short, in the wake of the emergence of the early agricultural sedentarization, the territoriality of the Azazme Bedouin evolved dialectically in the first half of the nineteenth century from within the group, without significant external intervention. Elsewhere in the Negev similar processes took place presumably for the same reasons. The recurring intertribal and interclan wars and hostilities throughout the nineteenth century (Bailey 1980) were rooted, *inter alia*, in these processes—particularly the increasing value of land for dry-farming. These wars, especially during the first half of the century, were another indication of the Bedouin response to the temporary political instability throughout the Ottoman Empire.

However, the political situation changed during the second half of that century. In light of the growing involvement of European powers in the Suez Canal zone, the Ottoman government sought to tighten its control over the Negev and to stabilize it politically. Pacifying its Bedouin population became therefore an urgent objective. One of the means of achieving this objective was the promulgation in 1858 of the Ottoman Land Law. Under this law—which related to areas beyond Palestine as well— all Bedouin lands in the Negev were defined as *mawat* (dead land), i.e., irrespective of their actual use by the Bedouin, they were considered unused and therefore state property. This was a significant decision for the Bedouin, who feared the possible loss of their grazing territories. Indeed, as Ashkenazi (1957) has suggested, desire for land has since become a prevailing Bedouin state of mind. Its significance derives also from the fact that for the first time an external factor was intervening in Bedouin land affairs. Bedouin tribes in the Negev—as well as throughout the Ottoman Empire—perceived the Land Law as their last opportunity to strike roots permanently. Hence they attempted to seize as much land and as soon as possible. This triggered wars not only among Bedouin tribes but also between the Bedouin and rural frontier settlements (Baer 1970). However, the promulgation of the Land Law also accelerated stronger territorial reactions among the Bedouin at both the macro and the meso levels. Hence, 1858 marks the onset of accelerated territorialization of Negev Bedouin society.

At the macro level, it was probably about then that the Bedouin began to realize the need to formalize their tribal or clan territories. In fact, the term tribal or confederation territory has often been used with reference to nineteenth century Negev Bedouin (e.g. Marx 1973; Marx 1974; Marx 1978; and Bailey 1980). However, the exact boundaries of these past territories were not specified in these studies nor the method of their determination or formalization. Yet, it now became necessary to establish means of classification and communication of tribal land possession, those criteria that, according to Sack (1986), would evolve first in a territorialization process.

This, however, does not imply that the Negev Bedouin were unacquainted with the notion of a formalized tribal or clan-confederate territorial boundary. In fact, there is evidence that an initiative was adopted in this direction by the neighboring Bedouin in the Sinai in the 19th century. A detailed discussion of this process there, pertaining to the Ahaywat of central Sinai, is provided by Stewart (1986). As indicated in Chapter 2, Stewart's assumption is that—in bringing the notion of formal tribal boundaries into practice—the Ahaywat were influenced by the growing involvement of the Egyptian and Ottoman governments in this area in the second half of the century. He suggests, however, that they apparently became familiar with this notion even before its later initiation into the region through the formal demarcation in 1906 of the Ottoman-Egyptian international boundary (see Figure 4.1).

In describing this process, Stewart provides a detailed account of a document—presumably dated around the mid-19th century—regarding an agreement between the Ahaywat and the Tiyaha. He also draws maps including specific place names, showing the exact agreed boundaries of the Ahaywat territory. Within this territory, resource utilization was similar to that described previously for pastoral nomadic Bedouin elsewhere in the region: pasture, water, and jobs were claimed by all Ahaywat tribesmen with little differentiation. Through the power of the agreed, defined, and clearly demarcated boundary, however, these resources of the Ahaywat were denied to the Tiyaha.

The very process suggests that the Ahaywat territorial boundary case was a major event within Bedouin circles. Consequently, the idea of macroscale tribal territorial boundary must have become known to the neighboring Bedouin in the Negev. Tribal territories began to take shape there too, and seizure of grazing resources—customary in the past—was no longer possible. This process culminated in the fixation of tribal territories by the Ottoman government in 1890 and their formalization in a tribal territory map in 1906 (see Figure 4.1).

The significance of this process is that once territoriality was adopted at the macro tribal level, it almost inevitably began to infiltrate lower levels of the Bedouin sociopolitical organization. The process thus developed internally within Bedouin society both from below and above without external intervention. Indeed, after 1858, the embryonic processes described earlier at the mesolevel—that is within the tribe—began to accelerate among the Azazme as well as other tribes in the Negev. Kressel et al. (1991) provide a detailed account of changes in land use in the region since the mid-19th century. Information from their study relevant for growing territoriality among the Bedouin is again extracted and interpreted here accordingly.

Basically, the processes were similar to those described above for the embryonic stage: tribal grazing lands were transformed into arable land by undergoing first a process of parcellation into small family units, which were then privatized. The intensification of this emerging land use pattern is, however, explained by factors which are associated, at various degrees, with the growing political stability and better economic prospects in the Negev. Firstly, following the relative stabilization of intertribal political relationships, an atmosphere of greater political and economic security developed among the Bedouin. This atmosphere encouraged investments in agriculture. Secondly, the same process of geopolitical stabilization also triggered the beginning of a prolonged process of deterioration in the political status, importance, and hence also size of the tribe. Consequently, its responsibility and authority in guaranteeing equal and exclusive grazing rights to all its members also begun to diminish. Thirdly, there was a growing demand for Middle Eastern barley in the European beer industry. Concurrently, export in commercial quantities became possible through the establishment of steam boat lines during the 1870s. Merchants in Palestine responded to this demand, triggering the development of these crops, particularly in the northern Negev. Finally, the emerging agricultural nature of the region—associated with political stabilization—began to attract landless fellaheen (peasants) from other areas in Palestine and elsewhere, particularly the Nile Valley. A process of migration of fellaheen into southern Palestine and the northern Negev begun in ever increasing numbers (see also Grossman 1994b).

These processes suggest that demand for and competition over farming land in the Negev intensified considerably. This previously free commodity began to be valued in market terms by a growing number of Bedouin. Furthermore, it is significant from a territoriality perspective that land in the semiarid and arid zone began to assume formal and legal status within internal Bedouin circles. This is reflected in the growing role of tribal judges in arbitration in land ownership disputes. Consequently, the *dira* further forfeited its traditional significance and begun to assume a stronger meaning of more fully privatized land and resources. The significance of these processes is that they implied the beginning of an ideological change among individual Bedouin with regard to territory and territoriality.

This change in the nature of the *dira*, as Kressel et al. (1991) suggest, further affected the already diminishing status of the tribe. Gradually becoming property owners, tribesmen began to challenge the traditional notion that cultivated land like grazing land should be treated as though it was still common tribal territory. Consequently, the status of the tribe—previously linked to its size in population and territory—was weakened. Privatization of land was thus becoming inimical to the concept of tribalism and political unity.

The latter two reasons suggested by Kressel et al. (1991) for the emerging status of the land were relevant particularly for those tribes whose habitat was in the northern Negev, on the edge of the settled frontier. As indicated earlier, ecological conditions there—in terms of precipitation and soils—were superior, and agricultural resources were denser and more predictable than in the central and southern Negev. Therefore, competition for these resources grew fiercer not only among the Bedouin themselves, but also on the part of those fellaheen who began to gravitate into the region. Although there are indications that some fellaheen had lived among the Bedouin previously, the massive arrival of these migrants began in the late 18th century, and the major waves occurred primarily from the late 19th century on (Grossman 1994a; Grossman 1994b).

These fellaheen were annexed to Bedouin economy as client tenants on Bedouin lands. The annexation of this social element triggered the emergence of an ethnically-based division of labor within Bedouin society: the Bedouin themselves continued to engage in livestock production, while their plots were leased to and cultivated by the fellahi tenants as sharecroppers. Toward the end of the 19th century, several consequences ensued as this sociospatial process accelerated. The first of these was the widening of the economic gap between families who adopted such division of labor and the majority who did not. Consequently, social stratification within tribes, which had previously been determined through agnatic relationships, now began to assume an embryonic landed capitalistic nature. Secondly, the fellahi population generated an increased population pressure on land. This further enhanced the drive toward privatization of cultivable plots and land valuation in market terms. Toward the end of the century land gradually became a market commodity far more than in their pastoral nomadic phase. Thirdly, an internal semilegal system of quasi-official procedures for land inheritance was adopted, based on those practiced in the neighboring sedentary villages. These indications of increasing territoriality among the Bedouin developed under conditions of increasing competition for relatively dense and predictable resources. Although these circumstances pertained particularly to the northern Negev, Bedouin elsewhere in the region were reacting similarly.

Yet, there was another important condition which affected the trend toward greater territoriality. Until about the turn of the century, these trends originated dialectically within the Bedouin population. From about that time, the direct and indirect activities of the various governments had a growing impact on Bedouin affairs, which later even intensified. This enhanced the attraction of the Bedouin to the land and the intensification of the territorialization process. The impact of the formalization of tribal territories in 1890 and the 1906 tribal map have already been discussed. In addition—seeking to increase its hold over the Negev desert—the Ottoman government established the town of Beer-Sheva in 1903 as an administrative center for the Negev (see Figure 4.1). The strategic objective was to cope with the growing interest of European powers in the Levant, particularly British interests in Egypt and the Suez Canal.

In terms of direct settlement Beer-Sheva proper was not attractive to the Bedouin. Indeed, very few of them—mainly sheikhs—moved to this town. However, Beer-Sheva naturally evolved as a market town for the

Bedouin, especially for surplus agricultural yields which began to accumulate in commercial quantities. This opened up an important outlet for a growing external demand for Negev agricultural products (Ben-David and Kressel 1995). The evolving functional role of Beer-Sheva affected the Bedouin in several ways. First, the flow of capital gradually but intensively introduced monetarization into their economy. Second, the Bedouin were becoming an integral part of the local, regional—and to some extent even the international—market economy. Third, it generated prosperity for their agricultural and to some extent also their livestock economy. Finally, these economic impacts contributed significantly to an increase in the standard of living of many Bedouin, and consumption of many previously unfamiliar goods became possible. The establishment of Beer-Sheva is therefore justly regarded by Ben-David (1989) as a milestone in the further shift of the Bedouin toward sedentarization.

However, from the perspective of the present discussion, the indirect impact of Beer-Sheva on the already growing territoriality trend was even more significant. Land transactions became a common phenomenon, first among Bedouin who were engaged in farming. Some of them contracted debts to merchants in towns and were forced to pay them off with parcels of land. This phenomenon legitimized land transactions by many other Bedouin who were not necessarily engaged in farming but were anxious to keep pace with the rising regional standard of living. Thus, the outcomes of the spatio-economic change reflected in the evolution of Beer-Sheva as a regional center indicate that the Bedouin attitude to land changed further and adopted a new dimension.

Further capital inflow into the Negev was encouraged by additional labor opportunities, which promoted Bedouin economic growth. A regional labor market evolved during the 1900s and 1910s, launched through Ottoman government-initiated projects such as road and railway construction. During World War I various other earning opportunities—such as harnessing camel "fleets" as transportation and supply means for British troops—became available. At the macropolitical level, the British and French conquest of the Levant brought the entire region into the sphere of influence of the Western economy. The economy of the entire region thus gradually opened up, particularly during the British Mandate over Palestine (1922–1947). This entailed a further inflow of capital to the Negev Bedouin (Ashkenazi 1957).

Although the Bedouin in general benefited from these processes, their gradual integration into the capitalistic economy had repercussions in terms of pressure on their farming and grazing lands. Old as well as new sources of pressure on land now participated in the process. On the one hand, migration of fellaheen into the northern Negev continued. On the other hand, merchants and other capitalists from Beer-Sheva, Gaza, and neighboring towns increasingly purchased or otherwise gained control of Bedouin land. As indicated in the previous chapter, however, in addition, the Jewish Zionist movement began demonstrating a growing interest in purchasing land in the Negev. These attempts—which had begun at the turn of the nineteenth century—accelerated during the 1930s and 1940s.

The growing pressure on Bedouin land had three interrelated results: intensification of agriculture at the expense of pastoral activities, further parcellation and privatization of tribal lands into household ownership, and further legalization of land issues. Dry-farming activities further intensified and were estimated to cover about 500 square km (=500,000 dunams=50,000 ha.) by the end of the British Mandate period (Porat and Shavit 1981). This growth may be attributed to two processes. First, the Bedouin were beginning to realize the opportunities associated with agriculture. Therefore—rather than assigning cultivation to their tenant fellaheen—a growing number became directly involved in dry-farming themselves. A side benefit was of course that farming became now an important source of supplementary fodder, enabling the sustenance—albeit at a smaller scale—of pastoral activities under conditions of internal land-use competition. Second, the amount of investment capital flowing into Bedouin hands increased significantly. This was the outcome of their growing integration into the regional labor market through British Mandate government-initiated public projects, such as erection of army camps or railway and road works. The increased capital inflow enabled them to purchase new types of seedlings, tools and machinery, stimulated gradual technological progress of dry-farming agriculture, and improved its economic prospects.

These activities were integrated into the previous pastoral nomadic economy to such an extent that the notion of a locality as a permanent return base became a state of mind among the Bedouin (Ben-David 1989). This required consolidation of existing facilities and adoption of new ones. In addition to the growth in private water sources (wells or cisterns), storage facilities, and cemeteries, as described above, permanent domiciles begun to appear in the 1930s (Bar-Zvi and Ben-David 1978). In particular, the *baika* (a thatch)—previously performing a storage function—was gradually transformed into a residence. The *baika* was significant in the emerging sedentary state of mind due to its fixed nature. Yet, it emerged as most important to the evolvement of the *dira* into a fixed immutable and permanent household spatial entity, and was hence crucial to Bedouin society in its becoming territorial. Thus, the territorial encapsulation that had begun in the late 19th century now intensified even further.

In order to further shape-up the household domestic unit as a spatial-territorial container for its social and economic properties, the trend toward parcellation and privatization of tribal lands increased. During the British Mandate period this trend penetrated further into the desert expanses. Pressure toward land parcellation and privatization came now from another source, in addition to the real estate market. Kressel et al. (1991) note that the government sought to dissolve the *musha* (communally collective land ownership) system that prevailed in villages throughout Palestine and therefore encouraged land privatization. This system did not exist among the Bedouin as such (Baer 1970), yet the government also encouraged further privatization of their version of tribal collective grazing land ownership. Consequently, previously-adopted patterns of privatization, that is privatization of plot possession on hill slopes, were intensified. However, while the status of existing water wells and grazing lands remained open and free tribal resources, old and new cisterns collecting run-off water were privatized. The justification for private ownership of these and other water installations (such as water reservoirs, albeit few and small) was the considerable amount of labor invested in building and maintaining them. This tendency was followed by the gradual abolishment of the traditional practice of land gifts. These major changes from the previous patterns are considered by Kressel et al. (1991) to be a milestone in terms of attitude toward land tenure issues and a sharp socioeconomic turnabout within Bedouin society.

The third effect of the growing pressure upon Bedouin land was accelerated formalization and legalization of its status. This trend had previously been internal to Bedouin society. The emergence of the regional real estate market in an as-yet unstable tenure pattern generated a growing number of land tenure conflicts (Al-Aref 1937a). The British Mandate government considered the internal system of conflict resolution to be no longer sufficient and sought therefore to regulate land transactions. These goals were facilitated through the establishment of a land court in Beer Sheva in 1921 (Levi 1969). Following this administrative act, land holding and selling became increasingly formalized through written land sale contracts (Ashkenazi 1957). This process required the adoption of more innovative territorial demarcation methods, the previous one (the *r'jhum*) having proved inadequate. For example, Al-Aref (1937a) mentioned the planting of squills *(el basul)* in the presence of two witnesses as one of the principal methods of demarcating plot boundaries. Kressel et al. (1991) describe various kinds of land sale agreements, land mortgaging, and land tenancy. The significance of these agreements is that they contain information not only on various objects within plots (e.g., cisterns, caves, trees, etc.), but on exact plot boundaries as well.

In the context of the present discussion, this may be considered proclaimed territorial information which reflects clearly an evolving territorial ideology and tendency of the Bedouin at the micro-level. This is so because a clearer distinction now became possible between two concepts of land tenure: tribal communal *possession* of grazing and water resources, and household private *ownership* of cultivated land and self-developed water resources and other facilities. As this distinction grew, so did the erosion of the traditional concept of *dira* into its new modern version. Ben-David and Orion (1990) indicate the increase of private household farms in the 1930s and 1940s. Each of these was an integrated household *dira*, containing both grazing and dry-farming cultivated lands and privately developed cisterns, storage facilities, and primitive domiciles. Some wealthy sheikhs even built estates equipped with designed homes, large barns, flour mills, mechanically-pumped water wells, and even irrigated agriculture. The tendency to own private cultivated plots adjacent to the household residence also made it difficult to maintain the traditional large and densely inhabited camps. These processes thus had their effect not only upon the traditional *dira* but also—as suggested by Ashkenazi (1957)—upon the dissolution of the traditional pastoral camp.

In summary, embryonic territoriality in the early nineteenth century emerged dialectically from within Bedouin society. However, its growth since the mid-nineteenth century is underlined by two major interrelated structural processes: penetration of governmental administration and of capitalistic economy into Bedouin life. These were manifested—both spatially and functionally—in three effects: the establishment of Beer Sheva as an administrative center and later the establishment of its land court; the establishment of several more government centers in Bir-Asluj, Hallasa, and Auja (see Fig. 4.1); and the emerging, still smallscale, process of externalization and proletarization of Bedouin economy in terms of real estate and labor markets. These processes had strong effects upon the territorialization of Bedouin society down from the tribal to the household or domestic level.

The Sociopolitical Dimension

Most of the discussion so far has focused on the spatial process of territorialization through land privatization and plot demarcation. Little has been said about its internal political and social consequences. Politically, one of the most important consequences was the impact upon the status of the tribe as a sociopolitical entity, and the eventual collapse of traditional tribal forms of political authority. It was indicated earlier that control of pastoral resources—which previously was possible on an exclusive tribal basis—began gradually to be expropriated from the tribe and transferred down to the household domestic level. Although embryonic indications of this process emerged during the Ottoman period, it accelerated during the British Mandate. Ashkenazi (1957) indicated the disappearance by then of higher-tier levels of this authority (the clan, *qabila*, and the tribe, *ashira*) whose roles were transferred to the extended family *(hamula)* and the family *(ailah)*. This assertion is shared by Kressel et al. (1991). Marx, however, maintains that for the purpose of maintaining kinship ties, affiliation, and traditional economy, the Bedouin tribe in the Middle East in general—and in the Negev in particular—still remains a large scale operation (Marx 1978). Yet, as shown above, the economic function was taken over by the domestic group. Fabietti (1986a; 1986b; 1991) indicates that, among the Saudi Arabian Bedouin, ties between members of this 'social body' had indeed been consolidated—but for the purpose of controlling its territorial resources rather than for conserving tribal identity, solidarity and affiliation. Hence, in Fabietti's terms the domestic group remains the principle unit for the Bedouin community's material and ideological reproduction.

We may now look upon the issue from a social perspective. Within the classless and relatively socially-homogeneous pastoral nomadic Bedouin society, this process actually became one of class-structuration and social differentiation. Rather than communal tribal resources, growing importance begun to be assigned by individual domestic units to their own, private, spatial and nonspatial resources. Furthermore—rather than to their large tribal sociopolitical organization, which previously determined their rights in and access to communal resources—Bedouin identity and social relationships began to relate more to their private territory and to whatever it contained. The significance of these processes is that the Bedouin began to cross the dividing line from a society in which territory was socially and politically defined through tribal affiliation into one in which social relations are defined by private territorial property and resources within it.

These processes developed internally among the previously pastoral nomadic Bedouin. Yet, there were already external factors involved during the 19th century, with the accelerated migration of fellaheen into the Negev. The fellaheen adopted certain traditional Bedouin economic and social traits and thus underwent a process of partial Bedouinization. However, the differences in the freedom of choice of survival strategy between the Bedouin and the fellaheen remained and explain the emergence of social differentiation between these groups. Grossman (1994b) suggests, therefore, that the penetration of fellaheen into the Bedouin milieu, and the emergence of these differences is one of the causes for the emergence of nonegalitarianism within Bedouin society.

In order to distinguish between the Bedouin and the fellahi survival strategies, Grossman employs the term "minimum discharge." Accordingly, the pastoral nomadic Bedouin adopted a strategy of "minimum discharge," namely, disregarding benefits of years of abundance to ensure survival even in times of shortage. At least part of this strategy could be achieved through spatial flexibility based upon grazing. This provided some kind of "insurance" against total failure at times of drought or political unrest and was the main factor in the survival of pastoral nomadism at the desert frontier (see also Sandford 1983; Scoones 1994). Such a strategy was not available to the same degree to the fellaheen in general and those living among the Bedouin in particular. This choice—which was ecologically and hence economically constrained—is responsible for the social inferiority of the fellaheen within Bedouin society because sedentary farming was more vulnerable than pastoral nomadic livestock production to the afflictions of drought, economic crisis, or political unrest. It generated, therefore, a larger economic gap between good and bad years among the fellahi peasants than it did among the pastoral nomadic Bedouin.

The pattern of social stratification that emerged has been the preferred one from the perspective of the strategy of pastoral nomadism. In this sense this process is Bedouincentric. However, as shown above, many pastoral nomadic Bedouin in time became involved in agriculture. The very penetration of the fellaheen into Bedouin society also generated the counter process of fellaheenization of the pastoral nomadic Bedouin themselves, who became socially differentiated according to their degree of departure from pastoral nomadism. In this process, further social differentiation and stratification evolved because a fellahicentric element had now been introduced into the social system. Consequently, a sociocultural and spatial continuum evolved along with a dualistic sense of social class (Havakuk 1986; Meir and Ben-David 1989). Those Bedouin who are closer to the pastoral nomadic edge claim social superiority by virtue of their adherence to a pure nomadic culture, while those closer to the sedentary edge regard themselves as socially superior to the more nomadic Bedouin by virtue of their technological and economic progress. However—despite Bedouin fellaheenization—this distinction cannot conceal the fact that social stratification is now rooted in the major historical dimension, which draws a distinction between "real" Bedouin and the fellahi Bedouin (see also Boneh 1983). Nevertheless, this social distinction suggests that the dual sense of class draws now ethnocentrically from both edges of the nomadism-sedentarism continuum (see also Grossman 1992; Johnson 1969).

Beyond the internal political significance of this social process, it is also significant from the perspective of territoriality. As time went on, the fellaheen began to organize themselves in co-liable groups based primarily but not exclusively on lineage relationships. By so doing they adopted the sociopolitical organizational pattern of their host Bedouin society.

However—despite this social initiative—their annexee status remained unchanged, at least in the eyes of the real Bedouin. As such, social separation between the Bedouin and the fellaheen has been almost total. This is manifested by several crucial issues. For example intermarriage, particularly between Bedouin women and fellahi men, but not vice versa, is prohibited. Furthermore, from a political perspective, fellahi groups could in principle be distributed among several tribes according to land leasing agreements and were not necessarily linked permanently to any Bedouin tribe. This implies that spatially, a fellahi group would spend most of the year in its own camp—separated from that of the host Bedouin tribe—since actual labor required for cultivation of leased land consumed only a few weeks annually. Even those fellaheen that maintained some livestock tended to have spatially separated patterns of migration from those of the Bedouin. Being landless and having no fixed land base, they retained their intergroup relationships by spatially gravitating toward each other—concentrating their dwelling units into large dense camps away from those of the Bedouin (Marx 1974).

While political and economic structures have been responsible for spatial separation between the Bedouin and the fellaheen, the role of cultural-ideological ones was no less important. These cultural structures and values implied that life without livestock would be detrimental, culturally-speaking, for the Bedouin as would relinquishment of farming for the fellaheen (Marx 1974). Preservation of each group's dominant cultural values was possible only through sociospatial separation. While in its simplest meaning, territoriality refers to maintaining a separate spatial unit with its physical material resources, here we are confronted with spatial separation aimed at preservation of nonmaterial resources, that is cultural, ideological, social, and political resources as well (see also Casimir 1992). It thus transpires that spatial separation between the Bedouin and the fellaheen amounts to a special kind of territoriality. Separate spaces have become necessary as containers for the nonmaterial properties of their inhabitants. This strategy was never resorted to at the time when Bedouin pastoral nomadic society was culturally and socially homogeneous.

In essence, then, the territorialization process—described earlier as originating dialectically from within Bedouin society, and later accelerated due to external economic, geopolitical, and administrative forces—repeats itself but with an additional external force at work, this time a social one. Territoriality—emerging during the rural phase of shifting away from nomadic pastoralism—has thus become also a vehicle for distinguishing between the seminomadic real Bedouin and the annexed tenant fellahi sociocultural group. From this perspective, an interpretation of these processes is now possible in a similar manner to that suggested earlier: sociospatial separation reflects further the transition of the Negev Bedouin society from a social definition of territory into territorial definition of social relations.

The State of Israel Period

These processes and their resulting practice of territorialization intensified considerably after 1948, with the establishment of the State of Israel. The major difference that emerged now was the highly intensive governmental involvement in Bedouin affairs. The previous chapter revealed the harsh context, circumstances, and process of the Bedouin encounter with the Israeli state during the late 1940s and 1950s. We recall that for political and military reasons many of those Bedouin who chose or were allowed to remain in the Negev were relocated from their traditional habitats into the militarily administered *sayig* (enclosure, see Figure 4.2). This area constituted only about twenty percent of the previous Bedouin territories in the Negev. Their population was reduced by a similar proportion. Despite this decline, however, relocation to the *sayig*—in close proximity to those tribes which remained in their previous territories—implied a dramatic reduction for the entire population in pasture and water resources and a considerable increase of pressure on those available. This obviously had a detrimental effect on the ability of the Bedouin to foster their already declining pastoral economy. In addition, the Israeli government—by inheriting many elements of the Ottoman Land Law—classified all Bedouin lands in the Negev, previously considered *mawat* (uncultivated land), as state-owned.

In the past, government administrative and legal measures had been followed almost always by typical processes. The Bedouin reacted now in similar ways. These included involvement and investment in agriculture, willingness to fragment and privatize land—even grazing land—and demarcation of their private plots. The major difference was not in the type of processes but in their magnitude and nature. All these processes were now heightened to such an extent that plot demarcation began to be conducted relatively openly, something which they had been reluctant to do previously (Kressel et al. 1991). More sophisticated and accurate methods for measurement and demarcation of plot boundaries were adopted, while some of those employed earlier were now improved. These included the planting of Arab thorn bush, stone fencing, engraving agnate group signs onto rocks, plowing deep furrows, or burying burnt stones in the ground (when concealment of the event was desired). For purposes of future conflict resolution, the presence of witnesses was again required in some cases. New methods included planting of trees, particularly olive

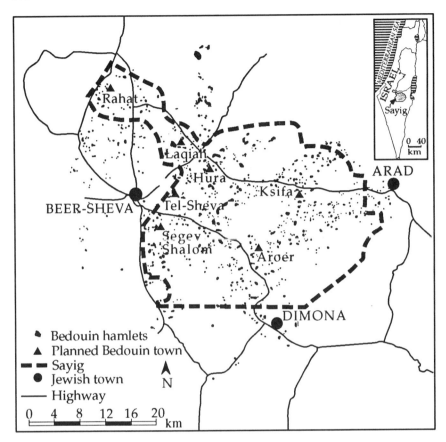

FIGURE 4.2 Bedouin hamlets and planned towns, 1990 *(Source:* Adapted from Meir and Ben-David 1990).

groves, construction of terraces and small earth dams, and erection of permanent domiciles. These methods became quite common under the State of Israel, particularly the last—which was considered by the state to violate the Ottoman Land Law of 1858, the Planning and Construction Law of 1958, and the Land Law of 1969. The Bedouin were thus reacting to the latter laws which regarded as state-owned those lands previously regarded as *mawat*—but for which they claimed ownership by virtue of their traditional possession customs.

Thus, the balance of forces which previously dictated the privatization and demarcation of plots and Bedouin territorialization was now reversed. Hitherto, these processes had been influenced mainly by the relatively free land market forces and less by governmental intervention. Now they began to assume a new dimension of intensive state intervention within a political conflict context, while the relevant real estate market for t Bedouin no longer existed. In fact, Bedouin land ownership rights were never legally recognized by any regime. The Bedouin for their part—acting as *de facto* owners—never felt any need to legally effectuate those rights, even when given the opportunity in 1921 by the British Mandate authorities to gain recognition of their attachment to their *mawat* lands by virtue of their farming activities (Ben-David 1989; Kressel et al. 1991). On the other hand, under the new state land laws, the government refused by and large to recognize Bedouin land ownership claims based upon prior possession. Hence, informal privatization of land from tribal territorial possession and its demarcation were now further intensified internally among Bedouin, who feared further state encroachment.

Maturation of Territoriality—The Semiurban Phase

The Transition to Semiurbanization

Some of the processes that intensified the territoriality trend among the Bedouin during the early years of the State of Israel have already been described. In fact, these processes have been accelerated during recent decades in the wake of fullscale sedentarization, which became the most powerful process. The modern sedentarization of the Bedouin took place, however, in two major phases: the so-called spontaneous rural sedentarization and government-planned semiurbanization.

Relocation of the Bedouin into the *sayig* implied in fact the abolition of the previous tribal and clan territories crystallized under the Ottoman government. Consequently, land-tenure patterns which had begun to shape up earlier, were now considerably reformulated (Ben-David 1986). Landlessness was previously an exclusive characteristic of the fellahi tenants, although some managed to acquire land. Due to spatial reorganization, however, those relocated real Bedouin tribes became landless too and were now spatially interspersed among landed tribes with the fellahi Bedouin. The increased proportion of landless Bedouin caused, as shown above, a dramatic change in sources of livelihood and dwelling patterns and initiated the process of what has been generally accepted as "spontaneous sedentarization."

The "spontaneous" nature of sedentarization—carrying with it the connotation of a natural and voluntary process—is, however, debatable. Contrary to Fallah's contention (1983; 1985), sedentarization per se was not imposed upon the Bedouin. On the other hand, neither can the opposite position—i.e., that it was indeed a fully voluntary process (e.g., Soffer and Bar-Gal 1985)—be accepted. Genuine spontaneity can be assigned only to those processes of sedentarization that took place before 1948, or to those Bedouin who chose to settle afterwards. In general, a very narrow latitude of choice of survival strategy has been available to the Bedouin since the late 1940s, either from the ecological perspective of land and water resources or from that of a governmental regional development policy. The Israeli government, like other governments in the Middle East (Bailey 1971; Havakuk 1986) and elsewhere, made this choice a constrained one. It is within this directly imposed constrained range of options that Bedouin choice of sedentarization was spontaneous, other alternatives being virtually unavailable.

As grazing and water resources within the *sayig* became extremely constrained, the already reduced role of livestock in Bedouin economy declined further, while dry-farming agriculture alone could not provide sufficient subsistence. During the 1950s the government began to realize the problems of Bedouin economic survival and gradually enabled them to seek additional income within the regional labor market outside the *sayig*. Thus the process of proletarization of the Bedouin—indications of which had emerged previously—was set in motion. The Bedouin were drawn toward Jewish settlements, first as seasonal farm laborers, and later as tenured blue-collar job holders in construction, transportation, and industry. At a later stage—primarily from the 1960—a process of entrepreneurship, albeit on a minor scale, began, primarily in agricultural and construction sub-contracting. General occupational figures (Zohar 1982) suggest that by the late 1970s about 63 percent of Bedouin adults of working age were involved either as laborers or as entrepreneurs in secondary and tertiary occupations. A survey conducted in 1991 (Ben-David 1993), which sampled several hundreds of households (Table 4.1), suggests that these proportions have not changed considerably for household heads. However, among young employees, secondary and tertiary occupations increased to 91 percent.

TABLE 4.1 Bedouin employment structure, 1991 (in percentages)

Branch	Family Heads	Young & Educated
Non-professional, manual, & construction	46	35
Manufacturing and industry	12	12
Services (government and public)	6	27
Services (tourism and catering)	--	5
Commerce	5	9
Medical, para-medical, and others	--	2
Agriculture	31[a]	9[b]

[a]In traditional farming. [b]In modern farming.
Source: Adapted from Ben-David (1993).

Despite the process of integration into the regional labor market, pastoralism and dry-farming were never entirely abandoned. Many Bedouin households have simultaneously maintained small flocks and dry-farming plots. As described by Marx (1981a), the Bedouin have adopted this dual economy as a defensive strategy against the uncertainties of their integration into the modern market economy. This dual economy has been adopted as a safeguard mechanism by Bedouin in other regions in the Middle East as well, but among the Negev Bedouin uncertainty derived primarily from the unique political context of their sedentarization.

Nevertheless, these economic changes triggered a process of spatial gravitation by Bedouin towards the main employment foci in the Negev or towards main transportation arteries. This process was enhanced with the abolishment of the military administration in 1965. The Bedouin gravitated particularly toward the city of Beer Sheva, which had become a center for the diffusion of many social and material innovations (Meir 1983). Their dependence upon this regional city as a focus of economic, administrative, and service activities increased to such an extent that they gradually became not only a labor-market dependent society (see Table 4.1) but—as will be demonstrated later on in this book—a public-service dependent society as well.

The shift in the balance of dependence away from internal traditional economic and sociopolitical structures toward external and modern ones, constituted a continuation of processes begun earlier. From a spatiopolitical perspective, the process of alienation from tribal structures and territories accelerated. Besides the fact that the tribal structure was almost completely destroyed during and after 1948, the government denied formal leadership to some hostile sheikhs and awarded it to more obedient and cooperative ones. The government also reorganized tribal structures under newly nominated sheikhs (Mor 1971), by awarding tribal status to some extended families as well, some even of fellahi origins. Consequently, by the early 1990s, the number of formally recognized tribes had increased to forty eight. The inflated number of sheikhs and tribes and the manner of their nomination and formation, contributed significantly to their already deteriorating status. Thus, separation from tribal control and institutions increased and the obligation balance shifted down further towards the *hamula* and extended and nuclear household units (Soen and Shmuel 1985; Meir and Ben-David 1990).

This process of sociopolitical individualization—accompanying the proletarianized economic process—promoted processes of territoriality. At the mesoscale—that is, within tribes—numerous tiny hamlets began to form within the *sayig*. These were either permanent tent encampments or clusters of wooden huts, tin shacks, or few concrete block houses. These hamlets had already begun to form in the 1950s, but their number increased significantly after an amnesty on illegal construction was declared in 1967. Amiran et al. (1979) suggest that—in anticipation of future expropriation of their land by the government—the Bedouin took advantage of this amnesty and speedily erected new dwelling structures, resulting in fast proliferation of hamlets within the *sayig*.

With reduced ability of the tribe to protect its own as well as its tribesmen's interests, and in the context of the ideology of land privatization, the proliferation of numerous small hamlets further signifies the tendency of the Bedouin toward territoriality. However, once again external factors accompanied internal ones. Land ownership and possession now became important not only due to government pressure on Bedouin land but also due to the Bedouin's own demographic pressure on their land resources. Demographic pressure had begun to increase earlier, primarily due to fellaheen migration. Yet—as will be seen in the next chapter—the Bedouin population grew tremendously, particularly during the 1960s and 1970s. By the late 1980s it had reached its lowest estimate pre-1949 size but now with a fivefold population density.

As pressure on land increased in the 1960s to degrees unprecedented in Bedouin society, the Bedouin were faced with a new spatial reality. Economically, they had now to compete harder for two types of resources: reduced ecological resources (water, and grazing and farming land), with more competitors from within both Bedouin circles and public and state agencies, and external labor-market opportunities where they faced Jewish competitors. Socially they had now to confront immeasurably more personal encounters within a drastically limited space. In Rapoport's theoretical terms (Rapoport 1978), nomadic-derived mobility mechanisms for distinguishing members and nonmembers of a group, and therefore group identity, were beginning to dissolve, as were social mechanisms for spatial order. This required further substitution of social boundaries by spatial ones, that is, new means of space management in order to restore social order. Consequently, sociospatial separation between various groups now became even more acute. While previously this territorial mechanism had been relevant for the landed real Bedouin versus the landless fellaheen, it now became relevant also for the new class of landless real Bedouin. The latter, as well as the landless fellaheen, spontaneously erected hamlets on government-owned land in the inner areas of the *sayig* and these were separated from one another and from those of landed tribes in the eastern and western parts of this region.

Even groups within landed tribes—whose processes of tribal land privatization were already several decades old—found sociospatial separation into small hamlets necessary under the emerging unfamiliar spatial reality. The household or extended family *dira* now assumed an even greater significance vis-à-vis the tribal one. Data from Ben-David (1982) suggest that—among the landed tribes—the number of hamlets increased and their size declined considerably compared to those of landless fellaheen and real Bedouin tribes. For similar reasons, sociospatial separation as a territorial mechanism was also adopted at the micro level. Each hamlet was composed of several expanded families of the same agnatic origin. Amiran et al. (1979) have found that distances separating expanded families from one another are considerably larger than those separating nuclear families within each expanded family.

These meso and micro scale spatial differentiation processes were interpreted by Meir (1988) also as a centrifugal reaction by the Bedouin to centripetal pressures applied by the state. In the early 1960s the government realized that the extensive dispersion of Bedouin hamlets within the *sayig* was beginning to conflict with public development plans. Consequently it endeavored to reduce the vast numbers of small hamlets and replace them by seven towns, each with several thousand Bedouin. The towns were to be dispersed throughout the *sayig*, each located close enough to existing major concentrations of spontaneously erected hamlets to minimize further relocation (State of Israel 1974). A process of planned sedentarization and semiurbanization thus began, with the town of Tel-Sheva in 1966, followed by Rahat in 1972, and other towns in the following decades (see Figure 4.2). By the early 1990s about 45 percent of the total Bedouin population (estimated officially at 75,000) had already moved to towns.

The penetration of territorial ideology into Bedouin society is reflected in the degrees of failure and success of the semiurbanization process. It is suggested that the transition of the society to semiurbanization was largely made possible by the fact that it became previously territorially-based, but also that becoming semiurbanized further enhanced territoriality among the Bedouin. In other words, land ownership with fixed abode and sociospatial separation became valuable in Bedouin ideology to an extent that conditioned their willingness to defy or adapt to the new environmental scheme offered to them by the state. This territorial scheme, however—as could be inferred from Sack (1986)—intensified these territorial values among them and caused further reshaping of the semiurban environment.

Bedouin formal land ownership issues in the Negev have not yet been settled completely. In the 1950s about 55 percent of the land within the *sayig* was declared state land (Zohar 1982) and leased to resettled Bedouin on an annual basis. Since then, the implementation of the planned towns program—as well as other public projects—have required either expropriation of land or revocation of leasing agreements, each of which raised strong objections among the Bedouin (Marx 1981b). The first reaction of the Bedouin to the program was therefore an almost total reluctance to yield land rights and to move to towns. The reluctance of the Bedouin in the early stages to move to towns stemmed from the siting of towns on lands that, in their eyes, belonged to absentee Bedouin or had been expropriated from resident ones. Settling on such land—though legal under state law—would still constitute a violation of Bedouin traditional law. Furthermore, according to state law, the government was able to offer residential land in towns only on a 49-year lease basis. Having become accustomed to living in fixed dwellings within a defined territory that, according to their concepts, is under their ownership, and—being unacquainted with this regulation and its true meaning—the Bedouin became skeptical about their present and future ownership rights.

More important for the territorial issue, the town planning concept that guided governmental town planners disregarded informal territorial rules that had developed among the Bedouin, real and fellaheen alike. At the meso scale, in particular, spatial separation between agnatic groups and between fellaheen and real Bedouin was not taken into account. Furthermore, the planning concept of the 1960s, as described by Frenkel-Horner (1982), called for a European-style linear village with single standard housing units, each on a one-eighth of an acre land lot, closely bordering and facing each other. Even the desire for privacy—that was apparently beginning to evolve at the individual family microscale—was not taken into consideration.

For these reasons, early development stages of the first town (Tel Sheva) proved a failure. The town was originally planned to accommodate 1,200 families. In fact, over the first twelve years, only twenty seven nuclear families—mostly landless fellaheen of different agnatic origins—moved in. The consequences of nonterritorial planning for a society with evolving territorial rules, under circumstances of sharply increased density, soon became evident. According to Lewando-Hundt (1979), Frenkel-Horner (1982), and Al-A'finish (1987), the heterogeneous composition of the population became a source of friction and violent conflicts between different groups within the town.

The experience with the first planned town sharpened territorial ideology among the Bedouin to such an extent that its realization became an informal precondition for further settlement in towns. Consequently, from then on town planners consulted the Bedouin over some issues pertaining to territoriality. Due to this enhanced participation of the Bedouin themselves in the planning process, other towns were planned and settled with considerably greater success (Fenster 1991). It is noteworthy that fellahi Bedouin perceived the semiurbanization program as a vehicle for realizing their territorial desires and upgrading themselves from their landless status in particular and inferior social status in general. Government efforts were therefore directed at these groups first, in anticipation of their becoming a model group for obstinate landed and landless real Bedouin.

According to the new town planning territorial concepts that emerged in the early 1970s (Kaplan et al. 1979; Lerman and Lerman 1987; Oron 1987), land lots were owned by the inhabitants and were at least half an acre in size, capable of accommodating two or three household units each. Architectural standardization was replaced by response to specific family desires, subject to building codes. Most important, however, the main planning principle was a hierarchical spatial division of social units. More specifically, there was spatiosocial matching between neighborhoods, main streets, alleys, and lots and the spatial units of the respective tribes, *hamulas*, extended families, and nuclear families. Such a spatial definition of social relations was necessary in order to achieve the balance between minimal social friction and maximum town communal life under conditions of higher population density than within hamlets in the periphery.

Although the entire town, composed of several neighborhoods, was perceived as the planning unit by the planners, it was the neighborhood which constituted the widest spatial reference system for the Bedouin. They tended to regard their neighborhood as their own settlement and other neighborhoods within the same town as entirely separate settlements. Therefore, mixing groups of different origins in a single neighborhood was unacceptable to them. Even trespassing by members of an external group was seen as undesirable. Consequently, not only did spatial separation become a major territorial principle but the town street system was planned with minimal direct linkages between neighborhoods. Even at the town mesolevel, major streets within the neighborhoods were planned as dead-end roads, as were branching-off alleys.

These planning principles were adopted to cater for Bedouin territorial desires, and proved socioculturally relevant. Indeed, the process of semi-urbanization gained strong momentum from 1972, with the establishment of Rahat and, in the 1980s and 1990s, of the other five towns. Henceforth, further development of Tel- Sheva also became possible. The town of Rahat became the first Bedouin incorporated local council (municipality) in the Negev, with an elected mayor and council. Upon reaching a population of 25,000 in 1994, it was officially declared a city by the government. The town of Tel-Sheva has also been declared a local council. The other five towns are split between two incorporated regional councils (municipalities), and plans are presently underway to change their status too into local councils.

Territoriality in Town

Being the largest Bedouin town in the Negev, with about one-quarter of the total Bedouin population, Rahat was chosen fin 1988 or an in-depth study (Bar 1989; Meir 1992) designed to examine attitudes of the inhabitants towards issues of territoriality within the new semiurban environment. Rahat is composed of twenty-six neighborhoods spread over a total area of 8,800 dunams (2,200 acres) and planned to accommodate a population of 35,000. At the time of the study, there were fifteen different fellahi groups and ten real Bedouin ones, with 59 percent and 41 percent of the population, respectively. The annual natural increase rate of Rahat's population was about 5 percent, compared to 3.5 percent for the Israeli Arab population and 1.7 percent for the Jewish population.

Rahat is sited on state land expropriated from the real Bedouin tribe of Al-Huzayil. Early settlers came from the fellaheen of the tribe of Al Oubra, whose members had previously been tenants of the Al-Huzayil, and received its protection in conflicts with other tribes (Kressel 1982). The Al-Huzayil strongly opposed the idea of settling in towns and in particular the attempt by their fellahi tenants to settle on the expropriated land. Being one of the senior Bedouin tribes, they regarded this act by fellahi Al-Oubra as a serious challenge, a violation of Bedouin traditional law, a threat to their sociopolitical hegemony and domination, and an indication of a new sociopolitical hierarchical order. Early stages of settlement in Rahat were therefore accompanied by conflicts and violence between these tribes. Although the Al-Huzayil yielded at a later stage and began themselves to settle in town, relations between the real Bedouin and the fellaheen have been marked by sociopolitical tensions and conflicts over issues of communal life in Rahat and elsewhere (Fenster 1991). This tension culminated in violent incident sin 1985 (Bar 1985) and during the municipal elections in 1989 and 1994. Nevertheless, in the early 1970s the government endeavored to encourage the Al-Oubra to settle in Rahat, by providing them with protection, by enabling them to participate in siting their neighborhoods, by selling them land lots at low prices, and by leasing to them out-of-town state land for farming.

The anticipated population density of Rahat was 4,000/sq. km., compared with 70/sq. km. for the total Bedouin population within the *sayig* had the semiurbanization program not taken place. Careful planning of neighborhoods was therefore required to guarantee a degree of territoriality sufficient to maintain normal communal life. Neighborhoods were planned so as to maintain communal life without interference from outsiders. Direct passage between various units of the same neighborhoods—as well as between neighborhoods—was barred as far as possible by abstaining from completion of the main and local street system as originally planned. The idea was to allow the resettlers sufficient time to adapt to the new reality and to decide on the future nature of their socio-spatial relationships. At a later stage the resettlers indeed chose to transform roads and streets into dead-ends to bar unwanted trespassing (see also Jakubowska 1984).

The conceptual framework that guided the Rahat study was based on articulation of previous processes analyzed above and territoriality concepts described in Chapter 2 and elsewhere (e.g., Stea 1965; Rapoport 1972; Altman 1975). As noted earlier, processes of territoriality among the Negev Bedouin resulted in sociospatial encapsulation of territorial behavior from the tribal down to the household level. Accordingly, during settling in a town, this behavioral pattern is carried over into the semiurban environment, and a hierarchical territorial division into three tiers develops. The primary territory includes the private lot and its nearby environment where members of the nuclear household reside. The secondary territory in general overlaps the neighborhood or part thereof which, in Rahat, is tribal or sub-tribal. It is a semipublic territory where routine social encounters are conducted. The tertiary territory includes all other areas and can be referred to as public territory.

Each of the above territories has a different meaning for the individual Bedouin with regard to the major issue of the study—sociospatial relations. This issue was broken down in the study into aspects related to desires regarding spatial separation at the nuclear and extended family, *hamula,* and tribal levels. More specifically, detailed territorial issues referred to the following aspects: the importance assigned to the identity of neighbors; the necessity of separation between extended family and *hamula* units within the neighborhoods and between tribal units, or between real Bedouin and fellahi Bedouin groups within town; barring access and trespassing by outsiders at the various levels; preferences with regard to acceptance or exclusion of *hamula* and tribal members as neighbors; preferences with regard to acceptance or exclusion of nonmembers as neighbors; willingness of individuals to reside in a foreign spatial unit; and acceptance of the latter desire by the kin group.

The study was conducted within the socially dominant tribes of Al-Huzayil (real Bedouin) and Al-Oubra and Al-Qrinawi (fellahi Bedouin). A sample of 230 household heads from these tribes (10 percent of Rahat's total households) were surveyed with a questionnaire that included the above aspects, covering equally the real and fellahi Bedouin. Their attitudes towards these aspects (on a yes-no basis) are summarized in Table 4.2, which is divided into Bedouin versus fellaheen responses (in percentages) in each level of territory.

In general, both groups assign great importance to the identity of their neighbors at their primary territory (A_1) but considerably more so among

TABLE 4.2 Attitudes toward territorial aspects in Rahat (in percentages)

Territory	Group	Territorial Aspects						
		A_1	A_2	A_3	A_4	A_5	A_6	A_7
Primary	RB	93	70	70	11	41	69	68
(A)	FB	71	48	64	32	42	48	42
		B_1	B_2	B_3	B_4			
Secondary	RB	82	79	31	82			
(B)	FB	57	40	12	52			
		C_1						
Tertiary	RB	78						
(C)	FB	48						

RB – real Bedouin; FB – fellahi Bedouin.

A_1 – importance of neighbor's identity.

A_2 – necessity of separation between extended families / *hamulas* within neighborhood.

A_3 – objection to trespassing on the private lot by other tribal members.

A_4 – objection to members of extended family as next-door neighbors.

A_5 – objection to members of another *hamula* as next-door neighbors.

A_6 – objection to other members of the same tribe as next-door neighbors.

A_7- objection to members of other tribes as next-door neighbors.

B_1 – necessity of separation between tribes.

B_2 – objection to trespassing in the neighborhood by nontribal members.

B_3 – objection to a son living away from extended family in the same neighborhood.

B_4 – objection to a son living outside the neighborhood.

C_1 –necessity of separation between real and fellahi Bedouin within town.

Source: Meir (1992) (compiled from data in Bar 1989).

the real Bedouin (93 percent) than among the fellaheen (71 percent). The former also are more in favor (70 percent) of spatial separation between extended families and between *hamulas* within the neighborhood (A_3) than are the latter (only 40 percent). Both groups (70 percent and 64 percent respectively) forcefully object to trespassing in their private lots by other members of the same tribe (A_3). Regarding objection to (or exclusion of) neighbors, the more remote the social circle of a person (A_4, A_5, A_6, A_7) the greater in general the opposition to accepting him as a next-door neighbor. This tendency is stronger among the real Bedouin than among the fellaheen.

At the secondary territory level, 82 percent of the real Bedouin desire separation between tribes (B_1) compared to 57 percent of the fellaheen Bedouin. Both groups put more emphasis on this type of sociospatial separation than upon separation within the neighborhood (A_1). The real Bedouin's objection to trespassing in their neighborhoods (B_2) is even stronger (79 percent) than at the intraneighborhood level (A_3), whereas that of the fellaheen is considerably lower (40 percent). As for the residential pattern, the questions now refer to adult sons. Due to possible future shortage of space in the town, and given the extremely high natural increase rate, they will encounter housing difficulties in the future and will have to chose between two alternatives: residing at higher density levels within the same neighborhood or seeking residential space in other neighborhoods. Jakubowska (1984) has also indicated the desire of many younger individual Bedouin to move away from their extended families in order to avoid taking responsibility for them although admitting that emotionally it would be difficult to live without them. The data show unequivocally that opposition to the second alternative (B_3, B_4) sharply increases among the real Bedouin (31 to 82 percent) and the fellaheen (12 to 52 percent) as spatial remoteness from the primary territory of the basic social circle increases. Such objection is, however, less pronounced among the fellaheen. The implication is that the real Bedouin are more willing to live at higher residential density within their neighborhood than are the fellaheen.

The pattern at the tertiary territory—that is at the town level—reveals that the real Bedouin manifest a stronger desire (78 percent) for spatial separation between them and the fellaheen (C_1) than do the latter (48 percent).

Several general patterns can be extracted from these data. The real Bedouin demonstrate a strong tendency to intensify their territorial behavior within the town of Rahat. This is shown in the great emphasis they put upon the identity of their neighbors at all levels; in their strong desire for complete spatial separation within neighborhoods and between themselves and the fellaheen; and in their desire to avoid unwanted social encounters by barring access and trespassing within and between neighborhoods. Their objection to neighbors increases as the social circle of potential neighbors is more remote. All these patterns are manifested in general more strongly than they are among the fellaheen. Also, the real Bedouin's desire for sociospatial separation between tribes in separate neighborhoods is stronger than their desire for such separation within the neighborhoods, and such desire is stronger than among the fellaheen.

This latter pattern, which re-employs the tribal framework as a vehicle for enhancing territoriality, is perhaps a spatial response by the real Bedouin to the sociopolitical challenge of the fellaheen, who—we may recall—regard the process of semiurbanization as an opportunity to upgrade their inferior social status. In turn, the fellaheen's tendency toward the same territorial indicators that are strongly manifested by the real

Bedouin is considerably weaker. Their more liberal attitudes are interpreted here as an attempt to blur social and spatial boundaries in their effort to gain sociopolitical hegemony within Bedouin society. This effort by the fellaheen has generated what has been regarded previously (Meir and Ben-David 1989; 1990) as dual social stratification. That is, both groups now claim social superiority as each regards its own status ethnocentrically as superior to the other's.

These processes indicate that settling in Rahat in particular—and semiurbanization in general—have further intensified territorial behavior within Bedouin society, particularly among the real Bedouin. The tendency towards territoriality within town entails recruitment of the tribal framework, that has already largely forfeited its importance. This spatial strategy has also been manifested politically in the local municipal arena, in the struggle for control and hegemony within the local council (see Al-A'finish 1987). These trends cast some doubt on the viability of Rahat as an integrated community because, as indicated above (see also Jakubowska 1984), each neighborhood regards itself as a separate community competing with others over allocation of resources by the municipality.

Yet, this phenomenon cannot overshadow the strong tendency to continue the pattern of intensified territoriality at intratribal social circles—that is, the extended and nuclear family levels. The strong trends towards spatial separation between groups belonging to the same tribe or *hamula*, to exclusion of neighbors whose origins are in other social circles, and to barring access and preventing trespassing, indicate the desire to protect the primary territory in order to avoid loss of social identity and to foster the emerging desire for privacy. This desire is also relevant at higher spatial organization levels within town.

These tendencies fed on trends to territorial individualization that began with the process of land parcellation and private ownership. Within the semiurban town environment this trend has for the first time become openly recognized. As will be seen in the next chapters, this process was followed by growing social and economic individualization toward the nuclear family in various respects. These imply that traditional status indicators—which were based upon social affiliation—are beginning to lose their meaning and significance and give way to territorial ones. In other words, the process of territoriality that began at early stages of sedentarization, when the Bedouin first became involved in agriculture, and continued in later sedentarization phases before and after statehood, matured at the semiurbanization phase. Throughout these processes, Bedouin society has been transformed from a society in which social definition determines territorial relations into one in which territorial definition is used to determine social relations both within and outside planned Bedouin towns.

Conclusions

This chapter has shown the close linkage within the Negev Bedouin society between the process of rural sedentarization and semiurbanization on the one hand and territorialization on the other. Early and intermediate stages of this process—that is, the shift in balance from pastoral nomadic production to agriculture—were voluntary and to a large extent were a matter of choice. Given the changing economic and geopolitical circumstances, they opted for the farming strategy because it was an "institutionalized alternative," without perhaps being aware of its possible socioterritorial concomitants. Once these became mandatory, however, they did not hesitate to adopt them. In time, the territorial strategy itself became an institutionalized alternative. Hence later, in the new state of Israel, this strategy began to condition nonvoluntary phases of sedentarization, particularly acceptance of the ecological framework of semiurbanization.

Early stages of territorialization can well be framed within the context of competition for physical and ecological resources. At later stages these ecological resources no longer played a major role, yet territoriality was enhanced. How can this be explained? What kind of resources have the ex-nomadic semiurbanizing Bedouin been competing for and protecting territorially? Meir (1995) submits that these resources are social identity and social hegemony (see also Casimir 1992). Territoriality is enhanced due to competition over these resources because of the growth of social differentiation and class stratification within the previously classless Bedouin society. These social processes are the outcome of the annexation of an external ethnic group (the fellaheen), articulated into the emerging landed capitalism, and integration of Bedouin society into the capitalistic economy and labor market.

This process greatly intensified within the sedentary and semiurban environment, due primarily to demographic pressures and state politics. These created a spatial reality with which the Bedouin were unfamiliar. Increasing population size and density—particularly within planned towns—entailed a sharp increase in undesired social encounters and reduced ability to distinguish oneself from other group members, and social groups from one another (see also Ben-David 1994a). Under such conditions it has become increasingly difficult to maintain social identity, previously possible through the nomadic alternative. New means of space management have become necessary to regain social order. This is achieved by spatial classification at the various levels of aggregation that is communicated to outsiders by overt and covert means of sharp separation or barring access and banning trespassing, and by developing an appropriate ideology of class consciousness.

Such an ideology is an articulation of two types of social structures. On the one hand, there is the Middle Eastern social structure based primarily on agnation, which does not yet allow accumulation of wealth to fully and exclusively determine social hierarchy (Kressel 1991). On the other hand, there are the Western capitalistic ideals—to which the Negev Bedouin have been exposed for nearly a century—which encourage individual social status mobilization,(see also Kressel 1976). This articulated ideology is the root of the conflict between the real Bedouin and the fellahi Bedouin, the latter exposing and yielding more liberally to the latter structure.

Territoriality, through redefining social identity and relations, thus becomes a vehicle in the sociopolitical struggle for control and domination. Spatial separation at all levels—but particularly between the real Bedouin and the fellaheen—is desired and practiced more by the former group than by the latter. It serves them to preserve their Bedouin culture which they regard as unique and different from that of the fellaheen. When manifested through territoriality, this attempt by the real Bedouin becomes an important channel, among others, of manifesting social hegemony within the newly urbanizing Bedouin society.

5

Demographic Dynamics

In the previous chapter we showed how the Bedouin society in the Negev has adopted elements of territorial behavior in the course of its process of sedentarization and semiurbanization. In line with the conceptual framework suggested in Chapter 2, this process contains elements of both spatial and social change but has become itself a trigger, among others, for further spatial and social change processes. We are concerned here with processes of demographic change, primarily those that have taken place since the late 1940s. While some demographic changes took place earlier under the British Mandate (Muhsam 1950; Muhsam 1956a,b), these were minor—reflecting the relative socioeconomic and ecological stability of this society in that period. As shown above, however, the major changes in its ecological relationships began to be evident under the Israeli state and it is in this period that demographic changes have been most intensive. Several aspects of demographic dynamics that are of critical social significance will be considered here. These include general demographic trends, child mortality, fertility behavior, and aging.

General Demographic Trends

Our analysis of general demographic trends among the Negev Bedouin is conducted at the macrolevel. It is based on official governmental data, which—as is the case with other pastoral nomadic societies as well–are problematic. This is one aspect of the more general problem of relationships between these peoples and governments and the degree of their cooperation with authorities. The situation vis-à-vis the Bedouin is particularly so, given that—as shown earlier—strong military-political tension prevailed between them and the state in early years of statehood. Therefore, the accuracy of official governmental data on the Bedouin population was relatively poor during the 1950s and 1960s compared to later years, when they were more closely integrated into state systems.

Hence the discussion of the early years should be treated with some reservation, although in general, as will be shown below, the data do not contradict the demographic processes outlined in Chapter 2.

Trends in crude birth and death rates within Bedouin society for the period between the mid-1950s and early 1990s are shown in Figure 5.1. The data are presented in three-year moving averages to smooth out annual deviations. To take mortality rates first, these are considerably low throughout the period, declining from a level of about 7/1,000 in the late 1950s to about 3/1,000 in the early 1990s. The latter rate is lower than the mortality rate for the Jewish population (about 6/1,000), a fact which casts doubt on the reliability of these official mortality data. It is quite possible that reports on death are withheld by Bedouin for various reasons, one of which may be reluctance to lose state benefits for elders. These false reports may, therefore, drive mortality rates down. However, even if the real rates are, for example, double those reported, they are still considerably lower than those recorded for sedentarized pastoral nomads elsewhere (Meir 1987a). Presumably, Bedouin mortality rates were considerably higher during the 1940s because only in the 1950s did the Israeli authorities launch a mass campaign for eradication of tuberculosis, the disease then responsible for a significant proportion of deaths among the Bedouin (Ben-Assa 1960).

The general decline of mortality rates since the 1950s was accompanied by a gradual increase in life expectancy towards 68 years in the late 1960s and 73 years in the late 1980s (Meir and Ben-David 1990). Nevertheless, throughout the recent decade there has been a considerable stability in mortality rates. From the perspective of demographic transition dynamics, the Bedouin have reached about the lowest mortality rate possible. This is a consequence of two processes: first, the gradual general increase in standard of living and in household income, as shown above; second—and more important—the introduction of public health services and modern medical technologies by the Israeli government on the one hand, and the beginning of adoption of new public health and medical behavioral norms by the Bedouin on the other hand. The latter issue will be dealt with separately and in more detail in Chapter 7.

The dynamics of fertility are considerably more complex. Fertility rates in the mid-1950s—when the Bedouin were still under military administration and at the beginning of their accelerated sedentarization— were in the range of 35–40/1,000. In comparison with data assembled by Meir (1987a), this rate is closer to the rate of the general range of pastoral nomadic groups than to that of seminomadic groups in Africa and the Near East. From then on fertility rates rose quite rapidly, peaking in the early 1970s at a level of 62/1,000. At that time, it will be recalled, the mo-

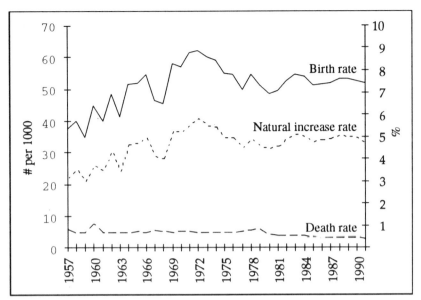

FIGURE 5.1 General population dynamics of the Negev Bedouin: 1957–1991
(*Source:* Data are from the *Statistical Abstract of Israel* for the various years).

mentum of sedentarization and settlement in planned towns was already
accelerating. Therefore, this level is somewhat higher among the Bedouin
than among other sedentarized pastoral nomads.

Unlike mortality rates, the time-trend of rising birth rates has been
highly unstable, particularly during the recession in the Israeli economy
in the mid-1960s and its recovery after the 1967 war. One may be tempted
to cite these events to explain the sharp decline followed by sharp increase in birth rates in these years. Accordingly, these fluctuations could
reflect the high demographic adaptability of the Bedouin to major external economic events. This explanation seems logical, particularly at this
sensitive stage of their sedentarization and early integration into the labor
market economy. Thus, their emerging "double-footing" in both the
modern market economy and traditional pastoral and dry-farming ventures (Marx 1981a) could facilitate a quick shift between modes of production and demographic regimes. However—given difficulties with the
data—this explanation requires yet further substantiation. Furthermore, it
is questionable whether there is an immediate responsive relationship between the economic and demographic systems. This is particularly so if
the prevailing low fertility-control behavioral norms and practices among
the Bedouin in those years are taken into consideration.

The relationships between mode of production and demographic regime is more clearly manifested in the longer run. The gradually rising
fertility between the mid-1950s and early 1970s is indicative of the grad-

ual change in mode of production. It is within this time-range context that the Bedouin strategy of a dual economic system—adopted so as to reduce uncertainty—is demographically manifested. This perhaps is a more reasonable explanation of the fluctuative nature of rising fertility throughout this period. Apparently the Bedouin have an unrealistic perception of the potentialities and miscalculate the uncertainty inherent in integration into the modern market economy. The gap between subjective perception and objective reality begins to narrow only at more advanced stages of this integration as uncertainty declines, entailing perhaps a more realistic appreciation and evaluation. It is noteworthy that at these stages (from the 1970s onward), accuracy of official data begins to improve significantly due to the increasing tendency by Bedouin mothers to give birth in the regional medical center in Beer Sheva and become thus eligible for state maternity and child benefits.

Indeed, from the early 1970s there is a reversal of the trend and fertility rates begin to decline (see Figure 5.1). Although this is a slow process, it is considerably more stable and less fluctuative. The slow pace of this process, in its third consecutive decade, still indicates the uncertainty of the Bedouin situation. On the other hand, however, its very nature may imply a growing—though not yet complete—economic certainty and security with their integration into the external economic system. This process is associated in general with the economic growth that has taken place within Bedouin society. However, at the macro scale it is primarily related to the process of social modernization that was a consequence of accelerating urbanization in the mid-1970s, as shown earlier. The section on fertility behavior below will elaborate further on these processes.

In summary, Bedouin society is now in the midst of a unique demographic transition process which has recently become typical of many Third World societies. Unlike the more conventional process typical of Western nations—in which fertility declined from its high levels following a decline in mortality—here mortality decline was followed first by rising and only then by declining fertility. The implication is that—given the low and relatively stable mortality rates—natural increase rates have also been rising and then falling (Figure 5.1). At their peak, in 1972, they reached 5.8 percent with doubling-time of about twelve years. Indeed, it is only through these rates that the Bedouin—who numbered about 12,000 in 1948 (Amiran 1963)—have been able to approach their lowest prestate population estimate of about 70,000. They now comprise about 20 percent of the total population of about 365,000 in the Southern District. Yet, even under declining natural increase rates, the Bedouin are still within the explosive stage of the demographic transition process, with a current fifteen years doubling-time for an official 1991 population estimate close to 75,000 (Central Bureau of Statistics 1993).

The Nomadism-Sedentarism Continuum:
A Methodological Note

The previous section demonstrated general demographic dynamics among the Bedouin of the Negev at the macroscale. This portrayal may be misleading, particularly as it ignores the cultural-ecological continuum which is likely to exist in many pastoral nomadic or exnomadic societies, including the Bedouin. A special methodology is therefore required for studying these processes among pastoral nomads.

The important point for the present discussion is that the process of sedentarization does not merely constitute an economic change in mode of production and a resulting change in social organization. Rather, it is an ecological change, with a dominant spatial-geographical dimension. Quite often a significant locational change is involved as the sedentarizing pastoral nomads move away or are removed from their grazing territories to other locations that are suitable for farming or other secondary and even tertiary activities. Thus, it is assumed that there is conformity between spatial-geographical change on one hand and phases of change from pastoral nomadism to rural sedentarism on the other. That is, a pastoral nomadic society, which is relatively unidimensional in functional and spatial dynamics terms, now becomes multidimensionally stretched along the nomadism-sedentarism continuum. This continuum contains several phases of socioeconomic development, each assumed to be characterized by a dominant demographic regime that is a product of a dominant mode of production and its resulting set of social relations.

The concept of continuum adopted here is different from that of Grossman (1992). He refers to different constellations of relationships between economic mode of living, residence, and settlement of a pastoral *nomadic* population. These constellations imply the possibility of interchangeably bidirectional processes of nomadization and settlement. As noted above, processes of nomadization are not likely to occur in present political contexts. Therefore, reference is made here to unidirectionality of movement along the continuum from nomadic to urban end.

To describe the nomadism-sedentarism continuum as composed of discrete phases of development and change contradicts our earlier conceptualization of change processes (see Chapter 2 above). At least in the short-run, a sedentarizing pastoral nomadic group is not likely to develop an entirely different mode of production, social structure, and demographic regime. However, for analytical purposes we assume that—due to underlying socioeconomic processes—certain phases may evolve, within which there are highly typical demographic regimes and therefore between which change processes can be discerned. The significance of this phase approach derives directly from the unavailability of time-series demographic data. This is particularly so since the nomadism-sedentarism continuum may stretch into segments of the exnomadic society for which data may be available, but where different demographic regimes may be experienced. In this case a distinction is necessary between the demographic regimes of the newly sedentarizing or urbanizing pastoral nomads and those of the rural or urban society into which they are being introduced during this process.

The phase approach, composed of spatial, economic, and social dimensions, is central to the methodology proposed by Meir and Ben-David (1991a) which is used below. The assumption is that a cross-section analysis of different segments of the same society along the nomadism-sedentarism continuum can serve as a substitute for the analysis of a single segment of this society through time. This assumption is required because, in contrast to other communities, in which the process takes place along the time dimension alone, the process here is two-dimensional. The pastoral nomadic society undergoes a spatial-geographical change concurrently with other processes, including demographic ones, that take place over time. On the assumption that the geographical phase dimension along the nomadism-sedentarism continuum already contains the temporal dimension inherent in change processes, the phases along the continuum thus replace the stages along the time dimension that are customary parameters in studies of spatially-fixed sedentary communities. Space (geographical phase) is thus substituted for time, a conceptual framework that is common in the social sciences—particularly in social geography (Kellerman 1994) but also in demographic studies (e.g., Tabbarah 1976). This is especially important given the usual lack of public official demographic information concerning pastoral societies in their most extreme nomadic state, let alone time-series data as they shift away from this mode of production.

For practical research purposes, however, the concept of a nomadism-sedentarism continuum must become operationalized. Although several subdivisions are possible, the society under consideration may be generally divided into four groups: pastoral nomads, seminomads, village-sedentary exnomads, and urbanized exnomads. Such division is appropriate for purposes of analyzing demographic dynamics because it represents phases of socioeconomic and cultural development within which relatively distinct demographic regimes may evolve (see also Meir 1987a). True, these are ideal types. Phases, as indicated earlier, are not absolute, and segments of the same group may pursue life styles and modes of production of adjoining phases. Accordingly, the demographic pattern of a certain phase may not be wholly typical and exclusive, as it may contain elements characteristic of the previous or the following phases. The proposed phases are therefore adopted here for analytical purposes only, in line with the theoretical discussion in Chapter 2.

However, there is another dimension to be considered. Many pastoral nomadic societies are characterized by a dual socioethnic class structure composed, as shown earlier, of original—often termed noble—nomads and annexed nomads. The latter group is made up of former farmers who voluntarily adjoined the nomadic society or were forcefully enslaved by it. Being often socially inferior to the host society and carrying with them nonnomadic cultural traits, they incline more toward sedentarism than toward nomadism (Grossman 1994b). Therefore, their particular social structure and relations may reflect a subtype mode of production within the general pastoral nomadic one. In each phase along the continuum they may demonstrate distinct demographic dynamics. Some evidence to this effect has been shown by Meir (1987a; see also Randall 1984; Randall and Winter 1986), indicating the methodological need to identify clearly the major social subgroups.

The main method for the analysis of demographic dynamics along the nomadism-sedentarism continuum is a synchronic cross-section of the various groups situated in different phases. The cross-section enables us to compare demographic patterns of the various groups and phases and draw conclusions about demographic dynamics along the continuum, without the need to resort to time series data as in diachronic studies. The first requirement is determination of a base-point about which change can be identified. This involves an analysis of the demographic pattern of the group situated at the most extreme, pure nomadic point along the continuum. Such groups are now rare and it is necessary to resort to data from past research on the same or similar neighboring nomadic societies. More often that not, however, such research is also rare. Therefore, it is quite plausible that the base-point along the continuum may be determined at seminomadic pastoralism—a mode of living still common in many regions worldwide.

The structural framework for the analysis of demographic dynamics is thus composed of two dimensions: the spatiogeographic-development (phase) and the socioethnic one (class). Official data on unidimensional pastoral nomads is rare, let alone data along these dimensions. Therefore, raw data required for this methodological design must be gathered through independent field surveys among the population in question.

In accordance with this framework, several Bedouin groups in the Negev were chosen for analysis. They include the two major social elements of this society—namely real Bedouin and fellahi Bedouin—as they are spread along the nomadism-urbanism continuum. At one edge of this continuum, however, stands the seminomadic group, as nomadic Bedouin no longer exist. The other edge is signified by the most semiurbanized group. Three groups of real Bedouin and three of fellahi Bedouin were selected from the respective segments of population situated in each phase. These groups were then analyzed synchronically in a comparative manner, on the basis of data derived from field surveys conducted between 1987 and 1990 (Meir and Ben-David 1989; 1990). Since then, many members of several of the groups studied have changed their positions along the continuum, moving ahead toward its semiurban edge.

The seminomad real Bedouin (henceforth referred to as group A) belong to the Abu-Rabia and Azazme tribes. They still live in tents in remote locations in the north-eastern Negev and central Negev Highlands (Figure 5.2), making a living from flock-grazing and primitive dry-farming. They are also eligible, as all Bedouin are, to state maternity, child and old-age social security benefits which often constitute a significant proportion of their income. Only a few adult males are employed in external blue collar occupations. All adults within this group have no formal education of any kind, and the younger generation is becoming integrated into this system only gradually due to distance from schools.

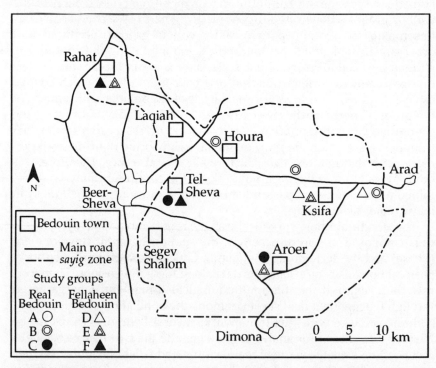

FIGURE 5.2 Location of Bedouin study groups in the Negev (*Source:* Meir and Ben-David 1989).

The rural sedentarized real Bedouin (group B) are so termed because they have been living since the mid-1950s in small hamlets of mostly wood and tin shacks with a few stone structures. Members of this group are from the Abu-Rabia and Al-Ataona tribes and their hamlets—which are inhabited by extended families—are located in the north-eastern and northern areas of the *sayig*. Although they still maintain flocks and pursue dry-farming activities, they have also begun some irrigated farming. However, a significant proportion of their income is derived from blue- and some white-collar employment in the regional labor market and from small entrepreneurship in the regional economy. Formal elementary education has been penetrating gradually into this group, and there is a small proportion of persons with high-school education.

Group C, the recently semiurbanized real Bedouin group, began moving into the planned towns in the late 1970s and early 1980s. They represent the Al-A'assem and Abu-Rabia tribes and reside in the planned towns of Tel-Sheva and Aroer respectively. A few households still maintain small flocks and engage in grazing and dry-farming in land plots leased from the government. These are, however, primarily supplementary to the main income derived from the blue-collar labor market into which many of them integrated even before settling in towns. As high schools are located in towns only, high school education has penetrated somewhat deeper into this group, especially into the younger generation.

The fellahi Bedouin have no nomadic section, as they began their processes of sedentarization and semiurbanization earlier than the real Bedouin. Their rural sedentarized group (group D)—who belong to the A-Nassasrah and Al-Qrinawi tribes in the north-eastern area of the *sayig*—has been living in wooden-shack hamlets for more than three decades. Although they maintain some flocks and dry-farming, being virtually landless they were obliged to resort to external labor market blue-collar occupations somewhat earlier than the real Bedouin. Although the fellaheen in general resorted earlier than the real Bedouin to formal education, as an alternative avenue of status mobility, this particular group is somewhat an exception, primarily due to remoteness from schools.

The recently semiurbanized fellahi group (group E) belong to the A-Jama and A-Touri tribes. They began their semiurbanization in the early 1980s in the towns of Aroer and Rahat respectively where many reside in two-storey homes. Their integration into the labor market and the regional economy became even stronger with the intensification of severance from dry-farming, their main traditional mode of subsistence. While educational levels among adults within this group are relatively low, exposure to formal elementary and higher education among younger adults and children within the semiurban setting is greater.

The final group of the fellaheen, representing the Al-Azazme, Al-Oubra and Al-Qrinawi tribes, are the early semiurbanized ones (group F) who settled in the towns of Tel-Sheva and Rahat respectively in the late 1960s and early 1970s. At that time they were already deeply involved in the regional economy, primarily in transportation and construction and in labor market blue-collar and some white-collar occupations. Their standard of living and rate of high school education are considerably higher than those of the other groups. The majority live in two-storey homes and have private cars, telephones, and modern utilities.

The guiding principle for gathering the necessary demographic data was selection of one or few extended families in each of these six subgroups. As is the case with many other pastoral nomadic societies (e.g., Cross and Kalsbeck 1983), it was extremely difficult to conduct a random sampling within the Bedouin population. This was due primarily to extensive geographical dispersion, wide variability in willingness to cooperate with outsiders, and particularly the outbreak of the Palestinian Intifada in the West Bank and Gaza, with which the Negev Bedouin sympathized. Therefore, extended families were selected on the basis of previous familiarity, or consultation with Bedouin informants themselves, maintaining as far as possible the criterion that the particular family be socioeconomically typical of its respective group.

All households within the selected extended families were surveyed, including information gathered from elder heads of the extended family concerning their parents' households. This enabled extension of the temporal dimension for each group beyond that of its living members. In all, 130 households were surveyed (between twenty and twenty-five per group), comprising about 2.5 percent of the total Bedouin households and of most of the respective groups. Structured questionnaires and tape-recorded in-depth open interviews were conducted with each household head and its adult (usually male) members, to derive the demographic and other data required for the study.

This methodological framework was employed to study several aspects related to processes of demographic and other types of change within the Bedouin society of the Negev. Some of the latter are reported in the next chapter.

Child Mortality

The discussion in the section on general demographic dynamics has demonstrated the relative stability since the 1950s of the already low mortality rates among the Bedouin, with only a minor decline. This portrayal of the demographic situation may be misleading. In addition to problems with the public official data, crude mortality rates usually conceal much information about age-specific rates that may be entirely different. Such is often the case with infant or child mortality, a well known indicator of the public health of a society and, indirectly, of its degree of socioeconomic development. This is particularly important within societies in cultural and socioeconomic transition, such as the Bedouin of the Negev. Therefore, the dynamics of child mortality at the microscale within this society is discussed here under the methodological design outlined above.

Child mortality rate refers here to children dying before the age of five. This definition is preferred over the common one of infant mortality rate (death under one year of age), which is more appropriate for Western societies than for Third World ones. Within the latter, causes of infant mortality apparently do not vanish after the first twelve months of life but continue to affect older children as well. The concept of child mortality rate within the less developed nations thus resembles the way Meade et al. (1988) have treated infant mortality, and is also symptomatic of the higher general mortality within these societies. As the data showed (Meir and Ben-David 1991b), child mortality rates in this age group among the Negev Bedouin have indeed been quite high.

Figure 5.3 presents the group specific percentage of both old households—i.e., those who completed their fertility cycle—and young households, who experienced at least one case of child death, along the continuum. The old families are those who pursued seminomadic and even nomadic life styles for their entire life cycle whereas the younger ones are

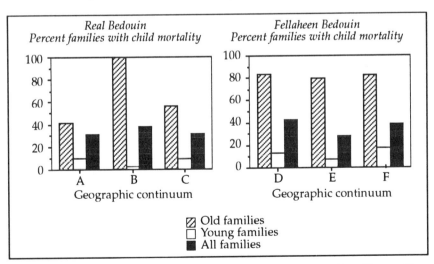

FIGURE 5.3 Negev Bedouin families affected by child mortality (*Source:* Data are from Meir and Ben-David 1989).

those who have already settled in hamlets or in towns. This distinction is made for the purpose of stretching further the implied temporal dimension of the nomadism-sedentarism continuum. The data for old households indicate that in the past most of the families (about 75 percent) suffered loss of young children, a reality characteristic of most Bedouin before 1948. This grief reality is no longer characteristic of young families, although it still persists for about 10 percent of them.

More important are group-specific child mortality data, which are presented in Figure 5.4. As is consistent with data shown in Figure 5.3, the old families suffered child mortality rates ranging from 127/1,000 to 269/1,000. The combined data for all old families, regardless of their group affiliation, suggest that at the seminomadic or nomadic phase about 20 percent of liveborn children did not complete their fifth year. These rates are comparable only to the infant mortality rates that prevailed until very recently in those countries in subSaharan Africa which still have relatively high proportions of nomadic populations. For illustration, infant mortality rates in Mauritania, Senegal, Niger, Somalia, Sudan and other countries in the mid-1980s were above 120/1,000 (P.R.B. 1989; see also Caldwell 1975). The Bedouin rate for old families is indeed extremely high, indicating their weak capability for coping with the harsh and underdeveloped environment in the past. Their neighbors in southern Sinai were living under yet harsher conditions and were situated even further on the nomadic section of the continuum. Their child mortality rate up until 1967—prior to the occupation of the Sinai by Israel during the Six-Day War—was calculated by Ben-David (1978) at about

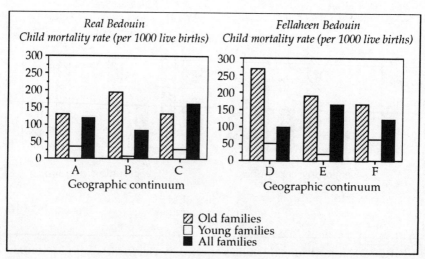

FIGURE 5.4 Negev Bedouin child mortality rates (*Source:* Meir and Ben-David 1994. Reprinted by permission of Magness Press).

325/1,000. It would not be unrealistic to assume that similar rates prevailed among the Negev Bedouin during the early decades of the twentieth century, under the rule of the Ottoman Empire.

The Bedouin were exposed to modern public health services only during the British Mandate over Palestine (1922–1947). This exposure—together with the considerable economic growth during those years—may have lowered child mortality rates to a level typical of the old families shown above, but perhaps not further below. It should be recalled that during this period the Bedouin were still extensively dispersed all over the Negev desert. Despite economic growth, they were living under comparatively poor nutritional levels and were mostly cut-off from the scant public health service centers. Presumably child mortality rates were therefore still extremely high.

While accelerated bifurcation of the Bedouin along the nomadic-sedentary continuum began soon after the establishment of the State of Israel in 1948, differences in child mortality rates between the real Bedouin and the fellahi Bedouin had existed prior to this year. The data on old households reveal that the fellahi Bedouin—who were more sedentary-oriented—suffered considerably higher rates than the real Bedouin. Apparently they were not as capable as the nomadic real Bedouin of escaping diseases or overcoming the poor hygiene and sanitary conditions that were typical of sedentary settings. The possibility of their higher child mortality rate is confirmed by Robof (1977) who suggested that nomads may in general enjoy better health conditions than their neighboring sedentaries, although this thesis is still debatable (see Swift et al. 1990). It also provides some indirect support for our previous proposition (see Chapter 2) that—upon sedentarization—nomads' health may temporarily deteriorate and child mortality may consequently increase temporarily, particularly given that the public health service environment is still underdeveloped.

This environment, however, has changed drastically in recent decades and Bedouin' accessibility to public health services—especially in the new towns—has improved considerably. This process, which will be discussed in more detail in Chapter 7, is apparently responsible for the considerable decline in child mortality rates within the younger families compared to the old families in all sections of the continuum. Child mortality rates have declined even among the old households. Furthermore, at present virtually all Bedouin births are taking place in the regional medical center in Beer-Sheva, since only thus do mothers become eligible for state social security maternity benefits. Presumably, therefore, Bedouin child mortality rates have in recent decades been converging on infant mortality rates as defined internationally in terms of duration. Yet, as Figure 5.4 reveals, they are still considerably higher than the infant mortality rate of the Jewish population of the Negev (about 13/1,000), implying that the public health service system is still inadequate as far as the Bedouin society is concerned.

The notion that at some point along the continuum health conditions may deteriorate—resulting in a temporary increase in child mortality—is highly significant from the perspective of general dynamics of child mortality among sedentarizing pastoral nomads. This is illustrated in Figure 5.4. Child mortality rates for both real Bedouin and the fellahi Bedouin young families decline in the transition from the most seminomadic phase towards the intermediate phase and then rise again towards their more advanced respective phase. Furthermore, in the respective comparable groups along the continuum, that is, rural sedentarized group D vs. group B and the recent semiurbanized group E vs. C, the general combined rates for the fellaheen are higher than for the real Bedouin. Yet, the rise among the latter in their later stage (that is, from group B to C) is considerably higher than that from group D to E among the former. This implies that the real Bedouin, who previously enjoyed relatively better health conditions and whose child mortality rates declined temporarily upon sedentarization, have been affected more seriously by the change in their life style as they progress toward semiurbanization.

Normally, child and infant mortality rates are expected to decline following economic progress (Woods 1982). The issue that is of particular interest here is that the process of economic progress is followed by rising child mortality rates. The process of economic growth and progress among the Negev Bedouin has been demonstrated earlier. In order to illustrate it, Bedouin respondents in each group were asked to rank their self-perceived economic standard of living on a scale of 1–5. Group averages were then calculated and are presented in Table 5.1. It transpires that—as the Bedouin shift towards sedentarization and semiurbanization—there is a general increase in the perceived standard of living. There is, therefore, some contradiction between the reversal of child mortality from declining to increasing rates on the one hand and economic progress on the other.

TABLE 5.1 Perceived economic standard of living of the Negev Bedouin

	Real Bedouin			Fellahi Bedouin		
Groups	A	B	C	D	E	F
Standard of living	2.00	3.30	2.81	3.05	2.57	3.26

A: seminomadic; B: rural sedentarized; C: recent semiurbanized.
D: rural sedentarized; E: recent semiurbanized; F: early semiurbanized.
Source: Meir and Ben-David (1989).

The major explanation for this contradiction is associated with re-placement of old methods of infant and child care by modern ones (e.g., breast-feeding by bottle-feeding) that has been taking place among the Bedouin. This shift has been taking place due to increasing adoption of new domestic and economic responsibilities by women as men enter the wage-labor market (Forman et al. 1990). As in many Third World nations, especially in Africa (Chetley 1979), there is often a time lag until mothers acquire dexterity in the new methods, during which child morbidity—and perhaps mortality—may rise. This issue is closely associated with the status of females. Lewando-Hundt (1980) has shown that Bedouin women's contacts with health service providers are mediated by their husbands as they are allowed no direct contact with strangers. Mothers are therefore deprived of direct instruction regarding proper medical care of children. In addition to this major explanation, the process of sedenta-rization and semiurbanization and the associated closer contacts with the regional human environment have exposed the Bedouin to a new bio-medical environment, and to new diseases with which their ability to cope is insufficient. Within the sedentary village and town settings, even the nature of their own environment has changed considerably, from a sparsely populated to a densely populated one, with consequent faster transmission of pediatric diseases compared to the previous seminomadic phase (Yagupsky et al. 1990).

The reversal in declining child mortality rates appears, however, to be temporary. The data in Figure 5.4 indicate that Bedouin society may have begun to emerge from the rise in child mortality. This is particularly evi-dent with regard to early semiurbanized fellahi Bedouin (group E). The improvement in public educational, health, and welfare service provision (see Chapter 7) has also considerably enhanced Bedouin ability to face the growing momentum of sedentarization and semiurbanization.

In conclusion, the application of the geographical phase approach, that combines the temporal and spatial dimensions, exposed the real dynam-ics of child mortality among the pastoral nomadic Bedouin during their process of geographical change. This micro-scale process was masked by the macro-scale analysis. The analysis revealed that child mortality rates of the Negev Bedouin indeed declined during early sedentarization, but rose temporarily only to be followed again by decline as the process of semiurbanization gains momentum.

Thus, the linear nature generally assumed to characterize the relation-ship between economic growth and declining child mortality may not necessarily be universal. Indeed Meade et al. (1988) noted that often mor-tality decline did not follow successful planned economic development programs, at least not immediately. In our previous general discussion of the relationships between pastoral nomads and the state (see Chapter 2),

we dwelt upon the misconception and misunderstanding of these societies by government officials. The issue of child mortality may be a case
in point. Officials may tend to adopt the accepted simple linear relationship between economic growth and declining child mortality and risk
overlooking the need to deliver extra health care to pastoral nomads,
especially during the sensitive transition phase from nomadism to sedentarism. Our analysis suggests that even in the developed, Westernized
context within which Israeli Bedouin have sedentarized and semiurbanized, this relationship is not necessarily simple.

From the perspective of general demographic dynamics, this refinement of our understanding of the demographic impact of economic
growth is consistent with an earlier refinement regarding the impact of
development on fertility decline. Tabbarah (1976) has postulated—and
many other studies demonstrated since (e.g., Bongaarts et al. 1984)—that
fertility decline may also be delayed and perhaps may even rise, during
early stages of development. The previous, macroscale analysis of fertility
trends among the Negev Bedouin has indeed substantiated this notion.
However, microscale patterns may still be discerned—particularly from
the more important perspective of fertility behavior—and these are the
concern of the next section.

Fertility Rationality and Behavior

An examination of the changing value of children is of particular significance to the analysis of current fertility behavior among the Negev
Bedouin. This issue refers not only to fertility patterns but to the entire issue of the value and status of children within Bedouin society. This, however, is discussed in detail only in the next chapter within the wider
framework of changes in the status of individuals within this society. At
this point suffice it to suggest that, at least from an economic perspective,
the value of children among the Bedouin has declined drastically in recent decades. A new socially-significant state of mind has emerged which
may be characterized as a latent surplus of children (Meir and Ben-David
1992). This lays the ground for an examination of the question of whether
the Bedouin have consequently begun to move from a rationality of high
fertility to one of lower fertility, and whether they have developed new
patterns of fertility behavior along the nomadism-urbanism continuum.

In attempting to answer this question, and under the same methodological framework outlined above, several indicators of household fertility behavior were analyzed for each of the six groups along the continuum. Here, however, both actual and desired patterns were included in
order to identify possible paths of change that may have emerged among

the Bedouin (Meir and Ben-David 1995). These indicators are presented in Table 5.2, showing verbally the general qualitative summary of quantitative trends, based upon detailed field data (Meir and Ben-David 1989). They represent group average household behavioral and desired trends along the continuum of both the real and fellahi Bedouin.

The trends in birth rates were presented above at the macro level, without accounting separately for the real or the fellahi Bedouin. In contrast, the trends in fertility patterns are not entirely uniform between these major social groups, nor are they entirely consistent within them. The first concern is the number of live-births. Among the real Bedouin, the number of live-births increases before beginning to decline along the continuum. Such growth in fertility during early stages of departure from seminomadic pastoralism is expected following improved nutrition, which increases a woman's chances to conceive and complete her pregnancy successfully (Frisch 1975). It may also follow exposure to public

TABLE 5.2 Trends in actual and desired fertility indicators among the Bedouin along the nomadism-urbanism continuum

Indicator	Real Bedouin[a]	Fellahi Bedouin[b]
Timing of first birth	Delay	Delay
Spacing of births	Decline followed by stabilization	Decline followed by minor increase
Number of live-births	Increase followed by decline	Decline
Number of children in completed family	Increase followed by decline	Decline followed by minor increase
Perceived social norm of family size	Stable	Decline followed by increase
Preference of male offspring	Decline	Increase
Desired family size:		
(1) under no constraint	Decline followed by increase	Decline
(2) under economic constraint	Decline followed by stabilization	Decline

[a] Real Bedouin continuum: seminomads; rural-sedentarized; late semiurbanized.
[b] Fellahi Bedouin continuum: rural-sedentarized; late semiurbanized; early semiurbanized.
Source: Meir and Ben-David (1989).

health services, which reduces the impact of environmentally-biologi-
cally- and behaviorally-suppressed fertility. In particular, it is associated
with the transition from prolonged breast-feeding—which could last as
long as three years and occasionally longer among the seminomadic
group—to bottle-feeding, which is a consequence of the growing tendency to give birth in the regional medical center in Beer-Sheva. This is
consistent with findings from nomadic societies elsewhere (e.g., Howell
1980). As the seminomadic phase no longer exists in the continuum of the
fellahi Bedouin, it is possible only to assume that they experienced a similar increase when shifting previously from seminomadism to early
sedentarization.

Differences in the number of children in the completed family between
these major social groups may be explained similarly. The minor increase
among the fellaheen may, however, be accounted for by both their drive
to improve their inferior social status and their earlier relocation into a
dense environment in towns. In this process, their need both to sustain
their improved social status and to achieve stronger deterrent demographic power has increased. The real Bedouin—who presumably do not
perceive any threat to their superior status—do not share this kind of fertility behavior. This explanation is supported by another indicator, the
perceived general social norm of family size. The real Bedouin perceive
no change that has taken place in the prevailing norm of family size within Bedouin society at large, despite the fact that the number of children in
their own completed families has declined. In contrast, the fellaheen perception reflects more realistically their actual family size trend as they
become semiurbanized, i.e., decline in the perceived norm of family size
followed by increase. Furthermore, preference for male offspring—which
is another indicator, and is related to the issue of sociopolitical value of
children (see next chapter)—increases along the continuum among the
fellaheen, while declining among the real Bedouin.

The major indicator is that of desired family size, the trends of which
are not entirely consistent with the other trends. For this reason it is presented here in more detail in Figure 5.5, showing actual and desired family sizes along the continuum. The notion of desired family size, as presented to respondents, refers to two alternative circumstances: (1) the
nuclear family has no economic constraint upon the number of children;
and (2) there is an economic constraint upon the number of children, a
consequence of both the decline in their economic value and the desire to
maintain the family's rising standard of living. The data reveal that the
constraint-free desired family size is similar in both groups at their respective continua are, however, different. Constraint-free desired family
size among the real Bedouin declines sharply followed by sharp increase

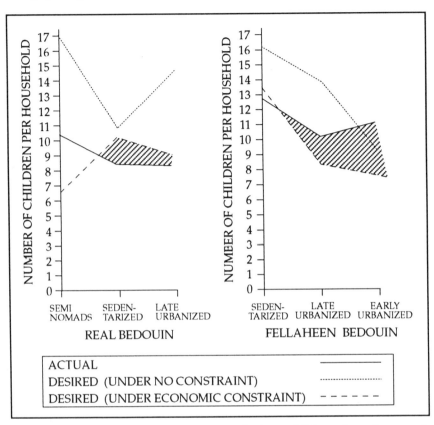

FIGURE 5.5 Actual and desired number of Bedouin children along the nomad-ism-sendentarism continuum (*Source:* Meir and Ben-David 1989).

toward the semiurbanized phase. This perhaps reflects their need for a larger family as they begin to realize the consequences of sociospatial friction within a denser space in towns. However, their preferences differ under an economic constraint. First, in their seminomadic phase they already begin to realize the economic constraint of maintaining a large family and would prefer a far smaller family. Second, such realization becomes stronger at the sedentarized and semiurban phases along the continuum.

There is greater consistency in the trend to decline between both types of desired family size among the fellahi Bedouin than among the real Bedouin, although the magnitudes and rates are different. These major social groups differ also in the values from which their economically constrained desired family size begins to decline. Among the fellahi Bedouin it declines from a higher level. Nevertheless, both groups eventually reach a similar level of desired family size. It is here that a major similarity emerges between them. Both are transformed along the continuum from a similar large family size—desired when no constraints exist—to a similar far smaller desired family size under economic constraint.

An examination of actual versus economically constrained desired family size yields further insights. As expected, the desired family size is lower than the actual family size, particularly at more advanced phases. Furthermore, there seems to be a partially inverse relationship between both indicators, supporting the earlier notion about the emergence of surplus of children. This is particularly so among the fellahi Bedouin, who have begun to realize the consequences of the conflict between the presently declining economic value of children in condition of high fertility on the one hand, and the desire to maintain an improved personal standard of living on the other. That Bedouin society has indeed raised its standard of living has already been shown above (see Table 5.1; also Abu-Rabia, A. 1994c).

However, the explanation for the emergence of a surplus of children assumes that such improvement in living standards, in association with exposure to "Westernization," has begun to encourage adoption of more modern values. These may affect the standard of living and quality of life more significantly than do traditional values. In order to substantiate this assumption, Bedouin respondents were asked to indicate in descending order of importance five indicators through which they would gain a reasonable quality of life. The replies were content-analyzed and then collapsed into two typical categories. The first category refers to traditional pastoral-nomadic indicators—such as pasture and water for livestock, residence in a traditional pastoral tent, freedom of movement and access to traditional grazing territories, nonintervention by government in their pastoral and tribal affairs, social acceptance, honor and dignity within the Bedouin community, and peaceful sociopolitical internal relationships. The second category—the modern one—refers to life quality indicators related to a modern materialistic standard of living, such as acquisition of modern education and professions, high income, and ownership of a home, an automobile, and home electric appliances and other related needs. Responses which initially specified one of the five original indicators as most important were assigned to the appropriate category. The percentage distribution of these categories within these responses is presented in Table 5.3 for each group along the continuum.

The data indicate clearly a strong infiltration of Western concepts of life quality along the continua of both the real and the fellahi Bedouin and a gradual decline in the dominance of traditional ones. While among

TABLE 5.3 Traditional and modern life quality indicators among the Negev Bedouin (in percentages)

	Real Bedouin			*Fellahi Bedouin*		
Life quality indicator	*A*	*B*	*C*	*D*	*E*	*F*
Traditional	100	69	69	63	84	53
Modern	0	31	31	37	16	47

A: seminomadic; B: rural sedentarized; C: recent semiurbanized;
D: rural sedentarized; E: recent semiurbanized; F: early semiurbanized.
Source: Meir and Ben-David (1995). Reprinted by permission of the *Journal of Comparative Family Studies.*

the real Bedouin there is a higher rate of increase, the absolute levels among the fellahi Bedouin are higher. A comparison with the trends in Table 5.1 reveals a certain parallelism: a decline or rise in dominance of these concepts along the continua is matched by a similar trend in the perceived standard of living. The implication is that a close link has emerged among the Bedouin between economic standard of living and Western concepts of life quality as their sociospatial trend toward semi-urbanization intensifies. This is especially evident among the fellahi Bedouin and partly among the real Bedouin.

A further implication of this linkage is the emergence of a more secular and materialistic Western-oriented fertility rationality. This rationality is reflected in the general economically-constrained desire for a smaller family. While hitherto the analysis of this process was conducted at the group level, the emerging rationality may have infiltrated also into the individual level, and may have been affected by several factors. Their relationships with the desired number of children (as a dependent variable) was therefore analyzed at the individual level (Table 5.4). These variables are: (1) perceived personal standard of living; (2) phase of the individual's respective group along the continuum; (3) educational level; (4) age; and (5) social group affiliation.

The analysis reveals that as the Bedouin advance along the continuum and as their educational level rises (negative signs of variables #2 and #3 respectively)—especially among the younger generation (positive sign of variable #4)—their economically constrained desired family size declines. However, there is still a conflict between findings at the group level and those at the individual level. In contrast to the group level, a larger family (a positive sign of variable #5) is more strongly preferred by the fellahi Bedouin than by the real Bedouin. Also, there is a positive relationship between standard of living and desired family size. Yet, as shown earlier,

TABLE 5.4 Summary of multiple regression analysis of desired number of children among the Bedouin (n=130)

Independent variable	1. Standard of living[a]	2. Phase along continuum[b]	3. Educational level[c]	4. Age	5. Social group affiliation[d]
B[e]	1.754	−1.905	−0.0307	0.091	3.285
Beta[f]	0.246	−0.267	−0.240	0.238	0.246

$R^2 = 0.27$; Constant=5.65; $p < 0.05$ for all variables.

[a]Measured on a scale of 1–5, based upon self-ranking of respondents.

[b]Ordinal scale: seminomadism=1; rural-sedentarized=2; late-urbanized=3; early-urbanized=4.

[c]Number of schooling years.

[d]Dummy variable: real Bedouin=0; fellahi Bedouin=1.

[e]Partial regression coefficient.

[f]Standardized regression coefficient.

Source: Meir and Ben-David (1995). Reprinted by permission of *Journal of Comparative Family Studies.*

it is widely accepted that the temporary increase in desired family size in early stages of development, due to increase in standard of living, tends to reverse at later stages. Indeed, a closer look at each Bedouin subgroup, via a simple correlation between desired family size and perceived standard of living (see Table 5.5), reveals that the relationships tend to become negative or nil from the less to the more developed phases along the continua. The conflict between the findings of the different levels of analysis suggest, perhaps, that the negative effect of the rising standard of living on desired family size has not yet become a reality affecting all individual Bedouin.

The implication of the above discussion is that Bedouin household heads, particularly younger ones who have been exposed to urban Western values and higher standards of living and levels of education, tend to

TABLE 5.5 Relationship between desired family size and perceived standard of living among the Bedouin

Groups	*Real Bedouin*			*Fellahi Bedouin*		
	A	B	C	D	E	F
r	0.65	−0.56	−0.22	0.23	0.28	0.05

A: seminomadic; B: rural sedentarized; C: recent semiurbanized;
D: rural sedentarized; E: recent semiurbanized; F: early semiurbanized.
Source: Meir and Ben-David (1989).

adopt fertility rationality in which modern materialistic components are more dominant than traditional ones. This indicates a process of individualization, whereby pluralistic behavioral norms emerge within the Bedouin society, replacing gradually the more uniform norm. In this process, the nuclear family's fertility decisions, at least from an economic perspective, are gradually less affected by those of wider social units.

However, even the norm of preference for male offspring, which is sociopolitically significant from the perspective of these wider circles in particular (see next chapter) has been changing. This is a consequence of the recent process of semiurbanization, which has often been cited as responsible for the declining importance of such wide social reference groups (Cole 1981; Frantz 1975). Table 5.6 shows the distribution of those respondents who prefer male offspring below or above the average desired number of children in the family in their respective subgroups. In contrast to Table 5.2, which revealed some mixed trends, here most of those who prefer male offspring are also those whose ideal family size is below their group average and these are situated at more advanced phases along the continuum (e.g., groups B=78 percent; C=75 percent; E=71 percent; and F=55 percent). Moreover, their rates increase with the advent of sedentarization and semiurbanization. This is particularly so among the real Bedouin and to a considerable extent among the fellahi Bedouin.

Thus—with intensified sedentarization and semiurbanization—not only the rising standard of living but also preference for male offspring is increasingly in conflict with the desire for a large family. It transpires that the balancing effect of the sociopolitical value of children upon the emerging materialistic-secular fertility rationality is still valid among the

TABLE 5.6 Distribution of respondents preferring male offspring below and above their group-average desired number of children (in percentages)

	Real Bedouin			Fellahi Bedouin		
Groups	A	B	C	D	E	F
Preference for male offspring	86	69	25	26	37	67
Desired number of children:						
-below average	50	78	75	40	71	55
-above average	50	22	25	60	29	45

A: seminomadic; B: rural sedentarized; C: recent semiurbanized;
D: rural sedentarized; E: recent semiurbanized; F: early semiurbanized.
Source: Meir and Ben-David (1989).

Bedouin, but has been weakening recently. Yet, the emerging fertility rationality—which implies a desire for a smaller family—has still to withstand another balancing effect, that of the gradual penetration of Islamic fundamentalism and its fertility implications into the modernizing Bedouin society. This trend, however, has been too recent for valid conclusions to be drawn regarding fertility rationality and behavior among individual members of this society.

Given that an awareness of the latent surplus of children has emerged within Bedouin society and that individuals have begun to adopt an alternative fertility rationality, the question arises of whether those who have adopted such rationality have also begun to resort to fertility and birth control methods. Evidence to this effect is as yet inconclusive. Table 5.2 implies that the Bedouin have perhaps begun to use family planning methods, which result in delaying the first birth and a minor increase in spacing of births at advanced phases along the continuum. Many individual Bedouin are generally aware of modern fertility and birth control methods, perhaps through the network of family planning clinics deployed by the government in some Bedouin towns and in Beer-Sheva, through couples who have resorted to these methods for medical reasons, or through rumors about individual women who used them for various other reasons. However, most respondents were reluctant to yield personal information regarding this taboo, and even data from the governmental clinics is as yet confidential.

Still, an unknown number of Bedouin wives—without their husband's consent or knowledge—as well as young Bedouin couples, have voluntarily used modern fertility control devices received from the clinics or from the regional medical center in Beer-Sheva. Obviously, such informal data—gathered through fieldwork and from numerous personal communications with officials and social workers—cannot be accepted for validating practice of fertility and birth control among the Bedouin. However, in line with the KAP (Knowledge-Attitude-Practice) formula (Nortman 1977), it could indicate that, to a considerable degree, the Bedouin's awareness of this behavioral option, their attitude toward this issue, and its practice, though still very minor, have become an important step toward realization of the newly emerging fertility behavior norms.

Early Indications of an Aging Process

The general conclusion that may be reached from the demographic processes discussed so far is that the Bedouin society of the Negev has been moving away from the demographic context of nomadic and rural societies in the Third World and approaching gradually the demographic context of the urban Western world. This possibly suggests that early indications of an aging process may have also begun to emerge. The significance of this possible process is not just demographic. If indeed there are such indications, they may have a bearing upon the status and wellbeing of Bedouin elders, an issue that will be discussed separately in the next chapter.

The processes discussed above have not by any means yet eliminated the typical Third World demographic nature of Bedouin population structure. Indeed, as Figure 5.6 illustrates, this is still a very young society, with at least half the population under age 15 and median age 13.2 (Central Bureau of Statistics 1994). Furthermore, Table 5.7 indicates that the percentage of elders has declined considerably in recent decades, implying that Bedouin society is becoming even younger.

However, a question may be raised as to the trends of the rejuvenation process evident within Bedouin society. A closer look at various data yields some insights into this issue. First, as shown above, Bedouin life expectancy has increased considerably in recent decades. Values are now very close to those of the Jewish and other Arab population in Israel.

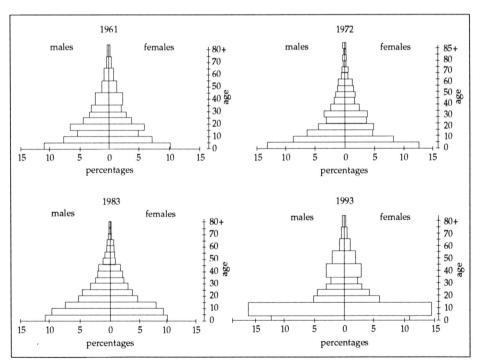

FIGURE 5.6   Age-sex structure of the Bedouin population: 1961–1993 (*Source:* Data are from the *Statistical Abstract of Israel* for the various years).

Table 5.7   Elders in Bedouin society, 1961–1983 (in percentages)

	Elders age >70[a]			Elders age >55[a]		
Year	1961	1972	1983	1961	1972	1983
Males	2.0	1.8	1.2	6.5	4.9	3.8
Females	1.8	1.6	1.0	5.6	3.6	4.0
Total	1.9	1.7	1.1	6.1	4.3	3.9

[a] The distinction between elders at ages >70 and >55 conforms to Bedouin's own distinction between biologically and socially old persons.
Source: Meir and Ben-David (1990).

Secondly, and more directly, the process of rejuvenation itself may be examined in more detail. Skewness *(Sk)* of age structures is a suitable measure for this purpose. A zero value of this index indicates an even distribution of age groups, and it increases positively or negatively as the population becomes younger or older respectively (Anson 1991). When applied to Bedouin age structures over time (Meir and Ben-David 1990), the values are as follows: $Sk_{1961} = 1.11$; $Sk_{1972} = 1.278$; $Sk_{1983} = 1.324$; $Sq_{1993} = 1.41$. Consistent with the high fertility rates, the increasing skewness values indeed indicate a rejuvenation process of Bedouin society. Yet, attention should also be paid to their growth rate. A comparison between the years reveals that the rates of increase of *Sk* for 1972–1983 and 1983–1993 (about 4 percent and 6 percent respectively) are considerably lower than that for 1961–1972 (about 15 percent), implying that the rejuvenation process may have been slowing down. However, one should still bear in mind the differences in quality of data between 1961 and 1993.

Third, and even more directly, an aging process may be discerned not only through relative rates but also from absolute numbers. This approach is particularly significant from the perspective of provision of public welfare services for Bedouin elders, which is the concern of the next chapter. Table 5.8 shows the number of Bedouin elders for the same period. Indeed, there is an increase in the number of elders aged >70, but it stops in 1983. This may be accounted for by life expectancy reaching its top possible level under the contemporary socioecological circumstances of the Bedouin society. However, it would not be unreasonable to expect the number of Bedouin elders aged >70 to continue to increase. Recent research has suggested that the annual growth rate of the number of Arab elders in Israel at large—forecasted until the year 2000—will be 3.8 percent, compared to 1.1 percent for Jewish elders (Be'er and Factor 1989). The implication of this forecast is that the elderly Arab population (of which the Negev Bedouin are part) will double itself by 2008, and will increase by about 50 percent by 2000.

Table 5.8 Absolute number of Bedouin elders, 1961–1983

	Elders age >70[a]			Elders age >55[a]		
Year	1961	1972	1983	1961	1972	1983
Males	194	267	266	631	730	854
Females	164	230	207	506	532	816
Total	358	497	473	1137	1262	1670

Source: Meir and Ben-David (1990).

While these rates may not necessarily be representative of the Negev Bedouin, a look at the category of elders aged >55 reveals that their trends may not be too far apart. The number of Bedouin in this age group has grown considerably in recent decades, with an average annual growth rate in 1972–1983 at about 3.0 percent. At this rate, it is not unrealistic to expect a doubling of the 1983 elderly Bedouin population within the next two or three decades. Even an assumption of sustained and perhaps accelerated increase since 1983 and in the coming decades may become realistic considering that the past high fertility rates will be reflected in future age structures.

In summary, this brief discussion—together with that of declining fertility rates—suggests that the typical Third World age structure of the Negev Bedouin society has begun to change. Early indications of an aging process have begun to emerge at both the base and the crest of the age pyramid. However, the full manifestation of this process has yet to be realized.

Conclusions

Several major processes relevant for population dynamics within the Bedouin society of the Negev were analyzed. These included general trends in birth and death rates, more specific child mortality trends, fertility behavior, and population aging. Several of these were analyzed along the nomadism-urbanism continuum that has emerged within this society in recent decades. While the first major demographic transition started among the Bedouin in the early 1970s—when fertility rates begun to decline—the present roots of the aging process may possibly signify the onset of a second major demographic transition.

Most significant from the particular perspective of this discussion, however, are changes in fertility behavior taking place along the continuum. The declining economic value of children for the nuclear family, due both to loss of control over them as producers of resources and their becoming consumers of resources in their own right, has generated a latent fertility surplus. This—coupled with adoption of a certain degree of Western-style economic fertility rationality and the desire to maintain a higher standard of living—is resulting in an emergence of new norms of family size. Perhaps the declining child mortality rates along the continuum have also had an impact on declining fertility rates, as households are presently far more assured of realizing their norms of desired family size. While there are some differences between the real Bedouin and the fellahi Bedouin in the nature of these processes, both groups tend to change their fertility norms from a large to a considerably smaller family size.

Thus, external pressures are responsible for the move across the ideological divide line between fertility ideals. This does not imply that the change in fertility behavior among the Bedouin has already taken on sweeping dimensions. Yet, fertility control has become a real and practical behavioral option. Obviously, the process has been gradual, and the various Bedouin subgroups vary in their tendency and practice. Consequently, a continuum of fertility rationalities, fertility behavioral norms and patterns and fertility variability has been emerging within this transitional society. Individual Bedouin households are thus becoming liberated from previous group values and norms of fertility. They tend now to voluntarily and independently adopt the new norms and practices for their own individual household's wellbeing, with considerably reduced commitment to that of their social group.

6

Social Status and Wellbeing
of Individuals

The discussion in the previous two chapters has revealed that the process of sedentarization and the changing socioeconomic ecological setting entailed also changes in the relationships between the individual Bedouin and his group. As the shift from pastoral nomadism via rural sedentarization to semiurbanism gained momentum, these changes were manifested primarily in two ways: in the tendency toward territoriality that has infiltrated down from the tribal to the individual household level; and in the emergence of variability in fertility norms and practice away from the previous uniform pattern. These spatial and demographic manifestations imply that a process of social and economic individualization of Bedouin society has been set in motion. As postulated in Chapter 2, individuals and nuclear households are now assuming greater responsibility for their own future than for that of their respective groups. Furthermore, the group is gradually losing its ability to be responsible for the individual and to shape his future.

The main implication of this change is that the status of individuals within Bedouin society may be undergoing change, entailing also changes in their wellbeing. This chapter will examine these changes with regard to the status of children, elders and women whose role has changed considerably. These changes are interrelated but those relating to children and elders are of particular interest. As will be shown below, to a considerable extent the economic wellbeing of children is enhanced at the expense of the elders.

The Status of Children

As demonstrated in the previous chapter, understanding of current fertility behavior among the Negev Bedouin derives chiefly from the issue of the changing value of children for both the nuclear family and society at large, which affects their social status. Few studies of social change within Bedouin society have paid attention to this issue, and then mostly in an indirect manner (e.g., Kressel 1982). Therefore, the discussion here is based primarily upon views and opinions concerning the value of children expressed in the open interviews conducted among the various groups along the nomadism-urbanism continuum (see previous chapter). Archetype patterns of each group were derived through an analysis of statements of individual respondents relating to perceptions and meanings of the status of children. As it turned out, these patterns have become more variegated the further away the various Bedouin groups have shifted from the pastoral nomadic mode of production. Therefore, a distinction was made between the traditional perspective and the newly-emerging one. The traditional perspective is referred to here as a normative one, exposing the prevailing norms with regard to the value of children in the seminomadic pastoral mode of production. This perspective, derived from group A, the seminomadic Bedouin (see above), serves as the basis for appreciation of changes along the nomadism-urbanism continuum.

The Traditional Perspective

The Theistic Dimension. The issue of value of children among the Bedouin seems to fall within three general dimensions (Meir and Ben-David 1989; Meir and Ben-David 1992). The first of these is a theistic dimension. The prevalent norm among the traditional seminomadic Bedouin is a large multichild family. This norm is anchored in a theistic reasoning, and is ascribed to the will of Allah as pursued by human beings who are his passive and submissive agents on earth. Their only role is to fulfill Allah's wish and beget children—his gift "without any reckoning"—as one of the interviewees put it. Hence, they reject any secular rationalization of the value of children, which could result in controlling family size.

In light of the view—once held by Western social scientist—that lack of Western rationality within traditional Third World societies implied irrational behavior altogether, this particular reasoning could also be perceived as irrational. However, in the contemporary pluralistic social science view, which legitimizes multiple rationalities, the Bedouin's reasoning of multiplicity of children, with no limit on fertility is therefore theistically rational. This norm, one of Allah's supreme goals, is also supreme, sanctified and universal. Thus, one of the interviewees argued that throughout their history Bedouin have always advocated a norm of maximum fertility. Therefore, the issue of supporting many children is not of much concern to the Bedouin. In their theistic philosophy, it is Allah's role to care for their basic needs and wellbeing.

These views are typical particularly of the elders of the seminomadic group. They are aware of other norms that are rooted in different kinds of rationality, in which human beings are regarded as more active and capable of controlling their affairs. However, even those elders who have already been exposed to secular rationality argue that social pressures within Bedouin society have so far left the individual with little choice but to adhere to the theistic norm of fertility. In their opinion, only a far reaching cultural change within Bedouin society will bring about a normative change in the size of the family. While some elders admit that such a change has indeed begun, they maintain that its consequences for the family still lie very far ahead. Yet, the significance of this view for the present discussion is that they acknowledge the possibility of a cultural change and hence also of change in the value of children.

The Economic Dimension. The theistic rationality vis-à-vis value of children is intertwined with two other practical dimensions—economic and sociopolitical. Economically, seminomadic Bedouin children are perceived by their parents both as a labor force and as supporters and hence as a resource—control and utilization of which should be maximized. This perception can be appreciated in light of the supreme status of elders on the one hand (see next section), and the subservient status of children and their lack of private status on the other. As in other pastoral nomadic societies, young Bedouin children of both sexes actively participate in all pastoral, farming and domestic labor assignments. They acquire their skills through the informal educational process (see Abu-Ajaj and Ben-David 1988) which socializes children into the pastoral-nomadic economic, social, and political fabric. The amount of material resources they produce directly for their parents via this channel increases with their number, although there is perhaps a ceiling in terms of marginal contribution.

Nowadays, however, there also occurs an indirect production process within which young and adult children are producing resources for their family. As fully fledged citizens of the state of Israel, the Bedouin are eligible for various state benefits under the Social Security Law. As far as young children are concerned, the social security maternity grant is about $250 and the monthly child allowances are about $30 per child under the age of eighteen, and increase progressively with the number of children, so that a Bedouin family of ten children may receive about $650 ($65 per child). On the basis of data from Ben-David (1988), monthly household income derived from livestock and dry-farming for the seminomadic Bedouin averages $200–250. At these extremely low income levels, the social security grants add significantly to the family's wellbeing. Adult sons, on the other hand, continue to pursue the role of resource-producers within the expanded family economic unit. They are expected to guarantee a secure old age for their parents and support them fully through their independent grazing and farming units which branch off from the father's unit (see also Boneh 1983). This issue is elaborated upon in more detail in the next section.

Gender is of particular importance in this context. As adult sons are expected to remain within the paternal expanded family, male offspring are of greater value and are preferred over females. From the perspective of fertility, this is another motivation for its maximization. The motivation of the Bedouin mother is also relevant here (Lewando-Hundt 1984; Marx 1986). She is confronted with the permanent risk of being divorced or taking second place to another wife. She wishes, therefore, to guarantee her wellbeing through maximizing her fertility so that her many male children will maximize her share in her husband's wealth (see also Kressel 1992a; Kressel 1992b).

These views of the economic value of young and adult children refer to their contribution to family income. From the perspective of cost of young children, the seminomadic Bedouin parents regard young children's needs as minimal. In their own words, these needs are well within the limits of "one piece of bread and one garment per child" and, hence, " a hundred children can be nourished by one dish." At this group's current traditional and under developed mode of living, other expenses associated with children are minimal. On balance, thus, it transpires that the economic cost of raising children to adulthood among the seminomadic Bedouin in the Negev is far exceeded by the economic benefits which accrue for their family.

Another issue associated with value of children among the seminomadic Bedouin is related to child mortality which, as shown above, is extremely high. In the other Bedouin groups—that are more advanced along the continuum—these rates are at similar yet somewhat lower magnitudes. However, their members have already become integrated in various degrees in the regional expastoral economic system. This being so, the economic value of their children, as will be seen below, is no longer as critical as it still is for the seminomadic group. Within the latter, the high child mortality rates may reduce the number of children available as a labor force within the completed family. Members of this group are well aware of this reality. Therefore, the spur for maximization of fertility is reinforced among them in order both to maintain the theistic norm and to guarantee the realization of the children's potential economic value in childhood and adulthood.

The Sociopolitical Dimension. The economic value of children was discussed above from their own nuclear family perspective. Their social and political value, however, extends into wider social circles. We recall the quasi-hierarchical sociopolitical structure of Bedouin society, which has traditionally been organized into clans, tribes, sub-tribes, co-liable groups, extended families, and nuclear families. In principle, a Bedouin individual is expected to express his loyalty toward all tiers within this system. This loyalty implies, in general, a total collective commitment for mutual defense of life, resources, and property, and this is brought into effect by male members of the group (see e.g., Stewart 1991). It appears, however, that due to recent processes of disintegration of the traditional political organization within the Bedouin society, the strongest loyalties are presently directed toward the co-liable group and more so toward the extended and nuclear families. The larger these groups are, the higher their sociopolitical status and their deterrence force. In the conflict-ridden Bedouin society, this enhances the value of male offspring and thus further reinforces the norm of fertility maximization. This role assigned to male offspring within their wide social co-liable circles is well rooted in Bedouin society, and it prevails even within the rural and semiurbanized Bedouin community (Marx 1974; Kressel 1982; Kressel 1992a).

The Emerging Patterns

The economic and sociopolitical dimensions of the value of children among the traditional nomadic and seminomadic Bedouin, articulated into the theistic dimension, shape the normative view of maximization of fertility within this society. However, an interpretation of views, opinions, and reasoning of respondents among the various other groups reveals that important changes have emerged in recent decades among the Bedouin along the nomadism-urbanism continuum. Their exposure to the Western rationality and its penetration—in various degrees along the continuum—into their Islamic theistic rationality is the most significant change. The emergence of this rationality is a combined product of the geographical, cultural, economic and political dynamics, particularly in the last five decades. The emerging conflicts between the present sedentary lifestyle and mode of production on the one hand and traditional fertility norms on the other, are well reflected in attitudes of Bedouin of all generations and all phases of the continuum toward the issue of value of children.

Economically, Bedouin of all phases along the continuum refer to the growing obstacles to pursuance of their traditional grazing and dry-farming sources of subsistence. Finding free natural pastures and water is highly problematic for those still maintaining livestock (see also Abu-Rabia, A. 1994c). As shown by Ben-David (1988), many are forced to reduce flock size due to growing expenditures on fodder and other livestock-related expenses. The livestock economy has been severely affected by market trends in the late 1980s and early 1990s, particularly by falling livestock and meat prices due to a decline in demand in the West Bank and Gaza Strip during the Intifada. Under such conditions, the potential contribution of children to the household production process, particularly among the semiurbanized groups, cannot be realized as in the pastoral nomadic phase. In these groups, old and young household-head interviewees often cited the argument that young children no longer produce economic benefits for their parents to the same degree as before. This implies that their value on the income side of the Bedouin household economic equation has fallen rapidly.

The economic value of adult children has also changed. The shrinking livestock and dry-farming economy and division of the family labor force within the regional wage labor market, have significantly contributed to fragmentation and individualization of the traditional extended family economic pattern. The traditional pattern of an extended family economic unit—in which the nuclear households share resources communally and adult children are responsible to the wellbeing of their parents—is no longer wholly characteristic of the Bedouin society. Less than half of the families (45 percent) maintain such a traditional economic pattern (Meir and Ben-David 1990; Meir and Ben-David 1993). This issue will be analyzed in more detail below. However, young parents are well aware of this, more individualistic emerging pattern and its bearing upon the economic value of adult children.

From the perspective of expenditures, it is most significant that the Bedouin across the continuum are adopting an economic terminology which examines the value of children in terms of revenues vs. expenditures. Even those seminomadic Bedouin who argued that Allah will ensure that "a hundred children can be nourished by one dish," now admit that they "calculate family economy according to one dish per child." More significantly, one respondent from a semiurbanized group indicated that—in contrast to the past, when only the very basic needs were fulfilled—children needs in the town environment are now considerably higher. He complained, therefore, that today "each child requires a separate budget to fulfill his needs."

Thus, the burden of children on the family economy is increasing. Statements that each child requires a dish and a budget reflect the increasing individualization of the Bedouin child, a process which encompasses a growing number of sedentarized and semiurbanized Bedouin households. It indicates a change in attitude from that in which the child is submerged in the general mass of children, with little privacy and fulfillment of individual personalized needs, to a state in which the boy (less so the girl as yet) receives more personal attention. To this may also be added the fact that concealment of personal identity—which was a common practice at the nomadic phase—is gradually disappearing as the Bedouin become integrated into the state bureaucratic system (Levi 1987). This process adds a further dimension to the individualization process. Thus, the needs of children as a group are broken down into individual needs which increases the overall burden on the family. Some Bedouin have commented that they are aware of the emergence of this rather different rationality, leading them to admit that—at least from an economic point of view—"Bedouin today desire fewer children."

The very emergence of such an ideal within Bedouin society is highly significant. The major factor in the changing roles of children—in addition to loss of their economic potential as producers of resources—is the intensive introduction of modern Western education by the government. This issue will be dealt with in more detail in the next chapter. Suffice it to note here that, in the past, whatever education was provided never interfered with the participation of children in the pastoral production process. Circumstances are now radically different. The growing awareness of the need to provide formal education to children, reflecting the newly-adopted understanding of the linkage between education and standard of living, is shared by all Bedouin across the continuum. Even the most peripherally-located seminomads do not rule out the possibility of pooling to transport their children daily to schools located in remote Bedouin hamlets or towns. This reflects their recognition of the dual damage which the family economy suffers through losing the labor of children and paying the cost of their transportation and schooling.

This awareness is even stronger among those Bedouin groups who have already sedentarized or became semiurbanized and for whom this is a pressing problem. As a safeguard against economic instability, about 10 percent of them, to various degrees, still maintain flocks and engage in dry-farming activities even while living in towns (Ben-David 1988; Abu-Rabia, A. 1994c). But they too are aware of the negative impact of schooling on the pastoral production process. Even for them, particularly those still living in hamlets, remoteness of schools and long school days leave their children with limited time for tending flocks. Thus, the shadow price of their economically valuable labor in terms of hiring extrafamilial herdsmen, with all its implications for the wellbeing of livestock and for household income, is suffered by their parents.

However, members of these groups relate more directly than do the seminomadic group to the role of modern education. Their children have not only been leaving the production cycle but have also been entering the consumption cycle through schooling and its related costs. Some older parents already wish that they had fewer children so that they could provide all of them with formal education. A few younger fathers have even admitted openly to practicing hitherto tabooed fertility control "in order to provide education and improved wellbeing for their children." Typical reasoning cited by members of these groups was: "an uneducated father cannot cope with too many educated children and even an educated one prefers fewer children in order to be able to devote more time to each"; "a couple will not be able to handle and care for many children attending school"; or arguments relating to the physical quality of life, namely "easing the burden of multiple childbirths incurred by the mother" through family planning.

These newly adopted attitudes are held as yet only by a minority within Bedouin society. However, as the educational process gains momentum, they reflect a growing dilemma with regard to value of children. From a sociopolitical perspective, the exposure of the Bedouin to social modernization takes place concomitantly with weakening of loyalty to traditional macro sociopolitical structures—such as the tribe and the authority of sheikhs—at the expense of growing individualization of loyalty to the micro levels of the extended and nuclear family (Ben-David 1992). In contrast, increased population density in hamlets or towns inhabited by groups that were previously overt or covert rivals may increase social friction and has often generated violent conflicts (Lewando-Hundt 1979; Meir 1984; Bar 1985). As shown earlier, sedentarization and urbanization may exacerbate internal sociopolitical tension, while depriving Bedouin of the option of nomadism which could relieve or lower this tension. While some Bedouin agree that "a multiple male-child family no longer constitutes an advantage since one can always resort to the state legal authorities in case of a violent conflict," the Bedouin by and large still reserve the option for conflict resolution of a variety of issues by traditional internal means. Accordingly, they still hold the view that the traditional deterrent sociopolitical power can be maintained only through a large, multimale group.

This dilemma is exacerbated further by religiosity. In principle, adoption of more secular attitudes towards various aspects of life is expected to follow the process of urbanization and exposure of the Bedouin society to social modernization. That such attitudes have, to a certain degree, indeed penetrated this society is evident, for example, from the growing readiness to control one's own and family future through family planning and acceptance of Western education. However, the Islamization of the sedentarizing Bedouin society (Layish 1981; Layish 1984; Layish 1991) and the recent penetration of Islamic fundamentalism into Bedouin society in the Negev—as into Israeli Arab society at large (Barzilai 1992—has begun to slow down the trend of secularization. This process encompasses a growing proportion of younger Bedouin, and is taking place particularly in towns where they are as exposed to the Islamic world as they

are to the Western one. They tend to interpret the demographic implication of Islamic fundamentalism rather stringently, i.e., that family planning is absolutely forbidden and to ignore the authoritative more liberal
interpretation (Weeks 1988) that fertility control does not necessarily contradict Islamic religious values. Although a trend to liberalization of population policies has recently begun even in the most fundamentalist
Islamic nations such as Iran (Omran and Roudi 1993), it is too early to
conclude yet whether this has had any impact upon fundamentalist
Negev Bedouin circles.

In summary, from an economic perspective the value of children
among the Negev Bedouin has declined drastically in recent decades
compared to their sociopolitical value. However, although at the normative level their sociopolitical value has not yet changed significantly, the
previous chapter has shown that its impact upon fertility rationality—as
judged by preferences for male offspring—has declined along the nomadism-urbanism continuum. Thus, the emerging state of mind characterized above as a latent surplus of children and the willingness to relin-
quish the norm of multiplicity of children within the family indicates that
their status in the society has changed. Within certain social circles they
no longer provide their families with the same type and magnitude of
rewards which previously won them a highly esteemed role in Bedouin
society. Rather, their multiplicity has in some respects become a burden.

The Status of Elders

The Traditional Perspective

Studies of the Negev Bedouin have not addressed directly the status of
elders as heads of extended families. In most cases the issue was indirectly referred to within the context of Bedouin law (e.g., Stewart 1987;
1991; Bar-Zvi 1991), intrafamily relations (Lewando-Hundt 1984; Marx
1986), and interfamily or intergroup disputes (e.g., Kressel 1982; Ginat
1987). Although there is no doubt that these are important issues, our
concern here is wider and relates to a variety of social, economic and
political aspects at the family, communal, and societal levels. An analysis
of the changing status of elders requires therefore an understanding of
their status within the traditional pastoral nomadic context. As was the
case with children, establishing a base model of the status of elders required in-depth open interviews with Bedouin elders who still practice a
seminomadic life style or did so in the recent past. These interviews were
conducted with nine elders and provided important information from
which three major dimensions of the traditional status of the Bedouin
elder were exposed (Meir and Ben-David 1990).

From a sociopolitical perspective, a Bedouin father becomes an elder at the earliest when his first-born son establishes his own nuclear family and production unit. From this stage on the elder father is gradually relieved of direct involvement in the production process. Thus the elder's status within the nuclear and expanded family projects upon his status within the wider social circles of the co-liable group and the tribe. The three dimensions of his traditional status, as extracted from the interviews, are authority and its sources, position within the housing unit, and role in external relations.

Authority of the Elder and its Sources. Since nomadic or seminomadic Bedouin society is a patriarchal and gerontocratic society, the elder is the central and supreme economic, social and political axis and is endowed with a certain degree of sanctity. This theistic source of authority is rooted in Bedouin custom and tradition according to which Allah awards the elder the role of transmitting cultural values and behavioral norms. However, beyond this spiritual perspective and from a more practical one, the elder's authority derives primarily from the traditional customary Bedouin law. This internal legal and judicial system regulates interpersonal and intergroup relations and formulates compensatory and punitive regulations regarding homicide, corporal and property damage, or violation of behavioral norms. Since the elders assume sole responsibility internally for their family members and externally towards the Bedouin community, they act as arbitrators and plaintiffs within the judicial system and are thus the exclusive carriers of this system.

An elder's authority is manifested first and foremost within his family, projecting upon all spiritual, material and social activities. His advice and experience—both vital for maintaining social order—are a considerable resource for his children to which they always resort. In principle he is a teacher of behavioral norms and of the historical heritage of the Bedouin community. The traditional extended family also operates as a collective economic unit (see also Jakubowska 1984) which is managed by the elder. He is the decision-maker of the pastoral and agricultural production unit, who controls, manages and allocates all family livestock, land, water and labor resources, as well as the family consumption process of production inputs and general family and personal individual needs.

Marriage of children is the most central social issue within the family onto which the elder's authority is projected. His wife may exercise some power in this issue (Lewando-Hundt 1984), but the elder in principle controls matchmaking for his children. It is his responsibility to ensure that the family's social, political, and economic interests are accorded supreme priority in this process. He seeks to marry off his first-born son as early as possible in order to acquire himself dignified social status as an elder. From among the various options, he still prefers to marry his children to their first cousins (see e.g., Natur 1991) in order to avoid any social uncertainty. Due to fear that refusal would entail the severe social sanction of outcasting and loss of family recognition and protection, the latitude of his children's choice in this regard is minimal. This sanction provides the elder with a safeguard over family development and reproduction process, guaranteeing his own and the family's status and honor within Bedouin society.

The Elder as a Focus of the Housing Unit. The extended family unit within the family housing range develops once children begin to establish their own nuclear families in order of seniority. The son receives then a certain minimal size flock to launch his own livestock unit. At that stage, the father usually retires from economic activities and the responsibility for his wellbeing as elder now falls on the son next in seniority, until he in his turn establishes his own family and receives an independent pastoral unit. Eventually, the elder remains under the care of the youngest son— even after the latter's marriage—while the remaining pastoral resources and property of the elder are handled jointly by all sons. This property becomes the family inheritance, the dual function of which is to guarantee the economic wellbeing and independence of the elder and to serve as a basis for the continuity of cohesiveness of the extended family.

The elder's need to control production and consumption as well as social processes within his family determines thus the layout of the family housing unit. Within the extended family, revolving around the elder's housing unit, namely spatial closeness, becomes normative for purposes of family cohesion and the wellbeing of the elder as its head. In order to achieve maximum protection for the elder, adult children avoid as much as possible extended absence from the family housing range.

Economic sustenance of the family's resources ensures its social reproduction. Daily unidirectional visits to the elder by his sons are mandatory both for management of family affairs and for maintaining the tribal and group cultural heritage. The elder is also a focal point for all visits from outsiders, even if these are directed to other members of his family. As he is the social focus of his family, his dignity and honor are symbolized through this custom, and manifested by the *shig*—the hospitality tent— which is also the elder's residential quarter within his nuclear family's tent. This institution assumes a central social role in Bedouin society, serving as a unique space where all family and external affairs are discussed, negotiated, and decided upon. The status of the elder derives thus from the social "weight" carried by the *shig* which is directly related to the size of the extended family and its wealth.

The Elder as a Focus of External Relations. The supreme authority and focality of the elder within his family and housing unit project upon its system of external relations. Due to relative spatial isolation of the traditional pastoral nomadic Bedouin society, three separate, yet interrelated circles are involved in the analysis of external family relations. The first is the internal circle, that is, relationships within the Bedouin society. Within each tier of this society (the tribe, the co-liable group, or the extended family) interfamily relations—including establishment of new ones—flow through the elder. His close familiarity with the delicate sociopolitical web of relations within the Bedouin society is greatly acknowledged and appreciated by members of his family. Children normally consult the elder in these matters, as this familiarity is an essential social resource for avoiding and preventing embarrassing and unwanted relations as well as encouraging and developing beneficial and useful ones for various purposes. The intertribal political "distance" is the major factor in the evolution of extrafamilial relations. There are intertribal political divide lines which generate major and secondary ones. Elders are situated at the base of each such social "basin," through which all social relations flow vertically or horizontally into other social "basins." Such relations persist firmly through time and members of different groups invest a considerable amount of time in maintaining them.

The second circle is relationships with the Arab society in Israel. In the past most Bedouin at the seminomadic phase had only sporadic relationships with this community, and these were drained through the most important tribes—and primarily through the elders or sheikhs. A similar pattern of relationships existed with the Jewish society, which is the third circle. As shown in Chapter 3, penetration of Jewish settlers into the Negev during the 1930s and 1940s was made possible largely by acquisition of land from certain Bedouin tribes. Only a few elders and sheikhs were the negotiators, and thus they developed relationships with Jewish society, from which most other members of Bedouin society were excluded. Even relationships with Jewish settlers developed primarily through tribal and group heads. Thus, external voluntary social relationships of family members were limited almost exclusively to the intra-Bedouin social circle and in this type of relationship the elder assumed a firm status.

Since he enjoyed absolute internal control over his family, the elder was accorded even firmer status with regard to its formal representation. He assumed external responsibility for his family in all social and economic matters and was thus required to represent them before other elders in all conflicts or confrontations. Resort to Islamic *shar'i* justice through *shari'a* courts or to state courts has become more common only with the growth of the sedentarization process (Layish 1984). In the traditional pastoral nomadic phase, however, all conflicts within Bedouin society were resolved through the Bedouin judicial system and traditional customary law, with which only the elder was fully familiar. Therefore, his representation was mandatory. Any commitment he undertook as a consequence of conflict resolution assumed validity by force of his role as family representative. Violation of such resolution would entail severe condemnation and imposition of social sanctions on the family and its head. Other members of his family would therefore never take the risk of assuming such responsibility independently because the consequences of the conflict resolution would have to be borne by the entire family. Such a joint commitment by the elder and his family members became possible only when the former—who controlled the family—was the conflict manager.

Formal family representation toward governmental authorities was also the responsibility of the elder. Here, however, the pattern was somewhat different. In Chapter 2, the unique nature of relationships between pastoral nomads and state governments has been elaborated upon. In the past, in order to maximize freedom of utilization of grazing and migration opportunities and to evade many civilian duties, the Bedouin laymen refrained from contacts with governmental authorities. Consequently, they rarely developed skills for negotiating with them. Instead, other middlemen, including sheikhs, were employed in such affairs (see also Abu-Rabia, A. 1994c). Yet, the representative's contact with the family was always made through the elder. This pattern was—and to a certain degree remains—acceptable to the authorities as well.

In sum, the elder assumed high and central status within traditional Bedouin society. The elevated status of the elders and social stability of Bedouin society were closely and mutually interrelated. As a social institution the elder constituted a means of generating and shaping social order which drew upon his absolute control over his extended family and its stability. Through their interfamilial relationships, elders projected social stability upon each other, thus enabling sustained general stability, or a return to stability after crisis.

Trends in the Status of Elders

The above discussion provided a model-type traditional perspective of the status of Bedouin elders in their pastoral nomadic environment. Clearly, there were variations on this model in both time and space. Nevertheless, it provides a sound basis for an analysis of changes in the status of elders. It is reasonable to suggest that the political, social, or economic destabilization of Bedouin society—which was discussed in previous chapters—was followed by a devaluation of their status. In analyzing this process, we again employ the concept of the nomadism-sedentarism-urbanism continuum now characterizing Bedouin society, with the same subdivision used in the previous chapter. The base point is the "model" status of elders within the seminomadic traditional Bedouin society as described above. The three major dimensions of the status of elders were each broken down into a number of specific properties. These were included in the questionnaires, within the same fieldwork described above, in the form of actual and desired patterns maintained by households. The replies—on a yes/no basis—enabled the identification of the dominant pattern of each subgroup with regard to each property and a comparison of subgroups along the continuum. It is worth noting that no specific weights were assigned to properties of the status of an elder. These could be helpful in assessing processes of change more realistically. Ideally, such weights should be assigned by the Bedouin respondents themselves. Given the large number of properties included in this study and difficult field conditions, this task was found to be largely impossible.

The specific properties in each of the three dimensions of the status of elders—totaling seventeen—are provided in Table 6.1. Given that each was analyzed twice (actual and desired patterns), detailed presentation would entail citing a great mass of data in percentage form and this is beyond the capacity of the present chapter (these data are presented in detail in Meir and Ben-David 1990). Instead, a single summary table is presented, showing change (positive/negative) or stability and relative magnitude of change (moderate/considerable) of each property along the continuum of each group (Bedouin/fellaheen) separately. This is followed by a comparison of the actual and desired patterns between the groups at their most urbanized edge of the continuum. It is useful to examine first the trends of the properties reflecting the status of elders by making some general observations.

General Trends. Looking at the actual patterns first, we discern that most properties (about 90 percent) exhibit only continuity or moderate (both positive and negative) change of traditional patterns along the nomadism-urbanism continuum. A closer examination reveals, however, that the number of properties displaying *moderate negative* change (that is, a decline in the number of respondents asserting that the property is still valid) far exceeds the number of properties with *moderate positive* change (seven vs. two respectively), and the number of these properties is slightly higher than the number of *stable* properties (six). The number of properties with *negative* change is even higher when we also take into account those few with *considerable negative* change. These trends are almost identical for the real Bedouin and for fellahi Bedouin. In particular, there is almost complete identity between the sectors in type of properties showing stability.

TABLE 6.1 Trends in the status of Bedouin elders.

Properties	Actual		Desired		Comparison of B and F	
	B	F	B	F	actual	desired
A. ELDER'S AUTHORITY AND ITS SOURCES						
Utilization of Bedouin judicial system	►	►	▼	▼	B=F	B=F
Elder as a historical source	▼	►	▼	▼	F>B	B>F
Elder as a behavioral guide	▼	▼	▼	►	F>B	F>B
Utilization of elder's experience	▼	▼	▼	►	B=F	F>B
Elder's role in matchmaking	▲	▼	▲	▼	B=F	B>F
B. ELDER AS A FOCUS OF THE FAMILY HOUSING UNIT						
Living with elder	▼	▲	▼	▼	F>B	B=F
Elder living with youngest son	▼	▼	▼	▼	B=F	B>F
Sons visits to elder	▼	▲	▼	▲	F>B	F>B
Elder visits to sons	▲	▼	▼	▲	B=F	F>B
Elder as focus for external visitors	►	►	▼	▲	B=F	F>B
The role of the shig	►	►	▼	▲	B=F	F>B
C. ELDER AS A FOCUS OF FAMILY EXTERNAL RELATIONS						
Contacts with Bedouin	►	►	▲	►	B=F	F>B
Contacts with Arabs	▼	▼	▼	▼	B=F	B=F
Contacts with Jews	▼	▼	▼	▲	B=F	F>B
Representation in intratribal conflicts	►	►	▼	▲	B=F	F>B
Representation in extratribal conflicts	►	▼	▼	▲	B>F	F>B
Representation towards authorities	▼	▲	▼	▼	B>F	B=F

B - Real Bedouin;   F - Fellaheen Bedouin

► - stable;   ▲ - moderate positive change;   ▼ - moderate negative change

▲ - considerable positive change;   ▼ - considerable negative change

Source: Meir and Ben-David 1990.

The situation is quite different with regard to desired patterns of properties. Among the real Bedouin, the same trend persists and is even magnified. Upon urbanization, more properties exhibit *moderate negative* change, and additional properties exhibit *considerable negative* change. Altogether, these properties encompass the large majority (twelve out of seventeen). Given that the real Bedouin do not desire continuity (that is, stability) of any property, the implication is that they are not satisfied with the traditional status of their elders. In contrast, sedentarization and semiurbanization of the fellahi Bedouin result in a considerable increase (from two to six) in the number of properties for which a *moderate positive* change is desired, compared to actual patterns. The number of properties for which a *moderate negative* change is desired is now smaller among them and is considerably lower compared to the real Bedouin. Furthermore, the fellaheen wish to maintain the continuity of far more properties than do the real Bedouin. In contrast to these trends (desire to maintain or strengthen some properties of the status of elders), there is an increase in the number of properties for which a *considerable negative* change is desired. In sum, however, as they move further towards urbanization, the fellaheen demonstrate a desire to strengthen somewhat the status of elders.

The degree of conformity among the real Bedouin between the actual and desired trends along the nomadism-urbanism continuum relates to about 65 percent of the properties, almost twice as much as among the fellaheen (35 percent). This implies that they are quite consistent in their belief that the actual changes in the status of elders conform with their aspirations. These aspirations indicate that they wish to sustain the desired trend to moderate change discussed above. The fellaheen are not as consistent in viewing this linkage and their general desire contrasts with that of the Bedouin.

This difference between the real Bedouin and the fellahi Bedouin is further substantiated when the left flank of Table 6.1 is viewed. Here a comparison is made between the groups in their most urbanized setting, by considering percentage of respondents in each who approve the prevalence of the various properties of status of elders, or desire to preserve them. The symbols in the table show which group has a higher such percentage or whether there is no difference. In comparison of actual patterns there are eleven properties regarding which there is virtually no difference between the Bedouin and the fellaheen in their maintenance. Differences become considerable when the desired patterns are considered. Regarding ten out of seventeen properties more fellaheen desire to preserve the status of elders than do the real Bedouin. This is a somewhat paradoxical finding given that—as shown earlier—in many respects the fellaheen have become more modernized and economically developed than the real Bedouin. One would expect them therefore to relax traditional aspects of their life to a higher degree than the latter. This paradox will be accounted for below.

At this juncture, it is possible to conclude that the dominant trend along the nomadism-urbanism continuum is *negative* change in the various properties reflecting status of elders, and more so among the real Bedouin than among the fellahi Bedouin. This trend—which is ascertained from an analysis of various property-specific trends—conforms to the view of respondents as to the general status of elders. Respondents in each of the six sub-groups were asked whether the general status of the elder in their family has deteriorated, improved, or remained unchanged, and to assess the magnitudes of deterioration or improvement on a scale of 1–5. Percentages of responses and average group magnitudes are given in Table 6.2.

The data reveal that the trends discussed above conform to the view of the Bedouin regarding the general status of elders. Less than half of the respondents (47.4 percent) maintain that the status of elders persists as in the traditional setting, and the rates decline consistently within each group as it becomes more urbanized. The rate of those who argue for a positive change is minimal, and falls again along the continuum. In contrast, close to half of the respondents (44.3 percent) believe that the status of elders has deteriorated, and the rates rise considerably along the nomadism-urbanism continuum. This trend is evident among both real and fellahi Bedouin, but more so among the former where almost all members of the urbanized group (87.5 percent) argue for a negative change.

TABLE 6.2 General status of elders along the nomadism-urbanism continuum

	Real Bedouin			Fellahi Bedouin			General
	A	B	C	D	E	F	
% Respondents							
Stable	86.7	38.5	12.5	52.6	47.4	46.7	47.4
Improvement	6.7	7.7	0	15.8	10.5	6.7	8.2
Deterioration	6.7	53.8	87.5	31.6	42.1	46.6	44.3
Magnitude of change[a]							
Improvement	0.33	0.31	0.25	0.63	0.32	0.20	0.35
Deterioration	0.13	1.38	2.18	0.58	0.68	1.00	0.96

A: seminomadic; B: rural sedentarized; C: recent semiurbanized.

D: rural sedentarized; E: recent semiurbanized; F: early semiurbanized.

[a] Mean group magnitude on a scale of 1–5.

Source: Meir and Ben-David (1990).

In a similar vein, the magnitudes of change in the status of elders con- form to the processes of transition from seminomadism to semiurbanism. The magnitude of negative change—which is asserted by almost half of the respondents—grows considerably along the continuum. This trend is evident especially among the real Bedouin, whose cited magnitude at the most urbanized edge of the continuum is more than double that of the fellaheen. In contrast, the magnitude of positive change declines consis- tently along the continuum, but at a slower rate.

It transpires thus that—as a consequence of their semiurbanization process—members of Bedouin society are well aware of the deteriorating status of their elders within both the family and wider social circles. The intensive destabilization caused by spatial, economic, and social processes affects precisely those status properties of elders which were central to traditional life within the pastoral nomadic setting.

Trends of Selected Major Properties. As shown above, in certain as- pects—both within Bedouin and fellahi sub-groups and between them— there is a considerable gap between actual and desired patterns of the status of elders. In certain other aspects the trends between the groups are consistent. The latter are exemplified in the utilization of the traditional Bedouin judicial system. This system has in principle remained intact, regardless of destabilization of traditional seminomadic life. Yet, both groups strongly desire to lessen—but not to abolish—its importance. This also implies the diminishing of the status of elders. There are both exter- nal and internal reasons for this evident trend. Externally, there is an emerging conflict between this system on the one hand, and state law and religious Moslem law *(shari'a)* on the other. In particular, as shown by Layish (1981; Layish 1984), Natur (1991), and Bar-Zvi (1991), recourse to the latter in internal affairs has recently begun to gain momentum and is even accepted by elders. Internally, the customary judicial system is con- trolled almost absolutely by the real Bedouin, with relatively little access to power left for the fellahi Bedouin. In a manifestation of social protest, the latter desire to diminish its importance.

The role of the elder in matchmaking for his children is another status property of major importance. The trends among the real Bedouin and the fellahi Bedouin in this regard are contrasting. The fellaheen's access to the real Bedouin marriage market is constrained by the latter's reluctance to give their daughters to them. Therefore, the matchmaking process among the fellaheen is loosening traditional bonds at a much faster rate. In this process, intergroup social barriers among them are gradually be- ing removed due primarily to the emergence of various aspects of social modernization (e.g., Western education, modern employment patterns, and division of labor), thus enabling a wider latitude of decision for in- dividuals. The role of the elder in this regard is now perceived by the fellaheen more as interactive consultation with his sons and less as absolute command and control as in the past.

Upon becoming semiurbanized, the fellahi Bedouin seek to lessen even further the role of the elders in determining such an important aspect of their lives. In contrast, the real Bedouin have not yet freed themselves from traditional bonds to an extent capable of lowering intergroup social barriers. Therefore, marriage patterns are still largely determined by elders in order to maintain the group's power. Some respondents as they semiurbanize even desire to strengthen the role of the elders in this regard—presumably in order to protect themselves in the social struggle within a denser and mixed urban environment. These conflicting processes exemplify one important aspect of the slower individualization processes among the real Bedouin as compared to the fellahi ones.

Utilization of the customary judicial system and matchmaking for children are major properties determining the authority of the elders. Given the above trends in elders' status and position within the family, it becomes clear why all other properties in this dimension display a declining trend or—at best—stability. The experience of the elder loses relevance within the new semiurban environment where major aspects of life are now external to the traditional Bedouin realm. Consequently, he is also less capable of acting as an instructor and educator in behavioral norms and historical heritage and less desired in this role by his children. These trends—like those discussed above—are indicative of the individualization process taking place within Bedouin society.

As a consequence of temporal and physical fragmentation imposed upon the family by division of labor and proletarization, the position of the elder within his family housing unit has also become less focal. While the extended family has not yet disintegrated, the magnitude of routine daily control by the elder over activities of his adult sons has largely decreased, even though they visit him whenever possible, a behavioral pattern which they would also like to change. His sons are thus more liberated in their own major decision-making processes concerning economic and social affairs. The elder's focal position as the recipient of all visits by outsiders is maintained now primarily for ritual purposes. Even the *shig* is gradually becoming an institution serving only the elders. Within the house in town, it has gradually been replaced by the *salon* (living room) of his adult sons, or by a neighborhood *shig* which the younger generation have established for themselves (Ben-David 1992). Except in ceremonial events, the traditional *shig* cannot compete with the new alternatives. This trend is desired by the real Bedouin as they semiurbanize. In contrast, the fellahi Bedouin desire to strengthen somewhat the status of the traditional *shig*.

The expanding web of activities within Bedouin society, as a consequence of semiurbanization, division of labor, and integration in the regional wage labor market, has contributed largely to a relative narrowing of the elder's role in external family relations and representation. His position in this regard is maintained within the internal tribal circle. The real Bedouin—as they semiurbanize—even desire to strengthen his position as generator of tribal relations in order to tackle the new social reality of potential friction in a denser environment. But, in matters of formal representation, the real Bedouin greatly prefer diversification of institutions and functionaries to the exclusivity of the elder in mediation in intertribal conflicts. In contrast, some of the fellahi Bedouin would like to somewhat strengthen the position of the elder in this regard and also to expand considerably his role in their relationships with the Jewish population. They view these relationships as a beneficial resource, expediting their integration into the labor market and regional economy. This is especially desirable within the semiurban context, where pastoral or agricultural opportunities have largely diminished, and where they would like to exploit the previously established contacts of their elders. In contrast, both the Bedouin and the fellaheen wish to oust elders from representative functions vis-à-vis government authorities, in the belief that they lack the qualifications for a semiurban labor market reality.

The contrast between the real and the fellahi Bedouin is thus quite evident. Moreover, internal inconsistency between actual and desired patterns among the fellahi Bedouin has already been noted above. With regard to certain properties they seek to weaken the status of the elders, which has actually gained force, and vice versa. In those matters that strongly affect individual life—such as matchmaking and representation toward government authorities—or issues affecting their status within Bedouin society—such as the role of the traditional Bedouin judicial system—they prefer diminished status of the elder. In matters that are related to external ceremonial manifestations—such as the formal role of the elder within the family (visits of outsiders, the role of the *shig*, etc.)—they desire to strengthen the elder's status. This is particularly the case within the denser and more outwardly visible semiurban environment where the influence of public opinion is increased.

These contrasting trends reflect internal class differences. As shown in the previous chapter, the fellaheen—whose processes of social modernization have been faster—strive for status legitimization and social equalization. One way of achieving these goals is by presenting themselves as culturally and socially similar to the real Bedouin in certain ways, even though these are actually unacceptable to them. The need to resort to this conduct becomes stronger following semiurbanization, which brings the fellaheen spatially under the close scrutiny of those whose image they wish to adopt. Being scrutinized puts pressure upon them, but they also feel threatened by the real Bedouin. They declare that the status of the elders in certain respects should improve, while in fact the opposite has occurred. They thus present themselves as "more Bedouin than the real Bedouin" and thereby reduce the sense of threat and the social pressure on them.

In sum, in absolute terms, the status of the Bedouin elder has deteriorated only to a minor degree. True, his roles within traditional Bedouin life are still quite prestigious. Bedouin society is still largely attached to tradition which is maintained and transmitted by the elders, because it has only recently begun to develop formal and ceremonial frameworks that are appropriate to the new semiurban environment. However, within this new environment, the status of the elder can be described as a static social enclave within an expanding sociocultural realm. The circumference of Bedouin life has greatly expanded, led primarily by the younger generation. The latter's exposure to traditional pastoral Bedouin life has been quite low while activity circles and forms of individual self-expression within the town environment are nowadays considerably greater than in the traditional pastoral nomadic environment. The elders cannot integrate easily into these circles. Therefore their relative status within Bedouin society has deteriorated quite considerably and this process is becoming an internal social dynamic capable of self-generation.

Impact on Wellbeing. We recall from the discussion above that in the traditional pastoral mode of production, the principles of the welfare support-system of Bedouin elders derived from the economic structure of the extended family, which performed as an economic enterprise with a completely collective fund. All earnings, incomes, and expenditures were transferred through this fund, which was controlled absolutely by the elder. The welfare support of elders was thus inherent within the traditional Bedouin social and cultural code. The system contained internal mechanisms that guaranteed provision for all the elder's needs (see also Marx 1967). One such mechanism was pooling of all family human and material resources with virtually no resort to external support sources. Another mechanism was the economic independence of the elder, which was made possible by the products of his remaining livestock and land property after his sons received their share upon marriage in order to establish their own production unit. Indeed, in this system, economic support of the elder did not constitute a problem. The question is whether the process of devaluation in the sociopolitical status of Bedouin elders has had any impact upon their wellbeing, primarily from the perspective of economic support. More specifically, our concern here is with the prevalence and desirability of the collective family fund and economic independence of elders.

The most important element in this system is the degree of stability of the extended family economic unit. As shown in this and previous chapters, the extended family is still a viable social unit. Yet, none of the peripheral hamlets and even towns contain an economic base. Jobs and sources of economic livelihood are now only infrequently found near the Bedouin settlements. Consequently, following the waning of the traditional livestock and dry-farming ventures, nuclear family heads have been obliged to seek external employment and income sources within the regional wage labor market. Hence, the labor force of the extended family—which was previously concentrated—has now become spatially and functionally fragmented. Many household heads are now responsible for their own nuclear family economy and—following the fragmentation of extended family economic ventures—are subjected to economic constraints that originate in fluctuations in the labor market.

As head of the extended family, the elder has thus been forfeiting control over its labor force, and external agents now determine its demand and value. Given that family material consumption has increased considerably, the likelihood of maintaining a collective fund within the extended family becomes constrained. Indeed, as revealed in Table 6.3, less than half of all families (about 45 percent) still maintain a collective family fund. The extended family's traditional nature as an economic system is thus no longer characteristic of Bedouin society. Such a process weakens the ability to maintain the traditional norm and principles of supporting

TABLE 6.3 Actual and desired patterns of traditional properties of family economic structure (percent respondents)

	Real Bedouin			Fellahi Bedouin			General
	A	B	C	D	E	F	
Actual							
Collective family fund	66.7[a]	61.5	31.3[a]	15.8[a]	42.1	66.7	45.4[a]
Economic independence of elder	66.7	69.2	87.5	94.7	63.2	86.7	78.4
Desired							
Collective family fund	80.0[a]	61.5	62.5[a]	52.6[a]	52.6	73.3	62.9[a]
Economic independence of elder	53.3	84.6	75.0	94.7	63.2	100.0	78.4

A: seminomadic; B: rural sedentarized; C: recent semiurbanized.

D: rural sedentarized; E: recent semiurbanized; F: early semiurbanized.

[a]Difference between actual and desired absolute numbers is significant at p>.05. Otherwise, there are no differences or differences are not significant.

Source: Meir and Ben-David (1993).

elders through this fund. This reduced ability is aggravated by the fact that for many elders—particularly within the semiurban setting—self-support through maintaining a livestock property is no longer a viable option.

Due to their higher dependence upon grazing and dry-farming, changes in the family economic structure have the strongest impact on the real Bedouin. Under the economic constraints involved in semiurban life, a heavy burden is placed on the ability of the individual household to contribute to the collective extended family fund. Indeed, the proportion maintaining the collective family fund has declined among them quite considerably during the process of sedentarization and semiurbanization. Only two thirds of households of group A (the seminomadic group) still maintain the practice, whereas among the recently urbanized group the proportion has dropped considerably to less than one third.

The fellahi Bedouin were better able than the real Bedouin to maintain their system of the collective family economic unit and collective fund within the modern labor market system. This is reflected in the entirely contrasting trend they exhibit. The proportion of families maintaining collective funds increases fourfold to about two thirds (from 15.8 percent in group D to 66.7 percent in group F). Given their historical economic inferiority, they began to seek employment within the labor market as early as the 1950s and 1960s. In those years, the extended family economic unit was still coherent due to low educational levels and standard of living. Consequently, the elder was still controlling his adult children as a family labor force. Hence, the search for external jobs—primarily as seasonal laborers in agriculture and construction—was conducted on an extended family labor pool basis. The fellaheen even reinforced this pattern before semiurban circumstances and modernization effects became strong enough to undermine it, as was the case with the real Bedouin. This is reflected first in the similar rates for group F, the oldest fellahi semiurban subgroup, and group A, the as-yet seminomadic real Bedouin. It is most clearly reflected, however, in the sharp gap between the rates for the subgroups which are most urbanized among the real Bedouin and the fellahi Bedouin (31.3 percent for group C and 66.7 percent for group F respectively). Yet, about one third of households within the semiurban environment (group F) no longer maintain collective family funds. This implies that even the fellaheen's success in maintaining this pattern has been limited.

The fact that the family collective fund has lost its importance, and that the elder has forfeited absolute control over family resources and over production and consumption processes does not imply that his personal economic independence has been severely hampered. Paradoxically, most respondents in the general category (see Table 6.3), and over two-thirds of each subgroup, argue that elders in their family are economically independent. With increasing semiurbanization, this attribute even tends to increase significantly.

To a certain extent the disintegration of the collective economic structure of the family is a stressful situation. Indeed, the Bedouin are not comfortable with it. The general proportion of families who favor a return to the traditional conduct of the collective family fund—even within a free labor market context—is significantly higher than the actual rate. Yet, over one third of respondents in the general category reject the idea of such a return. On the other hand, there are no significant differences within any subgroup between rates of actual and desired economic independence of the elder and the general rates are even identical. Nevertheless, once again the contrast between the real and the fellahi Bedouin is revealed. The real Bedouin's desire to maintain the collective family fund declines with semiurbanization, while that of the fellahi Bedouin increases. However, as they shift along the continuum toward semiurbanization, both groups generally demonstrate an increased desire for economic independence of the elder which is not based upon the traditional norm of the collective family fund. The Bedouin are thus aware of the reality that under semiurban conditions it becomes harder to maintain elders' economic independence in the face of the diminishing traditional income sources and increasing expenditures. Their major dilemma is therefore whether to seek an alternative to the traditional welfare and support system of elders.

Eligibility of the Bedouin for benefits originating in the National Social Security Law also encompasses old-age benefits. Depending on age, elders are eligible for a monthly old-age allowance. At ages 65–70 and 60–65 for males and females respectively, the size of this allowance depends upon the existence of other sources of income, but from 70 (65 for females) this allowance is given in full regardless of other income sources. In addition—if no other income is available, or if such income is low—elders are eligible for supplement of income up to a certain proportion (between 25–35 percent) of the national monthly average wage. A couple may thus receive about $500 monthly. Another benefit is monthly survivor's allowance, which is 25 percent of the national average wage, so that the survivor's total income is somewhat smaller than that of a couple. Finally, the survivor also receives a one-time death allowance equal to one month's average wage (about $1,100). All these benefits are paid by the Social Security Institute (SSI). In addition to the Social Security Law, the Welfare Insurance Law entitles all disabled elders to assistance and welfare services, which are provided through social workers. Although these laws apply to all Israeli elderly, personal communication with the Negev regional SSI office revealed that—due primarily to lack of proper information—only about one third to one half of Bedouin aged >65 have been receiving these allowances. Another major problem with Bedouin elders is that over the years many have not paid their monthly dues to the SSI as required by law, and these are now deducted from their monthly allowances, which are thus reduced significantly.

In numerous cases SSI allowances have become the sole source of income for elders and are perceived by many Bedouin respondents as sufficiently high to make the elder financially independent. The question is to what extent Bedouin elders have become totally dependent upon this external support, and how far it is being supplemented by internal support from their children. Bedouin responses to these questions are presented in Table 6.4.

The process already described above is to some extent reiterated here. It will be recalled that among the real Bedouin, traditional family economic structure has deteriorated seriously. Their qualifications for integration into the regional market economy are still relatively inadequate compared to the fellahi Bedouin. Therefore, there is a clear trend among them to considerable increase in the proportion of elders who are totally dependent upon external SSI support. The decline along the continuum in the proportion of families who provide this supplementary support from internal resources is minor, being low already. The increase in propor-

TABLE 6.4   Elders' dependence on SSI allowances and supplementary income by family: Actual and desired patterns (percent respondents)

	Real Bedouin			Fellahi Bedouin			General
	A	B	C	D	E	F	
Actual							
Total dependence upon ISS fund	6.7	15.4	56.3	63.2	26.3	6.7	30.9
Financial support from family	46.7	53.8	43.8	21.1	47.4	20.0	38.1
Desired[a]							
Total dependence upon ISS fund	40.0	61.5	87.5	94.7	84.2	93.3	78.4
Financial support from family	80.0	100.0	93.8	84.2	84.2	86.7	87.6

A: seminomadic; B: rural sedentarized; C: recent semiurbanized.

D: rural sedentarized; E: recent semiurbanized; F: early semiurbanized.

[a]Difference between actual and desired absolute numbers for both issues and for all groups are significant at p>.05.

Source: Meir and Ben-David (1993).

tions from group A on, and the higher desired proportions compared to the actual ones, imply that they would like to be able to increase this internal support, especially under semiurban conditions. However, aware of their inability to achieve this goal, they prefer the economic independence of elders (see Table 6.3) to be totally provided for by SSI allowances. The proportion of those expressing this desire increase considerably as they semiurbanize.

Somewhat opposing trends—which again conform to findings from Table 6.3—are evident among the fellahi Bedouin. The increase among them in the proportion of families still maintaining collective funds has already been shown above. Consequently, there is a considerable decline in the proportion of elders who are totally dependent upon external SSI support as they semiurbanize, and their actual rates of internally supported elders are considerably lower than those of the real Bedouin. While they still wish to provide elders with supplementary income from internal resources in case of need, they nevertheless would prefer considerably more elders to become totally dependent upon SSI allowances than do the real Bedouin.

The case of the fellahi Bedouin is somewhat paradoxical, as it was in some aspects related to the sociopolitical status of elders. The paradox is rooted in the fact that they are more able to support their elders in the traditional manner, but prefer to abandon this practice. This paradox may again be explained by the different socioeconomic paths taken by them, that is, earlier sedentarization and semiurbanization, earlier and more intensive exposure to the effects of social modernization, and in particular their deeper awareness of the role of the modern state in economic and social affairs. They are now ready to transfer responsibility for supporting the elders to the government. The real Bedouin's internal ability to support their elders has, in contrast, diminished considerably during sedentarization and semiurbanization, but they have not yet reached the same stage of social modernization or economic development. They thus regard as mandatory the transfer of responsibility for supporting elders to the government, while among the fellahi Bedouin this is largely a voluntary process.

It transpires thus that, within the context of an economically constrained semiurban environment, the ability of Bedouin society to economically support its elders has declined considerably. Among the real Bedouin—whose development is relatively slower—this process is in general more acute than among the fellahi Bedouin. It is, however, a somewhat paradoxical process. On the one hand, the traditional extended family economic structure has been disintegrating. On the other hand, the economic independence of elders is maintained through government welfare allowances. The paradox may be resolved by the possibility that economic independence does not necessarily imply economic wellbeing. Rather, it implies a growing detachment of elders from the internal support system which was once an absolute norm but has become constrained, and increasing dependence upon an external support which is determined by extraneous considerations. Furthermore—during the fieldwork—respondents revealed that, in many families, adult children demand these allowances from their elders on the pretext of continuity of the extended family fund, arguing that the material needs of the elder do not justify retaining such sums to themselves. Social workers interviewed confirmed their awareness of this practice. This problem may be further aggravated by the fact that unemployment rates among the Bedouin—particularly in the economically-baseless towns—is about 12 percent (Avni 1991) and may even be higher as many job-seekers are not registered, while traditional sources of livelihood have diminished considerably.

The growth of the Bedouin elderly population has already been dwelt upon in the previous chapter. The interaction between this process on the one hand and the weakening of the internal Bedouin support system and the desire to transfer this economic task to external agencies on the other hand have intensified particularly as Bedouin migration to towns continues. The direct implication is that the cost of living of the nuclear family, which has been rising due to growing material consumption, has risen further with the need to pay municipal taxes. The economic burden on nuclear families which were already economically distressed has consequently increased. Under the present circumstances these processes are likely to continue, the ability to support elders may further decline, and the tendency to transfer this responsibility to external governmental agencies is likely to increase.

Bedouin Women in a Changing Environment

The changing status of Bedouin women in the Negev has received extensive attention in the recent decade. There are contradicting trends, the interpretation of which can lead to different conclusions. In general, however—and particularly from the perspective of emancipation—the social position of Bedouin women has deteriorated considerably as a consequence of sedentarization and semiurbanization and may be epitomized paradoxically as regression into modernity (Tal 1995a). The issues that are of concern here are again women's involvement in the family production process and in public social life. More specifically, our concern here is with their economic and social roles and their spatial mobility.

In many respects, the economic roles of women in towns have contracted quite considerably. The decline in the pastoral production process within Bedouin society in the Negev has reduced the need for women's direct labor and indirect involvement in this process which previously awarded them certain resources and power. In contrast, Bedouin men have become the sole wage earners and therefore the decision makers over financial issues within the household economic unit. In the absence of these productive roles, the sole role left for a woman is to be a wife and a mother, functions which confine her to the home (Jakubowska 1984). In this respect her domestic sphere and power has been strengthened (Lewando-Hundt 1984).

However, loss of these economic roles does not necessarily imply that women are now financially worse off. As indicated earlier, all Bedouin mothers receive state maternity and child allowances from the SSI. In a certain respect, for settled and semiurbanized women, this income has become an economic resource substituting for those lost pastoral resources which they previously controlled. These women, however, have additional economic resources at their disposal. Lewandu-Hundt (1984) has dwelt on productive female labor, particularly that of married women, within the domestic sphere in towns. They produce embroidery, dresses, and head coverings which they sell informally to other women, thus earning money and gaining some economic independence and therefore power within the household. Such earning opportunities are far less available to those women in families that have not settled yet in towns and whose time is devoted more intensively to the pastoral or agropastoral production processes.

Unmarried young women in towns have also become exposed to external labor opportunities as unskilled laborers in nonBedouin industrial and agricultural enterprises in the region. As indicated by Jakubowska (1984), the women take this initiative in order to break the domestic routine and become exposed to the outside world. However, the jobs are subject to their father's or older brothers' approval and are usually arranged by their relatives who act as labor contractors and oversee their labor involvements. Normally, they return to their previous domestic roles upon marrying. The latter two restrictions reflect the limited degree of freedom these women have in this regard.

In general, however, women's external wage labor is as yet an unaccepted norm within Bedouin society (Tal 1995a). This issue is related to gender conflict, that is the manner in which Bedouin men view women's involvement in the public sphere. They justify their resistance to women's wage labor by various arguments such as remoteness of employment centers and lack of qualifications, but all these are apparently related to their desire to confine their wives and daughters to the domestic sphere for reasons of family honor and their own status, power, and authority as heads of the family (Rimalt 1991). Confinement of women to this sphere and their seclusion have thus become a typical process at the early stage of urbanization (see also Kressel 1976).

A closely related issue to that of women's wage labor is their education. Provision of public educational services to Bedouin society and problems associated with it are discussed in the next chapter. Yet, the discussion earlier in this chapter has revealed the general change in value of children in Bedouin society following sedentarization and the trade-off between this decline and schooling. While the norm of schooling and modern education has been penetrating Bedouin society in recent decades to a considerable extent, many individual Bedouin still question the value of education for male children, even more so for girls (Meir 1986b; Abu-Ajaj and Ben-David 1988). Gender conflict is reflected here as well. Even in towns, girls' schooling—particularly their exposure to male youngsters in schools as they approach adulthood—is still considered by many Bedouin fathers as a threat to their social image and family honor. Moreover, as shown by Tal (1995a), uneducated prospective husbands are reluctant to take educated wives for the selfsame reasons (suggested earlier in this chapter) that uneducated fathers find it difficult to cope with too many educated children. In these respects fathers and mothers have a common interest, the latter fearing that schooling will have a detrimental effect on domestic role sharing with their daughters and preparation for their future domestic roles (Hundt 1976).

Both wage labor and formal education are related to the issue of spatial mobility of women. Although important with regard to Bedouin women's emancipation from the confines of the domestic sphere, this issue has received little attention. Only one preliminary study on women's spatial mobility among the Negev Bedouin has been conducted to date (Tal 1993). Women in the traditional pastoral environment had quite an extensive degree of freedom in moving over space. The desolate desert space guaranteed both relative safety of the woman and control by her family of her whereabouts. Freedom in spatial mobility was made possible due to the existence of familiar space which was subject to behavioral codes, the purpose of which was to maintain social order (see also Rapoport 1978). These codes were designed primarily to ban unwanted encounters between women and nonagnate male strangers. Women moved freely and in routine tracks within the *dira* to perform their domestic and pastoral productive duties and to visit their relatives. Even young girls were able to move with flocks to distant pastures within the *dira*.

On the basis of preliminary research among three extended families, Tal (1993) reveals that at present many Bedouin perceive a growing threat to women in the new spatial circumstances that have evolved following sedentarization and semiurbanization. This threat therefore compels the family to tighten control over women. The extent of this control varies along two dimensions: the nomadism-semiurbanism continuum, and age and marital status. In the rural sedentarized phase, young girls enjoy quite considerable freedom of movement, as they are not considered sexual objects. Yet, as they grow up, their position as young unmarried women determines the strictness of the constraints on their movements. They are accordingly expected to stay within the domestic sphere with their mothers most of the time and their social networks are deployed in fact only within the extended family, even for those girls attending schools. Any departure of a girl from the home range must be approved by the male members of her family and she must be escorted by them or by her mother. The degree of freedom of movement is relaxed again when girls become wives and mothers, reaching its peak when they are elders. However, this freedom is never absolute, as they are allowed to leave home alone only for domestic and family reasons and only within the village. Visits to their own agnate families or to Beer-Sheva for shopping or medical purposes are allowed only in the company of their husbands.

The pattern of movement within the semiurban environment is quite similar except for the fact that the neighborhood within the Bedouin town, as indicated earlier, is considered by its inhabitants to be a completely separate settlement—the equivalent of the village or hamlet which is composed exclusively of agnate families. From the limited data gathered, Tal (1993) concludes that in this environment the freedom of movement of the respective age-set women is, to a certain extent, even more limited. This is due, perhaps, to the greater population density and more intensive public phase. Not only are many activities such as shopping alone in town or even accompanying their husbands to Beer-Sheva, in general denied to women, but they are expected to dress in a more modest manner (Tal 1995b).

These trends suggest that in these respects, not only has the process of settlement and urbanization not contributed toward modernization and the emancipation of Bedouin women from the traditional bonds, but it has even generated a regression in their status and social power. In the gender conflict men make every possible attempt to maintain their status, power, and authority at the expense of women's social marginalization. For women, the contrast between the domestic and the public spheres has only sharpened. However, this conclusion must be qualified. Jakubowska (1984) and Lewando-Hundt (1984) have revealed that in certain other respects women's power has to a certain extent increased in towns. Exclusion from the public sphere and confinement to the neighborhood have in fact intensified the strength of the all-female social networks. Through this network women are able to obtain—and become carriers of—relevant information on events and happenings within the neighborhood. Such information is a highly valuable resource because the high density within the neighborhood has increased the influence of public opinion on people's lives, with a consequent tighter social control over individual behavior. Women's improved access to and utilization of this internal resource (as against men who control external information resources) provide them with some power and authority within the gender power play. This power base of women leads Lewando-Hundt (1984) to suggest a paradoxical process. Increased segregation of women from men due to the latter's integration into the wage labor market limits women's extent of power and influence within their domestic sphere, but the process of settling in towns increases their access to other women and therefore to information (Lewando-Hundt 1984). In this respect, women's indirect involvement in the public sphere increases.

This paradoxical process raises the issue of wellbeing of Bedouin women, particularly in families that have moved to towns. They are exposed to—but have as yet limited access to—new education and labor opportunities that can emancipate them from the domestic sphere and provide them with greater involvement in the public sphere. These women are witnessing changes in the family economic structure in terms of their removal from power positions and their growing dependence on men. The social structure is also changing before their eyes as regards gender separation, due to men's integration in the wage labor market, changes in the value of their children, and the deteriorating status of elders. They are also exposed to the growing economic hardships entailed in surviving in the town environment while their potential contribution is as yet denied. All these carry seeds of individual frustration as the traditional economic and social systems have not yet been replaced by new ones that would provide them with the self-esteem and appropriate social roles and position they enjoyed previously. In fact, their access to these alternative systems has been largely barred so far by their society which to a considerable extent remains a male society. These alternative systems are, apparently, once again external to Bedouin society.

Conclusions

The changes in the status and wellbeing of Bedouin individuals—children, elders and women—which were the concern of this chapter, are a consequence of the trap of social modernization and economic growth which were triggered by processes of territorialization and sedentarization. For various communal sociopolitical circles the traditional economic and sociopolitical value of children has declined, whereas recognition of their individual inclinations, qualifications, and specialized personal needs has increased. While in the traditional framework, their value was rooted primarily in their nonpersonalized group mass, in the newly evolving framework their value is increasingly anchored in their individuality. From this individualized perspective, it might be suggested that their status as a mass has deteriorated while their status as individuals has improved.

The sociopolitical and economic status of Bedouin elders has also deteriorated. Previously central pillars of the economic, social, and political communal life, they now confront the evolution of new foci of economic, social, and political power which are alien to them as these are controlled increasingly by the younger generation. This newly emerging reality is thus composed of two parallel trajectories: the traditional one within which the status of the elder is still unaffected, and the modern one within which his roles are quite insignificant. The contrasting trends between the real Bedouin and the fellahi Bedouin reflect the class conflict between the groups. The fellaheen—traditionally inferior—wish to strengthen their social status by improving that of their elders, while the real Bedouin, in openly voicing their desire for further change, are giving vent to their social self-confidence. Either way, individual members of Bedouin society, by necessity or free will, are now ready to hand over the economic burden of supporting elders to external government agencies. Seen from this perspective, this can also be regarded as a process of individualization of elders.

There is a certain parallel between the trends relating to the status of elders and women. Both groups are unaffected by the progress that adult males have been enjoying. However, while the status of elders in traditional spheres is maintained to a considerable extent, that of women has deteriorated to the same degree. While the evolving duality in elders' status can be regarded as a natural outcome of previous economic and social processes, the declining status of women is the outcome of Bedouin men's choice and decision. In the final analysis, both women and those who are now elders (but began their life cycle as seminomads) remain within the traditional sphere, with relatively limited access to various aspects of the public sphere. However, while individualization of elders is quite evident and manifest, individualization of women is as yet only a latent process.

The analysis in this chapter reveals the conflicting trends between the status of children and that of elders within the expanded and even the nuclear family. Jakubowska (1984) indicates the conflict between the career of the father and that of his son. If the father adheres to the traditional pattern of family economic structure, he will eventually retire from active economic involvement and his sons will have to take over. This implies that their chances of controlling their own future are small. If, on the other hand, the father is willing to continue working and supporting his children, their chances of determining their future—for example, through education—are much improved. True, this does not imply yet that their obligations to their extended family are over. At present an individual's needs are still to a large extent second to those of the family, which still conditions his life (Jakubowska 1984). Yet, this dilemma has been gaining force particularly within the semiurban environment where, as shown above, young parents are becoming more aware of the increasing individual needs of their children and the difficulties of supporting a mass of children. This, perhaps, explains their greater willingness to transfer responsibility for the wellbeing of their elder parents to state authorities. In other words, not only is there a growing conflict between the social status of children and elders, but competition over resources seems to be emerging within the expanded family, which could affect the wellbeing of elders.

It transpires that Bedouin society has reached an important juncture in its social development. In the case of supporting elders it is adapting itself to new circumstances in which its ability to maintain the traditional system is considerably weakened. The Bedouin are being exposed to modern societies in which public care for elders becomes a major concern (Rudzitis 1984; Golant 1984; Rowles 1986; Warnes 1990; Wilson 1991). In more general terms—as will be seen in the next chapter with regard to traditional education, medicine, and welfare—the Bedouin are relinquishing highly important internal traditional social institutions to external agents. These institutions cater for the wellbeing of children, elders, and women alike. In other words, Bedouin society is becoming dependent on external public governmental goods for the wellbeing of its individuals (Meir 1990). From a public policy perspective, this process entails intervention by external agencies. The question is whether public service providers are themselves aware of these processes within Bedouin society and are prepared to assume the traditional tasks of providing for the welfare of its individuals and their wellbeing, as these are relinquished by the society. This question is the concern of the next chapter.

7

The Role of Public Services

The previous chapters have revealed that in the course of its transition from pastoral nomadism toward wage labor semiurbanism, the Bedouin society in the Negev has begun to give up its traditional economic structures. Its fragmentation within the urban labor market has generated dependence upon external economic resources that are beyond the direct control of its members. Such dependence is a far cry from the past when they were able to maneuver the balance between varying degrees of combinations of pastoral nomadism with agropastoralism, some limited trade, and wage labor—at their own choice. This system provided a considerable element of reliability, or what Salzman (1995)—in discussing the Baluch nomads of Iran—has termed "reliable uncertainties." It seems that among the Negev Bedouin such a shift is at present unidirectional and, economically, they have become highly constrained.

This process has entailed also social constraints. As shown in the previous chapter, traditional social institutions are gradually deteriorating, placing individuals at risk of being left without the internal social support that previously enabled their socialization and therefore wellbeing, thus contributing to social stability. This implies a growing individualization process within this society. In contrast to the previous reliable uncertainties, this social change has been taking place under conditions of what might be termed unreliable economic uncertainty. In fact, considerable unreliable economic and social—let alone political—uncertainties have characterized Bedouin society since the creation of the State of Israel in 1948.

Our concern in this chapter is with the alternative systems which are supposed to replace those internal ones that previously provided the necessary social certainty and wellbeing. While the Bedouin have been left to their own devices in integrating into the regional wage labor market in the Negev, those alternative social systems have been provided to them by the State of Israel in the form of public educational, health, and community welfare services. These public goods have long been considered in the literature on social and economic development as basic needs, vital for the wellbeing of a modernizing society (Seers 1977). Yet, the fact that these services are provided to the Bedouin as external public goods renders them, as already indicated in Chapter 2, especially problematic. This is particularly so given the crucial question of whether their delivery meets the requirements of spatial and functional availability and accessibility and of cultural relevance.

This question is critical in early and even advanced stages of sedentarization for several reasons. First, the roles of these public goods were previously filled by internal and "autonomous" social institutions within a pastoral nomadic context. At present they have begun to be perceived by the Bedouin as external resources necessary for adaptation to sedentary life, to be weighed against the parallel deteriorating traditional resources. Second, members of Bedouin society are being required now to cope with these external public resources individually. The very acceptance of the idea of resorting to the use of the new and complex consumption channel of a public good is potentially capable of generating stress, as the individual now has to cope independently with systems that are alien to him from the mental, administrative, and legal perspectives. Third, the strategic concept of provision of these services is inherent primarily within the context of the benefit to the state rather than to its clients. Given the Bedouins' growing inclination toward—and dependence upon—these public goods, these dialectics are discussed below, primarily within the context of degree of spatial, functional, and cultural appropriateness of such services which, in its turn may indicate the extent of Bedouin wellbeing during the critical period of change.

Educational Services

The inclination of the Bedouin to utilize formal educational services began to develop during the Ottoman and British Mandate periods (Meir and Barnea 1985; Ben-David 1994b). In these years, however, education was a privilege of the elite, primarily members of the close family of sheikhs. The growth and development of this service into a system that encompasses the entire community commenced only with statehood in the early 1950s. The problems of spatial, functional, and cultural appropriateness began to emerge at that time, generating various types of individual and communal stress.

Spatial Availability and Accessibility

Although the enforcement of the Compulsory Education Law among the Bedouin began only in the late 1960s, delivery of educational services to them began in the early 1950s. A major problem in those years was how to exert government control over the remaining seminomadic Bedouin in the Negev who, it is recalled, were relocated into the *sayig*. Such control was sought for political-military reasons, but also due to the policy aimed at removing the Bedouin from their seminomadic pastoral mode of living, settling them and thereby manipulating their locational patterns to suit state needs (Meir 1986b).

In order to achieve these goals, the government employed several political and administrative measures. Most important among these was the appointment of new sheikhs to existing tribes or to tribes newly established in the aftermath of warfare of 1948, and deposing of some existing sheikhs. In addition, the sheikhs were appointed heads of their "tribal educational committees." In light of the already emerging inclination of the Bedouin toward modern formal education, these measures provided the authorities with manipulative control over the availability of educational services to the Bedouin. Several considerations, tribe-specific or more general, were employed by the government in deciding to establish schools. Given the military and political tensions in the Negev during the 1950s, the degree of tribal loyalty to and recognition of the State of Israel were of supreme importance. Later on—during the 1960s and 1970s—the prime considerations were the degree to which a Bedouin tribe or group was willing to give up the pastoral nomadic mode of living and to move to the towns planned by the government. From a more general perspective, the Ministry of Education had to take into consideration economic and administrative efficiency criteria within budgetary constraints.

Even under the low demand for formal education that existed among the Bedouin until the late 1970s, these criteria resulted in constrained availability of schools to this community. The issue was not so much related to the number of schools—although significant in itself—as to the degree to which they catered to the Bedouin social-spatial-political tribal structure. In Chapter 4 we have described at length the process of territorialization of the Bedouin society, with the consequent sociospatial segregation between groups at various levels of aggregation. This has been manifested, *inter alia*, in the desire of tribes or groups within tribes to avoid a territorial and social mix that could revive dormant intertribal conflicts or generate fresh ones. In Bedouin eyes, one of the means to achieve this goal was to receive the public service on a tribal basis with minimal intertribal or intergroup mixture of students as well as staff. This desire implied maximization of the number of public schools to be established by the government. Such an ideal solution conflicted with state demands for security, political control, and economic and administrative efficiency in delivering this service, with consequent minimization of expenditures and hence of school establishments (Meir 1986b).

The demands and calculations of the authorities created constraints on availability and accessibility of school facilities. These constraints were significant for the wellbeing of children and parents alike both before and after the commencement of the massive settlement in planned towns in the early 1980s. Meir and Barnea (1985; see also Meir 1986b; Meir 1990) examined the indicators of tribal mix in schools and students' daily commuting distances to them during the late 1970s. In those years—it will be recalled—only two planned towns were in existence, and most of the Bedouin population still lived in hamlets of a spontaneous settlement nature. Hence, most of the schools were also located outside towns.

The situation that existed then with regard to tribal mix in elementary schools is shown in Table 7.1. It transpires that tribal mix was a characteristic of half of the schools, whereby in about 40 percent of them three and more tribes shared one school. Moreover, these schools encompassed 56 percent of all Bedouin schoolchildren (Meir and Barnea 1985). From the perspective of the tribes' desire for separate tribal schools, the vast majority of tribes–primarily the smaller ones—had to cope with the undesired reality of multitribal schools, two thirds of them within the highly stressful category of three and more tribes in a single school. From the government perspective there was no economic justification for providing each tribe with its own separate school facility, particularly as there were extremes of tribes with only a few hundred members. Still, as only the largest tribes enjoyed this privilege of separate schools, the majority had to suffer the cost of reduced social wellbeing by compromising between

TABLE 7.1 Schools and tribes by degree of tribal mix in elementary education, 1978–1995 (in percentages)

Tribal Mix[a]	1		2		3+	
	1978	1995	1978	1995	1978	1995
% schools[b]	50	25.8	11.1	6.4	38.9	67.8
% tribes[c]	20	31.4	13.3	14.3	66.7	54.3

[a] Number of tribes in school. [b] N(1978)=18; N(1995)=31.
[c] N(1978)=30; N(1995)=35.

Source: 1978-adapted from Meir and Barnea (1985); 1995-calculated from unpublished data of Ministry of Education, the Southern District (Courtesy of Moshe Schochat).

the wish to maintain the traditional tribal identity and integrity and the desire to achieve modern education via formal schooling for their children. Data for 1995—when the number of both schools and tribes was considerably larger—indicate that the situation with regard to tribal mix in schools has worsened, as two thirds of schools are in the highest category (3+), although there is improvement in terms of schools allocated exclusively to single tribes.

Spatial access of the Bedouin client population—that is schoolchildren—to educational services refers to their ability—or alternatively degree of physical difficulty—to commute to schools. By nature it is closely related to the availability of school facilities, because fewer schools imply lower accessibility. Accessibility of elementary schools was analyzed through daily commuting road distances, as shown in Table 7.2. In the late 1970s, 75 percent of the tribes were located more than 5 km from their elementary schools and 40 percent even over 7 km away. Most schools were also in these long-distance categories, as were about 37 percent of the students (Meir and Barnea 1985). The significance of this constrained access of Bedouin children to schools lies not only in the long daily walk to and from school under harsh topographical and climatic conditions, but is primarily related to the territorial codes and norms. These implied that the immediate space around schools that were established in tribal areas was capable of accommodating only a certain degree of population density if privacy and integrity—and hence identity—of the group was not to be disturbed.

Thus the conflict between state policy as regards service provision and Bedouin territorial norms imposes a physical burden on this population whose desire to provide its children with formal education has begun to grow. Yet, it is noteworthy that the stress is not an outcome of state policy alone, but also of internal Bedouin political processes. Quite often sheikhs have taken advantage of their power as heads of their tribal educational committees in order to determine the location of schools, usually to the benefit of their close family and relatives. Given the often sparse spatial distribution of population within tribal areas, other members—whether of fellahi origin or of rival groups—thus suffer internal discrimination.

TABLE 7.2 Schools and tribes by commuting distances, 1978 (in percentages)

Distance (km.)	<4	4–7	>7
	1978	1978	1978
% schools (N=18)	25.0	35.7	39.3
% tribes (N=30)	16.6	45.8	37.6

Source: Adapted from Meir and Barnea (1985).

Comparable data on present commuting distances to schools are not available. However, while the situation has changed, the problems endure. Indeed, data from the Ministry of Education (1995) reveal that since the late 1970s the total number of Bedouin schools has increased to 43, which is considerably more then proportionate (by about 40 percent) to the increase in population, but the vast majority of new schools were established in the planned towns. Due to migration of Bedouin to towns, about half of the total Bedouin population presently enjoy improved physical wellbeing due to proximity to schools within towns. Yet, the other half of the Bedouin population still reside in hamlets within the periphery (a recently-coined term in government circles for the spontaneous settlements). In fact, given the extremely high natural increase rates, the absolute size of the population there has remained virtually unchanged since the late 1970s, whereas the total number of schools has dropped dramatically to only ten. The direct implication of this drop is considerably diminished wellbeing of the Bedouin in terms of availability of schools and their spatial accessibility.

Functional Accessibility

Functional accessibility refers here to quality of educational services in terms of physical and academic functioning. Physical functioning is dealt with from two perspectives. The first is related to spatial availability and accessibility in terms of wellbeing of schoolchildren and schools within the educational process proper. Students in schools which are not conveniently accessible do not enjoy as normal and leisurely an educational process as in more accessible ones. This is because—in a society which is not accustomed to this new reality—detachment of children from the home and tribal environment for long hours is a rather stressful situation for both the school and the children and their families. As shown in the previous section, in the late 1970s a substantial number of schools were in the category of low accessibility, and consequently the social wellbeing of children and families in this regard was quite constrained. This generated disparities in wellbeing among tribes, intertribal jealousies, and tension, and a conflictual atmosphere (Meir and Barnea 1985). In order to reduce the physical stress associated with low accessibility, the Ministry of Education has been bussing students from the periphery since the early 1980s, particularly to schools in towns. However, this solution does not necessarily enhance the social wellbeing of children and their families for two reasons: first, bussing is provided only along main paved arterial roads, whereas a substantial proportion of families reside in off-road remote locations; second, it has provided the Ministry with the opportunity to extend commuting distances even further, causing thus further daily detachment of children from their home and tribe into an alien environment.

Physical quality of facilities is the second perspective of functional accessibility. Quality of educational facilities, along with their location, has been used by the state to manipulate the Bedouin into relocating into towns and thus avoid investing in fixed permanent hard structures in the periphery. Until the late 1970s, as revealed by Table 7.3, most school facilities were soft structures—usually small shacks with poor learning conditions—and were regarded by the authorities as temporary (Meir and Barnea 1985). One could argue—as officials often did informally—that the Bedouin were indifferent to the low quality of school facilities because these constituted for them an improvement over previous conditions. The fact is that by the late 1970s the Bedouin were already aware of the quality of educational services within the Jewish population. This resulted in low social wellbeing perception levels with regard to the educational process and also raised their expectation level. As will be shown in the next chapter, they exerted a growing pressure of protest on the government. Since the late 1970s there has been a considerable change in the attitude of the Ministry of Education. An Authority for Bedouin Education was established, whose activity resulted—among other things—in a change in terminology towards distinction between standard and temporary school facilities. Consequently, there has been a significant increase in the number of schools and classrooms, mostly in fixed permanent hard standard structures and primarily in towns, while the proportion of temporary schools and classrooms has declined considerably. In fact, Table 7.3 reveals a complete reversal compared to the late 1970s. This increase in functional accessibility notwithstanding, there has still been a slight (5 percent) increase in average classroom density, particularly in the peripheral areas.

Academic functioning is another aspect of functional accessibility of schools. The term refers primarily to achievement levels of Bedouin students, and is of particular importance during a process of social change because it determines, among other things, the prospects for transition

TABLE 7.3   Types of classrooms in schools, 1978–1995 (in percentages)

Year	Standard	Temporary
1978	21.1	78.9
1995	78.7	21.3

Source: 1978-adapted from Meir and Barnea (1985); 1995-Ministry of Education (1995).

from the traditional ascriptive status system toward acquired status mobilization, and for better integration into the labor market. Ben-David examines these issues from two perspectives. In the first one—relevant for elementary schools—he shows that in 1992 about 45 percent of Bedouin students failed in standard achievement tests in arithmetic and reading comprehension (Ben-David 1994b). This poor achievement level—when carried over to high schools—results in an extremely low percentage of students reaching the senior class level. On the basis of data from the Ministry of Education (1995) and the Central Bureau of Statistics (1994), it is estimated here that only about 20 percent (400 students) of the appropriate cohort reached this level in 1992. From Ben-David (1994b) it follows that only 28 percent of these students take matriculation exams in full and only eighty four students (about 5 percent of the entire cohort) within the entire Bedouin community were granted full matriculation certificates, a prerequisite for admission to institutions of higher education.

Thus, the modernization of the Bedouin educational system in academic terms is lagging considerably behind its partial physical modernization. This indicates, above all, the low degree of social wellbeing which the educational system provides for the Bedouin. This is reflected in the extremely high drop-out rates (see below), themselves reflecting the lack of confidence in the ability of the system to meet their expectations.

Cultural Relevance

Cultural relevance (Meir 1986b; Meir 1990) refers to the degree of compatibility of the public service with Bedouin norms and values. It is related to Bedouin society's receptivity to modern and formal education. As shown in Chapter 2, the process of integration of pastoral nomads into the system of governmental provision of this public good is destructive to their cultural and social structure. Several issues are relevant here as regards the Negev Bedouin. The first, discussed above, is the issue of school location and quality of facilities, which has been employed by the authorities to promote Bedouin relocation into towns. Its significance here lies in its conflict with the Bedouin nomadic ideal of locational freedom. The dialectics of the tension between the desire to retain the nomadic mode of living and the wish to integrate into the modern socioeconomic environment via schooling and education has resulted in deterioration of the traditional locational ideology. This causes considerable stress, particularly to adults and elders who were brought up within this ideology.

Secondly, schooling and formal education, as shown in the previous chapter, have strongly interfered with the household economic and domestic roles performed by children and hence have diminished their eco-

TABLE 7.4   Enrollment rates by grades, 1978–1994 (in percentages)

Grade	1978		1995	
	Boys	*Girls*	*Boys*	*Girls*
1st–5th	80	40	100	93
6th–8th	61	17	95[a]	68[a]
9th–12th	29	5	65[b]	34[b]

[a]Grades 6th–9th [b]Grades 10th–12th

Source: 1978-calculated from Meir and Barnea (1985);1995-calculated from un-published data of Ministry of Education, the Southern District (Courtesy of Dov Barnea).

nomic value. The Compulsory Education Law resulted in a considerable increase in enrollment rates in both elementary and high-schools during the 1980s and 1990s (Meir 1986b; Ministry of Education 1995). However, from a cultural perspective, Bedouin receptivity to this process has not yet matured. As shown in Table 7.4, in 1978 enrollment rates for boys were quite high in lower grades but declined considerably in higher grades, totalling less then one-third of the appropriate cohort by 12th grade. The situation was even more problematic for girls, whose already low enrollment rate in the low grades (less then half) dropped dramatically to about 5 percent in 12th grade.

Comparable data for recent years reveal that while there has been a great improvement throughout the years, the problem of high dropout rates persists. It is particularly acute for girls, because at about the age of thirteen their exposure to the male environment in schools becomes a threat to family honor. Thus—from a cultural perspective—modern education is still irrelevant for a considerable proportion of the Bedouin population and this situation becomes even more acute given the loss of opportunities to exploit children's economic value.

The last issue is that of ethnicism and relates to relevant implications of the pedagogic issues of curricula and teaching staff (Meir and Barnea 1985; Ben-David 1994b). Curricula in the Bedouin educational system have been culturally irrelevant. They emphasize mainly Western cultural values and are devoid of any Bedouin cultural heritage traits or applied knowledge relevant to the transition to the new semiurban environment (see also Abu-Saad 1991). This fact is rooted in the problem of recruiting teaching staff. Because of the immature educational system the educated class—from which Bedouin teachers could be recruited to produce a body of relevant authentic "ethnic" knowledge—is limited in scope. This problem is related to the number of university graduates and certified school teachers. By 1994, there were only 135 Bedouin university degree-holders,

TABLE 7.5 Teaching staff by origin, 1978–1994

Origin	1978	1994
Bedouin	100 (36%)	679 (63%)
Non-Bedouin	176 (64%)	398 (37%)

Source: Adapted from Meir and Barnea (1985) and Ben-David (1994b).

almost all of them males, a rate of 2/1,000 compared to the national average of 80/1,000 (Abu-Saad 1994). Table 7.5 shows the Bedouinization of teaching staff in the early 1990s compared to the late 1970s, when two thirds of the teachers were Arabs from elsewhere in Israel. The underlying reason for the turnaround has been the desire of both the Bedouin (for sociocultural wellbeing reasons) and the authorities (for political reasons) to create a culturally and socially more compatible and homogenous educational system. From this perspective, the cultural relevance of the Bedouin educational system and hence Bedouin wellbeing has improved significantly. To this one must add that in 1994, 164 Bedouin students were enrolled at universities in Israel and overseas (Abu-Saad 1994). However, the fact that about a quarter of the teachers are still uncertified—most of them in elementary education (Ministry of Education 1995)—may be, as suggested by Ben-David (1994b), the root of the low achievement levels shown earlier. Seen from this perspective, Bedouin society does not enjoy a high degree of wellbeing.

Health Services

In general, the nature, structure and methods of provision and utilization of health services differ from those of educational services. The difference is rooted not only in the type of public good concerned but also in the specific target population. Therefore, the effect of health services in terms of social wellbeing is more individually than communally oriented compared to educational services.

Yet, it is noteworthy that—from a communal and wide societal perspective—a process that was generally termed epidemiological transition by Omran (1971; 1977) has been taking place within Bedouin society in recent decades. One indicator of this process—the decline in infant and child mortality—has already been described in Chapter 5, in conjunction with the process of demographic transition. Another indicator is the emerging change in morbidity patterns. Although this indicator has not yet been thoroughly analyzed, it transpires from various sources gathered by Meir (1987b) that the high prevalence rates of infectious and respiratory diseases among the Bedouin in the past have been replaced by growing prevalence of degenerative diseases (Ben-Assa 1964; 1974; Zilber 1961;

Abu-Rabia, A. 1979 1994a; Berginer et al. 1982). Due to this change, prevalent diseases are more individually oriented than communally oriented. Seen from this perspective, the issues of availability, accessibility, and compatibility of health services to the Bedouin once again become relevant.

Spatial Availability and Accessibility

As in the case with educational services, there has been no overall coherent public health-service provision policy for the Bedouin. The only clear and long term guideline until recently was that the development of the services should follow the growth of Bedouin towns, with the exclusion of the peripheral population. Until the early 1980s in particular, with the onset of the massive migration of Bedouin to towns, this process was marked by inertia, ad hoc decisions based on imitation of the method of provision to the Jewish population, economic criteria and intertribal rivalry (Schreibman 1984).

In those years, the system of public health services comprised two elements provided by two separate agencies. The Ministry of Health deployed a network of seven preventive mother-and-child clinics for infant care and instruction in proper hygiene and nutrition. These clinics were located mostly in the new towns or the sites of future ones and in Beer-Sheva, the latter clinic serving the peripheral population. The second element—comprised of seven primary health clinics—was provided by the semipublic Sick Fund of the General Federation of Labor Unions (G.F.L.) which, until recently, was the main vehicle for provision of public primary health care in Israel. These clinics were also located mostly in towns or on their future sites. The medical center in Beer-Sheva, with its emergency room, ambulatory services, and out-patient clinics, has been supplementing these two elements.

Given that only two new towns had been established for the Bedouin by the early 1980s and an additional two were in the process of establishment, transportation constraints and distances have still had considerable impact on the spatial accessibility of health services. Thus, by 1983, the general utilization rate of mother-and-child clinics by pregnant Bedouin women was only 52 percent due to limited spatial opportunities. The rates among the still seminomadic groups living in the remote periphery were as low as 42 percent, compared to 52 and 62 percent in the hamlets and towns respectively (Naggan 1984). A study conducted by Rafiq (1985) revealed that—on a scale of 1–100 of accessibility of primary health clinics—only 30 percent of the Bedouin population received a score of 82 whereas the rest scored less than 31. Obviously, the high-scoring population resided in Rahat, the largest Bedouin town. This problem was acute particularly in the eastern Negev where large tribes resided.

While these rates illustrate the benefits of moving to towns, they reflect the contemporary low accessibility of health services for a significant proportion of the population. Furthermore, these data suggest low awareness of the Bedouin vis-à-vis health services due to poor spatial availability. As a partial solution, the medical center in Beer-Sheva initiated a mobile health unit in 1980, which has become the first specific Bedouin-oriented element in the health service system for this population. This outreach service is targeted primarily at the peripheral population. Its functions include identification of sick persons and referral to clinics and to the hospital, shortening of hospitalization periods and prevention of repeated hospitalization through follow-up of those released from the hospital, instruction of the population in the purpose and proper utilization of the various services, community instruction in preventive medicine, and instruction of medical personnel and staff in the unique cultural characteristics of the Bedouin so as to improve communication. The mobile unit improved the spatial visibility, availability, and accessibility of the services, quality of contacts with this population, and Bedouin awareness of various aspects of medical treatment. However, its contribution in quantitative terms was found by Meir (1987b) to be only marginal, particularly given the still relatively high child mortality rates. Two additional mobile units were established during the 1980s—this time by the Ministry of Health—aimed primarily at preventive medicine.

A significant improvement in spatial availability and accessibility of health services has been taking place since the mid-1980s. In particular, there has been a considerable increase in the number of clinics. Three new mother-and-child clinics have been established—making a total of ten—so that each town now has at least one clinic. Given the extremely high birth rate, four more are now planned by the Ministry of Health. Although these clinics serve also the peripheral population, accessibility of this service is still constrained. This fact is reflected in the higher infant and child mortality rate among them, compared to the town-dwellers, as revealed in Chapter 5. This population—it will be recalled—still comprises about half of the total Bedouin population and, as shown by Ben-David (1993), is little inclined as yet to move to towns given the present form of town physical and social planning and settlement of land-tenure issues. The implication, from the perspective of the present discussion, is that the health-related wellbeing of a considerable proportion of the Bedouin population is still highly constrained.

The urban-peripheral disparity is revealed again in the case of primary health clinics. True, their number has more than doubled to seventeen, to which can be added the two clinics in the Jewish town of Dimona which the Bedouin are eligible to use. This increase reduced the ratio of population/clinics from about 7,100 in the early 1980s to 4,700 in the mid-1990s.

This achievement is attributed partly to the response of the major provider, the Sick Fund of the G.F.L., to population growth but also to other semipublic health care associations which have recently grown and began to penetrate this population. However, fifteen of these clinics are still located in towns, and the two operating in the periphery have only recently been established on a partial service basis. This indicates once again the constrained situation of the large peripheral Bedouin population. In partial response to this stress, the Sick Fund of the G.F.L. has begun—for the first time—to include the peripheral population in its policy considerations and plans are underway to establish four more primary health clinics there in recognition of the fact that migration of the Bedouin to towns has been rather slow.

Functional Accessibility

Despite improvement of spatial availability and accessibility of health services, the problem of functional accessibility—that is quality of the services—has been acute. Proper functional accessibility is important, particularly given that the epidemiological transition process has not yet been completed and that infant and child mortality rates are still relatively high. Quality of services is judged here in terms of availability of medical personnel in primary health care clinics. Table 7.6 presents the ratio of physicians and other medical personnel (nurses and paramedical staff) per 1,000 population in Bedouin clinics in the early 1980s and mid-1990s. In the early 1980s, the rate of doctors/population for the urbanized Bedouin was nearly double that of the general rate. The latter figure indicates the extremely low rate for the peripheral population which—as shown in the previous section—enjoyed no separate services. In contrast, a comparison with the rates for the Jewish population in the Negev reveals, first, the wide gaps between the two populations and, second, that very small gaps existed between the rates for the Jewish urban and nonurban population. Meir (1987b) has found that only when the Jewish rural rates are considered does the gap with the Bedouin town population narrow (0.47 and 0.32 respectively). The general and town rates of other medical personnel for the Bedouin population are similar to that for physicians, indicating again the urban-peripheral gaps. These are considerably wider than for the respective Jewish rates.

It transpires that, in the early 1980s, the quality of health services—that is functional accessibility—for the Bedouin population was quite poor. However, at least with regard to physicians, the situation has improved considerably toward the mid-1990s. By 1995, the urban rate has increased by 56 percent to 0.50 and the general rate more than doubled to 0.37. The

TABLE 7.6   Medical staff per 1,000 population in primary care clinics, 1983 and 1995

Population	Physicians		Other Personnel	
	1983	1995	1983	1995
Bedouin-general	0.17	0.37	0.18	0.22
Bedouin-towns	0.32	0.50	0.33	0.31
Jewish-general	0.85	n.a.[a]	1.25	n.a.[a]
Jewish-towns	0.73	n.a.[a]	1.16	n.a.[a]

[a] Data for 1995 are not available in a manner comparable to 1983.

Source: For 1983-Meir (1987b), compiled from data of Sick Fund, G.F.L., Negev District; for 1995-compiled from data of Sick Fund, G.F.L., Negev District.

latter rate, in particular, implies indirectly a significant improvement in quality of services for the peripheral population, although they still suffer from constrained spatial availability and accessibility of the services. The major explanation for the increase in availability of physicians is that, during the 1980s and early 1990s, the growth in the Bedouin educational system—despite all the difficulties and problems discussed above—has produced a number of Bedouin physicians. These joined the medical work force and thus solved a major problem for service providers who previously found it difficult to staff Bedouin clinics.

The situation with regard to nurses and paramedical staff is still problematic. The rates have not changed since the early 1980s, yet it is precisely this kind of medical personnel that is crucial from a sociocultural perspective, serving as the middle layer between the highly educated doctors and the poorly educated Bedouin patients. Seen from this sociocultural angle, the functional accessibility of public health services for the Bedouin has been quite constrained.

Cultural Relevance

It was argued above that the effects of health services in terms of well-being are more individually than communally oriented, since the target population is only sick individuals (in comparison to all school-age children in educational services). In contrast to the latter, here the individual faces service providers alone, and the cultural gap is manifested most sharply. The issues at stake are Bedouin perceptions of the process of medical care, the socioethnic structure of Bedouin society, and the status of women and children.

The general problem among the Bedouin is related to the conflict between traditional and modern medicine. More specifically—as in many

Third World societies (Gesler 1984)—Bedouin traditional medical concepts and terminology are rooted in supranatural forces, in contrast to
modern medicine which is usually anchored in germ and molecular
theory. For this reason Bedouin unawareness of disease symptoms often
results in deterioration of even simple cases to emergencies (Lewando-
Hundt 1980). The Bedouin are also unaware of modern medical methods
and technology, as these conflict with their traditional perception of
medical treatment. A related problem is the Bedouin traditional perception of time which further conflicts with the demands of modern medical
care. Finally, to these one can add their unfamiliarity with administrative
requirements of health services such as referral, continual treatment by
the same doctor, follow-up, and documentation. These perceptual problems and administrative and technological demands generate a communication barrier between Bedouin patients and the medical personnel, and
restrict their readiness to use modern medical care. For this reason, medical treatment by traditional healers *(darwish)* is still prevalent, as shown
by Abu-Rabia, A. (1979; 1994a).

Evidently, the processes of urbanization, integration into the wage labor market, and growth of the educational system have narrowed the cultural gap between the Bedouin population and western culture, and
hence increased Bedouin receptivity to modern public health services.
However, as shown above, certain processes have also occurred within
the health service system itself, such as the improvement in spatial accessibility and the increase in Bedouin personnel. A project initiated in 1995
is recruiting young educated Bedouin women into a paramedical program to serve both in the clinics and in outreach services among the
peripheral tribes. All these factors have also contributed to improvement
in cultural accessibility of these services.

Yet, not all cultural barriers have been removed. As is the case with
educational services, lack of consideration by service providers for the
sociopolitical structure of Bedouin society and the status of women are
still hampering the prospects of drawing a fair level of cultural wellbeing
from these services. The sociopolitical structure, particularly intertribal
rivalries, has a bearing on proper functioning of clinics and personnel. As
they do with schools, each tribe demands a separate facility, in conflict
with any efficiency criteria of service provision. Due to the limited number of clinics which could be established, there have been conflicts over
their location both between the Bedouin and the medical authorities and
among the Bedouin themselves. These conflicts resulted in some cases in
new facilities being torn down by rival tribes (Meir 1987b).

With time, however, the Bedouin have begun to accept the constraints
under which the authorities operate and the latter have begun to realize
the stress generated among Bedouin by their policy, particularly its re-

striction of services to towns. As shown above, additional clinics are planned now for the peripheral tribes, and very recently, one of the new clinics was established specifically to meet the sociopolitical demands of one of the tribes within a town. It should be noted in this regard that a major incentive in adding clinics has been the implementation in 1995 of the National Health Insurance Law. Nevertheless, the addition of these tribal facilities—which is a culturally relevant act on the part of service providers—can help improve the cultural wellbeing of Bedouin patients. Yet, while the addition of Bedouin personnel has contributed to improved functional accessibility of the services, it has generated another problem— that of their tribal origin. Bedouin patients are not always prepared to accept and express confidence in personnel from other—particularly rival—tribes due to suspicion and hostility. This internal ethnic problem has been hampering the proper functioning of some of the clinics.

Another cultural barrier is related to the status of Bedouin females. Unlike educational services, successful provision of health service requires direct contacts of Bedouin women—patients and mothers alike—with the external society. Yet, Bedouin women are not allowed such contacts easily, being subject to the decisions of men in their family. Consequently, women suffer from a two-step instruction and information process transferred through men, resulting in deficient care for themselves or their children (Lewando-Hundt 1980). Given the high fertility and child morbidity and mortality rates, children, in particular, are the victims of this problem. It was found that 40 percent of sick Bedouin children were taken to the emergency room of the regional medical center in Beer-Sheva rather than to local clinics and that the chances of hospitalization of a Bedouin child were double those of a Jewish child (Naggan 1984; see also Carmel et al. 1990).

It thus transpired that the Bedouin were using the emergency room at the regional medical center as just another clinic, imposing considerable pressure on this facility and generating an intensive direct encounter with the highest level of public health services. This encounter exposes the cultural gap acutely: Bedouin patients, particularly children, are displaced from the tribal environment, a fact which generates bilateral language and communication problems, given the inadequate understanding of Bedouin culturally relevant issues by the medical and administrative hospital personnel. This was the major reason for the decision reached and implemented in 1987 to transform one of the clinics in Rahat, located some 30 km north of Beer-Sheva, into a day-care facility and smallscale frontline emergency room. However, Rahat and its peripheral tribes comprise only about one third of the total Bedouin population. While this form of outreach service has indeed been culturally relevant for a large proportion of Bedouin patients, the majority of the Bedouin still do not benefit from the improvement in wellbeing derived from provision of public health services. This situation clearly illustrates the notion raised in Chapter 5 that, in general, government officials tend to ignore the rather sensitive stage of transition from nomadism to sedentarism in terms of medical wellbeing.

Welfare Services

The informal internal welfare system among the traditional pastoral nomadic Bedouin was based on the tribal and family social structures. As noted in the previous chapter—and similarly to many other pastoral nomadic societies (see Chapter 2)—the overriding structural principle guiding this noncompetitive society was mutual responsibility between the individual and the group and fatalistic trust in Allah's generosity, both of which reduced the need to worry about future survival. Customs and rules were therefore evolved for bestowing free aid on those in various kinds of need, with the aim of maintaining social reproduction and continuity. In traditional nonmonetized Bedouin society, mutual aid was mostly embodied in goods and services. Earlier discussions in this book highlighted intergroup mutual aid in terms of grazing and water resources. At the intragroup level, Al-A'assem (1983) provides several examples of aid, such as in pastoral and dry-farming production, rehabilitation of ex-convicts or the impoverished, aid to impecunious newly wed young men, maintenance of the social custom of generous hospitality, gifts and assistance to new mothers, and various other types of mutual aid.

Social and economic changes among the Bedouin in recent decades, particularly the shift to an urban wage-labor monetized environment and the gradual deterioration of the traditional social structures previously concerned with the individual's wellbeing, also generated increased stress and uncertainty concerning future survival. As explained in the previous chapter (see also Al-A'assem 1983), individual Bedouin are facing a dilemma: whether to resort to government welfare aid at the cost of losing internal tribal or family support. It is only natural that, through time, their level of expectations from the public provision system will rise.

On a community-individual continuum of applicability of public services, welfare services may be located close to the individual's end. This implies not only that the target population of these services is considerably smaller than in educational and health services and that they are concerned with very specific problems of isolated individuals, but also that—historically similarly to Western societies at large—these services were the last to receive the attention of public authorities. Indeed, while educational and health services were officially provided to the Bedouin already in the early 1950s, provision of public welfare services began only in the late 1970s or early 1980s.

Whereas the Israeli law defines explicitly the responsibility of the state for full provision of educational services via the local authority, or health services via various sick fund associations, the provision of welfare services is not regulated in this way. Only a few spheres are under direct state responsibility by law, such as care for the mentally retarded, the mentally ill, elderly inmates, minors in need of protection, youth probation services, and adoption. All other areas of welfare for which state financial support may be given are subject to the decision and initiative of the local authority. This implies that availability of services to their inhabitants varies as it depends on initiatives of the authority as a whole or individual functionaries. It also implies potentially low awareness and uncertainty of inhabitants as to services available to them (Schnit 1988).

There are two types of officials in charge of welfare services. The first are social workers, handling areas defined by law for which slots are to be assigned and filled. The second are community workers, who pursue a variety of social welfare tasks which are not strictly defined in terms of legal authority, and whose appointment is also conditioned by local initiatives. In general, community work is aimed at dealing with problems of adaptation and social and economic stress that result particularly from social change. Its roles are to explain the nature of the community and its needs to the authorities, to explore and define areas of need, and to disseminate information on services and thus generate demand within the community. Historically, this kind of community approach in the Western world is an even later development than the more individualized area of common social work (Gidron 1979).

Until the late 1970s, the limited services provided to the Bedouin came under the local office of the Ministry in Beer-Sheva, which served the Jewish population too. Only in 1980 did the Ministry of Labor and Welfare establish a separate National Bedouin Bureau in Beer-Sheva. The Bureau was staffed by two Bedouin social workers with a budget that sufficed only to pay their wage. They were initially intended to serve the entire Bedouin population, but in fact only those who met the strictest criteria of the law and applied to the Bureau were dealt with. This passive approach by the staff was due not only to their being newcomers to the system, or to legal constraints, but primarily to lack of means for outreach action to explore and identify social problems and design preventive and care measures.

Even after the establishment of the Bureau, the ability of government agencies to deal with social problems was quite constrained. This was the case particularly with the 40,000 Bedouin living at that time in the periphery. According to the Ministry's standard of one social worker per 1,000 people, forty social workers should have served this population. In reality, in the early 1980s only the two social workers of the Bureau dealt with this large population (a rate of 1:20,000), and in fact they had to serve the entire Bedouin population (totaling then about 55,000), including those in towns.

The problem was aggravated by the spatial perspective. The Bedouin in the periphery within the *sayig* were dispersed over an area of more than 1,000 sq. km. with harsh terrain and long distances from the service center. This population was largely inaccessible to the social workers who were based at the Bureau in Beer Sheva, without transportation for appropriate outreach to conduct individual and communal activities. Vice versa, the Bureau was objectively quite inaccessible to Bedouin elders and—given restrictions on spatial mobility of women discussed in the previous chapter—the problem was relevant to them as well. To borrow a term proposed by Rowles (1978), the severance from services which were essential to them and for which they were eligible made many Bedouin elders and women the prisoners of desert space. The spatial perspective of this problem may also reflect the cultural relevance of welfare services to the Bedouin. Reluctance of Bedouin families in the periphery to relocate to planned towns reflects their defense mechanism against further cultural change but also hampers their ability to use welfare services to solve problems that have already emerged.

Indications of change have appeared only recently with the establishment of departments of welfare and social services for each of the Bedouin municipalities (whether local or regional councils). Even the Bedouin of the periphery are now receiving these services from one of the regional councils. The process began first in 1986 in Rahat, the largest town, although some welfare services were available there from the early 1980s and in all other towns from the late 1980s. This change signifies primarily the shift from the more common conceptualization of welfare services as defined by law to the more comprehensive one of community services in line with the concept described above.

The area into which these departments moved first was care for the mentally retarded and those with congenital defects due to genetic diseases. This problem was brought to the public agenda quite recently as it was revealed that the child mortality rate due to these causes among the Bedouin is 7.5/1,000 (compared to 1/1,000 within the Jewish population). These extremely high rates are attributed to the high rate of endogamous marriages (estimated at 80 percent) (EFSHAR 1992). Previously, the problem—attributed by the Bedouin to Allah's will—was dealt with within the family, and children with mild mental retardation or physical disability participated in simple tasks of the pastoral production process or domestic duties according to their capacities, without becoming a burden. Difficult cases were kept at home without care. The process of urbanization and loss of pastoral opportunities has brought the problem to the surface as even mildly retarded children have become a burden upon the family. To begin tackling this problem, social workers—mostly Bedouin by origin—had to struggle in two arenas: first, to persuade the welfare authorities that a major problem existed; and second, to persuade the families of the necessity to solve the problem via external aid that could entail even expropriation of care from the family. The authorities have gradually recognized the problem, and initiatives have already been launched in terms of allocation of funds for establishment and operation of day-care and treatment centers, special education classes and schools, and institutionalization. Also, a mobile unit has been operated in recent years primarily for identification of cases in the periphery. The main difficulty still lies with the families, much persuasion being required due to family shame, reluctance to give away the children to external agencies, and fear of loss of SSI child benefits.

Other areas in which community service departments have begun to take action cover problems that result from those changes in the status of elders, children, and women discussed in the previous chapter. With regard to elders, social workers now have to take interventive action in cases where elders need to be institutionalized, or when adult children deprive aged parents of their SSI elderly benefits. Also, in many cases these benefits are reduced considerably, as the SSI deducts social security dues that were not paid by the beneficiaries in the past. In these cases the elders approach the department for income supplementation in terms of municipal tax discount or home helpers. In some towns, establishment of a day-center for the elderly was initiated to solve problems of detachment of elders from family economic and social activities. This initiative has met with only little success as of yet, because these facilities still compete with the elders' *shig* as a social club.

Regarding children, many families are now faced with the problem described in the previous chapter of a latent surplus of children. This demographic situation implies that Bedouin society, particularly in towns, has reached close to its "social carrying capacity" in terms of its ability to channel the extremely large child and youth population into beneficial economic and social avenues. Consequently, many low income multichild families require child care assistance and economic aid in terms of, for example, municipal tax discount. In some towns, home helper, daytime foster-care and child-minder services have been initiated in order to help families dealing with physical and mental disabilities, widows, divorced mothers, etc.

Due to high drop-out rates from schools, and lack of local employment opportunities, this problem has become acute particularly among youth in towns, leading to an emergence of juvenile delinquency and even drug dealing and use. These problems are becoming a target for action by community workers in terms of information campaigns and preventive action and even provision of youth probation services, and by the municipalities—who are acting to provide youth with alternative activities such as social clubs, sports and so on. These initiatives, like many others, require of course special funds beyond those defined by law, allocation of which is a matter for negotiation with the state at the risk of furthering local dependence on external provision.

Bedouin women have recently also become the target of action taken by social and community workers. One area of action is care for needy widows. In the past a widow and her children always received economic and moral support from her husband's family. At present such support has become more problematic due to the general social and economic stress of many families in towns, and therefore resort to public welfare services has become more common. A similar problem is that of divorced wives who live in separate households but are still required to transfer the SSI child allowances to their husbands, or those whose exhusbands refuse to support their children, preferring those of their new wives.

More serious problems which have been brought to light in recent years are those of physical and sexual abuse of wives, daughters, and sisters, extramarital pregnancies, and female circumcision. The problem is not so much the issue of abuse itself—as this presumably existed before—but rather the emerging conflict with Israeli law and changing social norms. Social and community workers are faced with a dilemma of whether to report such cases to the authorities—putting the abused females at the risk of being further abused by husbands, fathers, and brothers—or handling the problems internally, informally, and confidentially, thus evading the law. At present the tendency is still toward the latter option, the prime concern being the desire to avoid further stress within the already distressed Bedouin family. However, social workers increasingly report on growing awareness of this problem and requests from within Bedouin circles for formal intervention (Dinero 1995).

Finally, the growing general concern with women is reflected in growth of initiatives by some community workers in towns aimed at replacing the lost economic roles which women pursued in the past with social and recreation activities. These initiatives are still limited as they still have to face the sociocultural problem of constrained spatial mobility of women, particularly in towns.

From the perspective of functional availability and accessibility, the above discussion reveals that the spectrum of social and communal problems handled by social and community workers within Bedouin society has increased immensely in recent years. This is due both to the efforts of the workers themselves to bring these problems to light and growing awareness of the Bedouin population. Yet, the burden of responsibility for welfare and social services borne by the municipal departments is tremendous, outweighing capabilities and resources. Despite the fact that all the Bedouin population is at present covered by such departments in the various municipalities, only 15–20 positions have been allocated by the Ministry of Labor and Welfare to these departments, including professional, paraprofessional, and administrative workers. Even if all of them were professionals, the rate for the entire Bedouin population would be one worker per 4,000–5,500 population. Although these rates constitute an improvement over previous years—reflecting increased allocation of funds from the Ministry—they are still considerably below the Ministry's own standard of 1:1,000 and the rate of 1:1,600 for the Jewish population in the Negev. The problem is even more serious for the Bedouin population in the periphery whose size has not changed dramatically despite migration to towns, due to the high natural increase rate. As shown above, despite being covered now by the regional councils they suffer from inferior spatial accessibility compared to town dwellers.

Furthermore, according to data of the Negev Center for Regional Development (1993), by 1993 the proportion of cases under care of social workers among the Bedouin was 15/1,000 compared to 53/1,000 among the Jewish population, indicative of low awareness of and low tendency to cooperate with these service systems. Yet, the ratio of cases/social workers among them is 93, about 20 percent higher than for the Jewish population. However, in contrast to the Jewish population—where both the clients and providers are part of a long-standing system—social and community workers within Bedouin society have to function under abnormal conditions. They not only have to provide routine services to the population but also concurrently to raise the awareness level of both the client population to their availability and the authorities for the growing needs. Given the time and effort needed in these arenas, the relative amount of resources allocated for pursuing these tasks within the Bedouin community is even more indicative of the constrained functional availability of these services to the population than is indicated above by the sheer manpower/population rates.

From the perspective of cultural relevance, many of the initiatives taken by the social workers—even the Bedouin among them—are conceptually rooted in Western ideas of social and community work and do not necessarily conform to Bedouin cultural norms and needs. They are aimed at solving emerging problems, many of which were previously unheard of, others unpublicized, in Bedouin society. While the underlying problem of Bedouin society is adaptation to the changing roles of individuals within the family and the community, a more difficult one is adaptation to the new circumstances of facing unfamiliar problems of individuals and families. The most serious problem is, however, the dilemma over whether to allow external public professional intervention. This dilemma is particularly serious when the handful of professional workers are most probably from alien or rival tribal circles or from the rival real Bedouin or fellaheen groups, and when some of them are Bedouin women who have to intervene in areas of patriarchal Bedouin society previously under absolute control of men.

From a cultural perspective, there is thus strong tension between the desire of the system of public welfare and community services to provide aid to the Bedouin and the preparedness of the Bedouin society to accept this system. Availability of professional manpower can also be looked upon from a cultural perspective. Although most of the social workers are Bedouin by origin, the government has formulated no policy of developing this professional manpower. In similarity with educational services indicated above, Bedouin society does not appear to have reached an educational threshold high enough to produce internal culturally relevant social welfare manpower. Even if it had—as recent educational indications suggest (Abu-Saad 1991)—governmental policy of allocation of resources has so far contributed little to the realization of the potential of this culturally appropriate social welfare manpower.

Conclusions

Several processes that followed sedentarization and semiurbanization have brought the Negev Bedouin to a unique juncture where public services have began to play a major role in their affairs. They may be characterized as externalization processes. Economically, Bedouin society has become highly dependent upon constrained external economic resources in the market economy, beyond the direct control of its members. Socially, due to changes in the status of individuals and deteriorating social systems, individual Bedouin have to search for external alternatives to internal ones that previously enabled their socialization and provided for their wellbeing. They face now modern public systems in which these alternatives are public goods that are supposed to be provided by the state as basic needs vital for the wellbeing of a modernizing society.

Members of Bedouin society are now required not only to adapt to the new idea of consuming a public good from an external agent, but to cope independently and individually (compared to coping cooperatively and tribally in the internal system) with systems that are alien to them. Furthermore—by resorting to the alternative modern systems—individuals risk the option of support from the remnants of the traditional social systems, the deterioration of which has left Bedouin society with highly constrained internal resources to offer its members. This process is reinforced by those discussed in the previous chapters in terms of rights over resources, economic fragmentation of family labor force, and changing roles of individuals within the family and society. Together, they contribute to an emergence of new rationalization concerning control over one's future, and furthers the growing individualization process within this society. This situation generates considerable stress individually and communally. Under such circumstances, individuals foster elevated expectations not only concerning replacement of traditional institutions by modern services but, primarily, concerning the spatial and functional availability and accessibility and cultural relevance of these public goods

These essential public services are necessary for adaptation in early and even advanced stages of sedentary life and are to be balanced against the deteriorating parallel traditional ones. As the above discussion has revealed, however, none of the public education, health and welfare and community services are spatially, functionally, and culturally capable of providing the Bedouin with the desired degree of wellbeing. Their provision—as in many other pastoral nomadic societies—has been inherent primarily within the context of the benefit to the state rather than to the Bedouin. That is, besides economic and efficiency criteria, the main motivation of the state has been to draw the Bedouin into towns and this dictated the strategy of service provision. Indeed, spatial and functional availability and accessibility and sociocultural relevance of services have improved considerably in towns, particularly since the 1980s. Yet, even there the improvement has not reached a level sufficient to generate the desired individual and communal wellbeing. Furthermore, close to half of the Negev Bedouin who still reside in the periphery do not enjoy even this level of public service provision. This implies that, not only for this segment of the population, but in fact for the entire Bedouin society, social and cultural wellbeing is constrained in varying degrees due to deficiencies in public service provision.

The discussion in earlier chapters revealed that since the early 1950s Bedouin society has been heavily permeated with state intervention in its affairs. Provision of public services has gradually made the Bedouin dependent upon the state and this has provided the latter with an opportunity to intensify its intervention within both communal and individual aspects of this society. Yet, constrained wellbeing of the Bedouin due to unmet expectations during a process of accelerated change has complicated their mutual relationships with the state. This issue will be the concern of the next and final chapter of this book.

8

The Political Dimension:
The Bedouin and the State

The previous chapters emphasized processes of individualization within Bedouin society in terms of gradual detachment from tribal institutions and obligations, resulting from the sociospatial transformation of this society. It was also shown that the Bedouin have instead become gradually dependent on external resources—controlled by the state—through public service provision. This development and others have introduced a strong political dimension into the process of change within this society, generating tension with the state. This tension began during the Ottoman period and the British Mandate, but turned most intensive after the State was established.

Two ideas will be recalled from the conceptual framework in Chapter 2. The first is that this tension originates in the conflict between traditional pastoral nomadic centrifugal ideologies and modern state centripetal concepts and tendencies. It may result in opposing forces of space production. The second idea, however, is that a process of change does not necessarily entail considerable discontinuity. Cultural elements which appear to have been abandoned may in fact be held in reserve as institutionalized alternatives to be reactivated if the need arises. Such is the case with the centrifugal force of pastoral nomads. In a strong modern state one might expect the centripetal force of the state to overcome the centrifugal force of the pastoral nomadic population, thus affecting their locational pattern at the macro level to the benefit of the state. However, due to the persistence of the centrifugal tendency as an institutionalized alternative in reserve, this society does not necessarily lose its power. It can withstand the centripetal power of the state, even at the post-nomadic sedentarized phase. Despite processes of detribalization, individualization, and dependence upon the state, it is capable of reactivating this centrifugal alternative at the meso- and micro-levels in various spatial and functional forms. Thus, the centrifugal-centripetal tension becomes a useful umbrella term to describe the articulation of the old and the emerging cultural and spatial patterns of ex-nomad pastoralists within a modern state.

This chapter examines this issue through highlighting the centrifugal-centripetal tension between the Bedouin and the Israeli government. Many elements relating to this issue stem from the general or more specific processes and problems discussed in previous chapters. These elements accumulated with time, however, and elevated the tension to the level of an ongoing conflict that generated growing Bedouin protest against the government. This protest, it is argued, has contributed to the weakening of the centripetal force of the state and to its balancing with the centrifugal tendency of the Bedouin. The following discussion will examine the major issues generating this tension in recent decades, the evolution of Bedouin protest and action over wider and more specific issues, and will trace the spatial and functional manifestations of centrifugality stemming from this tension.

Issues of Bedouin-State Tension

The theoretical discussion in Chapter 2 presented the relationships and tensions between pastoral nomads and the state in a rather universal manner. Chapter 3, however, highlighted the unique political context of the Israeli-Arab conflict within which contemporary Negev Bedouin society has evolved. The dual universalistic and specific dimensions are thus intertwined within the centrifugal-centripetal tension between the Bedouin and the State of Israel. It is therefore difficult to determine whether—and to what extent—a certain initiative or action taken by the Bedouin as part of their centrifugal tendency is not partly motivated by the Israeli-Arab conflict. On the basis of field experience it is the impression of the present author that although the Bedouin are reluctant to discuss this issue, it plays a role in their motivation. Hence, any interpretation of most, if not all, of the issues in the following discussion will have to bear this context in mind.

In a hierarchical system of issues comprising the centrifugal-centripetal tension (see Figure 8.1)—whereby each level is related to those above and below—the top tier includes the major issue of land ownership dispute. This issue originates partly in the specific context of the Israeli-Arab conflict but carries also a universal nature. The next tier includes the issue of governmental settlement of the Bedouin and official urbanization policy and implementation, a process that began in the mid-1960s. This leads to the next tier, which is related to allocation of resources to the Bedouin. It encompasses economic resources in terms of agro-pastoralism

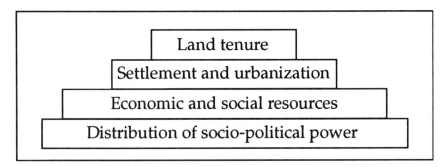

FIGURE 8.1   Major dimensions of Bedouin-state tension.

and employment opportunities and social resources in terms of public services. Finally, internal competition over these resources generates the tier of issues relating to the distribution of sociopolitical power within Bedouin society.

It should be noted that this hierarchy is only partly chronological, as the emergence of some issues at lower tiers to a certain extent predated those in higher ones. These major issues were discussed at various degrees of detail in previous chapters, but are reinterpreted here in terms of tension with the state. Each issue is composed of more specific and closely interrelated issues which originate in the same source, namely the centrifugal-centripetal tension.

Land Ownership

Land ownership became a major issue among the Negev Bedouin after statehood, but it began to emerge previously. As shown in Chapter 4, the process of privatization of tribal lands by individual families began in the second half of the nineteenth century under the Ottoman Empire, and continued through initiatives for formalization of ownership during the British Mandate in Palestine. Of the various categories of land defined by the Ottoman Land Law of 1856, the most problematic has been *mawat*, namely land which was not owned then either privately or publicly or was considered waste land. It therefore became state property, cultivation or grazing rights requiring state permission (Granot 1952; Graham-Brown 1980; Lewis 1987).

Despite the 1921 amendment of the law stating stated that cultivation of *mawat* land did not bestow ownership rights, the British authorities offered the Bedouin the opportunity of ownership recognition subject to registration in the Land Registry Office. The Bedouin, however, were reluctant to register their lands both because this move was at odds with their internal traditional system of ownership proof (see Chapter 4) and due to ear of taxation. Therefore, most Bedouin lands were classified as *mawat* but were cultivated without state interference (Al-Aref 1937b).

The major problems were that the British Mandate authorities never completed their initiatives—including surveying the Negev—and that the Israeli government adopted the Ottoman law. Relocation of the Bedouin after 1949 to the *sayig* therefore took place not only for security reasons but also in order to prevent their settlement on those *mawat* lands that now became state land administered by the Israel Land Administration (ILA). The ILA now holds about 90 percent of Negev lands and 55 percent of the land within the *sayig*. The Bedouin regard these areas— particularly in the *sayig*—as theirs by virtue of their customary ownership (see Fig. 8.2). In general, as shown in Chapter 4, there are two major categories of Bedouin land-claimers: those who were not relocated from their land since it was included in the *sayig*, and those who were relocated into it from other areas in the Negev. Both groups are involved in land ownership disputes with the state (Ben-David 1995). The first group—which claims land ownership by virtue of Bedouin customary traditional ownership—is primarily of real Bedouin origin. The second group—composed of real and fellahi Bedouin—bases its claim on power of possession of the land since the early 1950s. As will be shown below, land ownership has been a major issue of tension, carrying elements of fierce and bitter conflict with the government, particularly in the past two decades.

Settlement and Urbanization

The process of sedentarization accelerated during the 1950s and 1960s, once the Bedouin were relocated into the *sayig*. Settlement and urbanization first became an issue during the early 1960s, when Bedouin population pressure on land within the *sayig* began to conflict with government development policy. In order to protect state land from further Bedouin encroachment, a policy of planned urbanization was launched (see Chapter 4), calling for establishment of towns into which all Bedouin were eventually supposed to relocate. Nevertheless, since sedentarization had began some time previously, it became part of Bedouin society's arsenal of institutionalized alternatives. Hence, tension with the state was not over the issue itself but rather over the way it was implemented. This issue was viewed by the Bedouin in the context of two other issues: recognition of their land rights in their numerous dispersed hamlets in the *sayig*, and allocation of economic and social resources there. The former issue was highlighted above; the latter will be discussed in the next section.

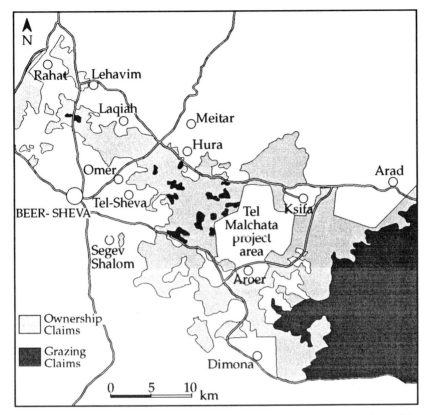

FIGURE 8.2 Bedouin land ownership and grazing claims (*Source:* Adapted from Steering Committee for the Negev Frontier 1991).

Despite the fact that settlement has been an institutionalized alternative, it constituted a major change in Bedouin life, particularly given its geopolitical context. It has been heatedly debated in recent decades by numerous academics and officials locally and internationally, in both the scholarly literature and the media. The present discussion is not aimed at reviewing this debate but rather intends to highlight the major dimensions of tension between the Bedouin and the state over the nature of the settlement process.

The most important issue here has been the nature of Bedouin settlements. The government—loyal to the centripetal raison d'être—sought to maximize Bedouin spatial convergence in order to enhance political control over them and minimize the cost of physical and social infrastructures. In the early 1960s it was therefore ready to allow only three settlements of a semiurban nature, each intended for several tens of thousands Bedouin. As shown previously, the Bedouin were reluctant to accept either the idea of high-density towns or their size and number. This reluctance is reflected in the fact that even today only about 50 percent of the Bedouin population—mostly of landless fellahi origin—live in these towns.

Furthermore, the Bedouin refusal to accept the initial concepts of internal planning of towns—related to the number of towns and their size—also impeded the process. Primarily for internal territorial and sociopolitical reasons, the Bedouin were concerned in particular with the tribal mix that would be imposed on them and its various consequences. In earlier years they were not overly concerned with the economic base of towns or physical infrastructure of the towns. These, however, have become important issues in recent years, emerging as agropastoral economic opportunities in towns have diminished without proper alternatives in situ, and as demands for modern elements of quality of life within towns have begun to replace pastoral nomadic traditional cultural values.

The problem of local government in these towns is associated with these issues, although it may also be categorized in the final tier in the above hierarchy. It surfaced as an issue when the semiurbanization process began to gain momentum and the population of Bedouin towns increased. The first town that became a municipality (a local council) was Rahat in the early 1980s. However, appointment of a Jewish mayor and officials ensured that its municipal management was retained by the Ministry of the Interior, with only a few local Bedouin representatives on the town council. True, this method of municipal management has been common in newly established Jewish towns as well, serving to position them on the proper development track until municipal autonomy and local elections are approved by the Ministry. Yet, in the case of the Bedouin, the government found this policy particularly convenient, presumably since it constituted a civilian control substitute for the military administration that was abolished in the mid-1960s. The government has been reluctant to renounce state control of this population and its affairs. Thus, this form of municipal management became the norm in all other Bedouin towns and regional councils (an assemblage of small towns in one regional municipality).

The issues of number and size of towns, their internal plan and economic nature, and local government, generated the issue of unrecognized settlements. This term has surfaced among the Bedouin in recent years with regard to many of the hamlets that were spontaneously erected during the 1950s and 1960s. It serves to distinguish them from towns which were planned, established, and recognized by the Ministry. In contrast to this term, as shown earlier, the previous use by government officials of the definition of "spontaneous" settlements has evolved in recent years—perhaps unconsciously and informally—first into "scattered" settlements *(pzourah)* and presently to "peripheral" settlements *(periferia)*. This terminological change may have been inspired by government attempts to enhance migration of Bedouin from these hamlets to towns. The authorities have thus been maneuvering to marginalize peripheral hamlets through stressing the higher quality of life in towns due to improved public services and residential facilities there.

However, the Bedouin still living in the periphery were aware of the many problems experienced by their kin living in towns (see also Ben-David 1993). These included, primarily, lack of local employment opportunities, higher cost of living due to municipal taxes and elevated material demands, increased intertribal tensions in a high-density environment, and the consequences of changes in the status and wellbeing of the elderly, women, and children. This awareness became associated with their refusal to evacuate the lands they claimed until the issue of ownership is settled. They believe that the drawbacks of life in towns outweigh the benefits. Consequently, they have scarcely responded to governmental attempts—through delegitimizing life in the periphery—to move them to towns. In fact, the Bedouin population of the periphery has grown and is now approximately the size of the entire Bedouin population of the Negev on the eve of massive migration to towns in the late 1970s. Yet, despite this considerable population growth, these peripheral settlements remain unrecognized by the government.

Allocation of Resources

The issue of allocation of resources is intimately interwoven with that of sedentarization and urbanization. It relates to economic resources in terms of agropastoralism and employment opportunities, and social resources in terms of public services. By maximizing Bedouin spatial convergence into towns, the government sought not only to minimize the costs of physical infrastructures but also to gain control of as much land as possible within the *sayig* and designate it for non-Bedouin military and civil projects. Consequently, in addition to regulating dry-farming, the state imposed severe restrictions on grazing territories and on livestock sizes and animal mix—particularly of black goats—that were mistakenly regarded as ecologically detrimental (see Perevolotsky 1991) until the early 1980s.

This policy has resulted in considerable contraction of these ventures in recent decades. Many Bedouin who use state land in the periphery, and others who live in towns and still conduct these economic ventures elsewhere, are required on an annual basis to renew grazing permits, licensing for the about 200,000–250,000 heads of livestock, and land lease agreements for dry-farming from the ILA and the Ministry of Agriculture (Abu-Rabia, A. 1994c). These permits, however, do not render them eligible for natural-disasters state compensation. In the case of dry-farming in particular, the Drought Line determined by the Ministry of Agriculture—south of which no compensation is paid—is demarcated north of Bedouin territories in the Negev. The Green Patrol, a special unit established in 1976 by the Ministry of Agriculture to supervise land usage in open areas in Israel, was given control of these agropastoral and other ventures of the Negev Bedouin as well. Its activities, which became notorious among the Bedouin, have been heavily criticized in the media and elsewhere (Maddrell 1990).

In addition to *mawat* land, water resources have also become state property under the various laws relating to water drilling and consumption, and allocation to the Bedouin has therefore been dependent upon the availability of water pipeline infrastructure. Obviously, supply of running water for domestic use in towns—which is regulated by law—does not constitute an issue, and residents are normally satisfied with the provision of this public service (see, e.g., Dinero 1995). Such is also the case with some of the peripheral settlements, despite the fact that they are unrecognized. Those hamlets located along highways are connected to the regional water infrastructure. Most of the remote ones also have access to special outlets along major pipelines, and haul water to their sites by private tractors and tankers. Yet, because of the prevalence of private smallscale irrigated farming, which is not officially recognized for water allocation purposes, water supply to the peripheral settlements remains quite problematic. It is also a particularly acute problem for those several hundred seminomadic Bedouin who live in the remote Negev Highlands. These Bedouin refuse persistently to evacuate this area despite repeated attempts by the government, which has been barring their access to local water wells over which they claim ownership.

Another type of infrastructural physical resource is electric power, the supply of which has been an issue in itself. As in the case of water, Bedouin towns are connected to the power supply network operated by the state-owned Electric Corporation. The problem persists in the case of peripheral unrecognized settlements, which are not eligible for this service. Their inhabitants resort to costly, unsafe, and unreliable private power generators for domestic use, usually operated and maintained on an extended family basis. Uses include lighting and water pumping from traditionally owned local wells and cisterns. The authorities have been slow to link to the grid even hamlets that have recently won recognition and been incorporated into one of the regional councils.

Another, newer issue is the lack of central sewage networks in towns. The towns are constructed according to a highly dispersed plan, which would render construction of a sewage system highly expensive, and the government has failed until very recently to provide municipalities with sufficient funds for this purpose. Thus, private homes still use domestic septic tanks. Under the prevailing demographic regime of extremely large families—and given the state policy of convergence of population in a few towns—these facilities are likely to constitute a serious health and ecological hazard.

As shown earlier, the state has never devised a program of employment for the Bedouin to compensate for the loss of pastoral and farming resources. In fact, in the early years Bedouin integration in the market economy outside the *sayig* was severely restricted by labor and travel regulations imposed by the military administration. When these were lifted in the late 1950s the Bedouin were left to their own devices in the search for employment in the Negev and elsewhere in Israel. Later on, the town planning concepts designated Bedouin towns as dormitory settlements (Kaplan et al. 1979), virtually devoid of any economic base. As shown above, separation of employment from home—particularly under conditions of restricted choice—has been highly problematic and detrimental to the Bedouin for social and cultural reasons (see also Dinero 1995). In addition, alleged discrimination of various kinds (e.g., Al-Huzayil 1994) and the slow development of the educational system, have resulted in inferior accessibility of Bedouin to the labor market, high unemployment rates, and constrained means of subsistence. The frustration caused by these drawbacks is particularly high in towns, where levels of expectations are elevated compared to the periphery.

Provision of public services as social resources for the Bedouin has been shown previously to have been highly problematic from the perspectives of spatial availability, functional accessibility, and cultural compatibility. It will be recalled that these services were supposed to replace the diminishing traditional institutions that provided for individual socialization and wellbeing. The problem has been particularly acute in the unrecognized peripheral settlements, as it was the stated policy of the government to provide them with only minimal services required by law. This policy has created wide gaps in quality of educational, health and welfare services—and hence in social wellbeing—between them and Bedouin town dwellers, let alone the Jewish population. The town-dwellers for their part, receive services inferior to those enjoyed by Jewish settlements. Thus, as the Bedouin have integrated into regional economic and social systems, and as more Bedouin have gained access to higher education, they have become increasingly aware of the gaps between their expectations vis-à-vis government provision of social resources and the reality that has been developing in this field.

Distribution of Sociopolitical Power

The limited scope of economic and social public resources provided by the state has generated strong internal competition and struggle over their distribution. This has replaced traditional competition that permeated Bedouin society over agropastoral resources which they perceived as provided freely and equally by Allah. In the past this competition was unidimensional, chiefly along tribal lines. However, due to the web of processes of change described in previous chapters, competition has evolved in recent decades along several dimensions.

In general, at the macro level, the major line of competition still coincides with tribal division. However, the War of Independence created circumstances which, in the eyes of the authorities, called for realignment of tribes and tribal remnants by the military administration (Marx 1974; Mor 1971). This process generated intratribal rivalries and competition, at times even along lineage lines. Furthermore, processes of individualization of rights over tribal and family resources, and social individualization of the expanded and nuclear family development process, led to the emergence of competition and conflict between individual families and tribal leadership. Competition has also evolved between the younger generation and the elderly. Finally, a line of competition has grown between the real Bedouin and the fellahi Bedouin. This originates in the historically inferior social status of the latter and their present quest for social recognition and perhaps hegemony.

It thus appears that the hidden agenda of Bedouin competition over internal distribution of resources has in fact been related also to the internal distribution of sociopolitical power. Therefore, this competition has itself become an issue of tension with the state. In early years the government exploited internal rivalries to enhance its control over the Bedouin population and gain its cooperation, primarily through co-optation (Lustick 1985). Hence, besides the general authority and responsibility allotted to tribal sheikhs in such areas as reporting births and deaths and heading tribal educational committees, they were selectively given control over state-installed water outlets, over permits for grazing, livestock, farming, labor, travel and other economic ventures, and permits for construction of homes and service facilities (schools and clinics). Many of these permit types were distributed by the sheikhs—usually also on a selective basis—to their close relatives and affines. Distant relatives were often denied permits or obliged to pay the sheikhs for them, a practice which proved to be lucrative.

Thus, internal discrimination in resource distribution—that began with agropastoral resources and continued with social resources—has evolved both between and within tribes. In time, this system of macro-

and micro-resource distribution generated internal tension that backfired upon state authorities and evolved into a major issue. Later, this issue became associated with conflict with the state over sufficient external allocation and proper deliverance of resources to the entire Bedouin community, as will be shown below.

A related issue has been state co-optation—usually also on a selective basis—by replacement or formal appointment of tribal sheikhs and tribal entities. This measure was meant to serve state interests, particularly in guaranteeing the security of the Negev during the 1950 and later in maneuvering the Bedouin into settling in towns. Such state intervention in Bedouin affairs, depriving them of access to their internal political resources, has become an issue of tension. An additional version of this issue has emerged in recent years in the case of self-management of Bedouin local and regional municipalities and official recognition of new ones.

The Evolution of Bedouin Protest

The issues discussed above reflect the attempts by the state to impose a centripetal force on the Bedouin. This force assumed spatial and functional forms. It affected both the ability of Bedouin groups to reside in a particular location, the nature of the settlement, and the manner in which they could conduct their life there comfortably. These issues—which originate primarily in the centrifugal-centripetal tension—considerably exacerbated the tension between the Bedouin and the Israeli government that originated in the broader geopolitical conflict. During the military administration, until the mid-1960s, the state was capable of suppressing manifestations of this tension. Therefore, with the exception of clashes with Bedouin infiltrators along the borders and with a few groups elsewhere in the Negev, and the appeal of certain tribes to their previous kibbutz neighbors for assistance (see Chapter 3), Bedouin civil protest in those years was quite minor.

The growth in Bedouin civil protest began in the late 1970s and is accounted for by several events and processes. First, the implementation of the state's urbanization policy began to gain momentum. This resulted in a second wave of spatial and functional turbulence in Bedouin society within three decades, the first wave having occurred during relocation into the *sayig*. Second, more than a decade of freedom from military administrative restrictions has contributed to increasing contacts of the Negev Bedouin with both the Arab and Jewish populations of Israel. Associated with this process is the minor growth of civil identity among the Bedouin at the expense of ethnic identity (Fenster 1993). This has resulted in growing assertiveness among them, particularly with the establishment of the Association for Bedouin Rights in 1974. This mood gained force especially since 1976, when the first "Day of the Land" protest by the Israeli Arab community took place. It took on particularly violent character among the Bedouin of the Negev. This protest, which was directed against land expropriation decisions taken by the government, became a turning point in Arab protest in Israel over various issues (Yiftachel 1995), becoming since an annual event.

In order to understand the evolution and dimensions of Bedouin protest and action, two types of preliminary surveys were conducted. The first (Ben-Dror and Meir 1995) concerns protest events as reported by the media since 1976, and the second (Seif and Meir 1995) refers to the emergence of voluntary organizations within Bedouin society. These processes are apparently associated. Despite the preliminary nature of the surveys and methodological problems with press reports, their results can provide a fair idea of the nature of the process of protest.

The Bedouin have been conducting various kinds of public protest, including press conferences, lobbying Arab and Jewish Israeli politicians, appeals to the Supreme Court, demonstrations, and schooling and sit-down strikes. They received external assistance of various kinds in their protest, but the role of the educational process—despite its various drawbacks—should not be underestimated. They have therefore learned with time to recruit the media to promote their cause. These types of public protest—as reported by the national and local printed media—were surveyed and broken down into the above major categories of Bedouin-state tension, except that the issue of distribution of resources was subdivided into economic and social resources.

Figure 8.3 shows the cumulative number of protest events by category since 1976. The issue of land ownership is the major one—as expected—accounting for about half of all cases and may be considered the engine of protest for all other types. Next in importance (about a quarter of all cases) is protest over allocation and internal distribution of public social resources. This is followed by issues of sedentarization and urbanization, allocation and internal distribution of agropastoral resources.

Bedouin protest in all issues combined has grown considerably and steadily in the last two decades. However, the evolution of protest over specific issues is of particular interest, reflecting processes of change within this society as described previously. The issue of land ownership has dominated the process of protest, with a consistent growth compared to the others. Despite various attempts by the state, this issue remains persistently unsettled, still capable of hampering the solution of other issues and evoking Bedouin protest. Particularly interesting is the growth in protest over land ownership during the late 1970s and early 1980s. This

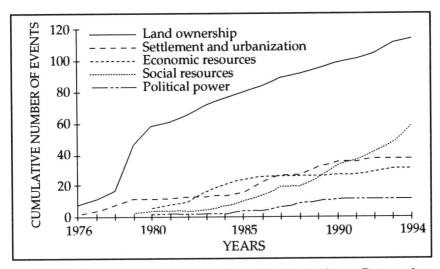

FIGURE 8.3 Bedouin protest events by issues: 1976–1994 (*Source:* Data are from Ben-Dror and Meir 1995).

is the consequence of government decision—following the peace treaty with Egypt—to construct a large military airbase in the northern Negev. The area most suitable was sited near Tel-Malchata, some 30 km east of Beer-Sheva (see Fig. 8.2), but this required evacuation of about five hundred Bedouin families (about 5,000 persons) from an area of about 30,000 ha. (Marx 1981b; Fenster 1995). This act created considerable turmoil among the Bedouin and in the media.

Bedouin protests over issues other than land have grown rather slowly, but their relative magnitudes have changed over time. Until the early 1980s, protests over issues of settlement and urbanization were quite dominant, reflecting Bedouin dissatisfaction with the nature of the settlements allowed by the state. Protest on these matters continued in later years, particularly over demolition by the authorities of illegally constructed homes in the periphery. Yet, the magnitude of this protest was gradually equaled by protest events over allocation of economic resources, primarily those related to agropastoral ventures. The latter are also related to the issue of the nature of peripheral settlements.

Yet, most interesting is the considerable growth in protest over allocation and internal distribution of public social resources. From the late 1970s, protest over this issue evolved slowly until the mid-1980s. However—again concomitantly with the accelerated process of urbanization in these years—its magnitude has been growing considerably, particularly since the early 1990s, outweighing the previous two issues. This change in balance between protested issues implies changes in preferences of the Bedouin (indicated in Chapter 5) toward more individualized elements of modern quality of life in towns and peripheral settlements alike. They replace those elements that originated in the traditional agropastoral nomadic and seminomadic more communal economy. To these we may add the emerging protest, since the early 1980s—albeit relatively minor and slow—over distribution of political power, particularly in relation to self-management of Bedouin local and regional municipalities and state recognition of new ones.

The gradual accumulation of Bedouin civil protest is associated with the emergence in the 1970s of voluntary organizations within this society. This process reflects an attempt by founders and activists—usually from the younger and educated generation—to fill in the void created between the deteriorating old system of internal care and support and the newly emerging one that has been provided by the state. It is also a response to the inability of individual Bedouin to cope alone with the issues and problems. Seen from the perspective of grass roots development, their prime purpose has been assistance to the Bedouin community in face of lack of sufficient governmentally originated development measures. In this sense, they constitute an act of protest against the state. However, they also constitute a protest particularly against the traditional tribal leadership which, in the eyes of their members, failed to handle Bedouin affairs properly vis-à-vis the state during a process of critical change. In this sense, the emergence of these organizations is another manifestation of the process of social and political change and particularly of social and economic individualization within Bedouin society.

Preliminary data on Bedouin voluntary organizations were collected from the Organizations Registrar of the Ministry of the Interior and from the SHATIL Project of the New Israel Fund. This project aims at guiding new Israeli voluntary organizations in their initial steps until formal recognition is granted for purposes of fund raising. These data were supported by interviews with organization activists. The first voluntary organization was the Association for Bedouin Rights, which was established, as noted above, in 1974. The founding of this organization became a milestone in this process, paving the road for additional organizations. By the end of the seventies three more were added, with an additional four in the 1980s and thirteen during the early 1990s until 1995. In addition, interviews revealed that beyond these registered organizations there are also unregistered ones, their number unknown. Some of the organizations concentrate on lobbying while others focus on action. Some are active particularly in the unrecognized settlements, viewing these as particularly needy.

Most of the Bedouin voluntary organizations were founded for long-range action. This, however, does not imply that all have lasted or remained active, a fact which reflects the objective and subjective internal and external difficulties, particularly within the previously pastoral no-madic Bedouin society. Although the tribal system has deteriorated con-siderably, intertribal competition and rivalry prevail within a constrained resource distribution context. One of the major difficulties is the persis-tent conflict between narrow tribal interests and wider communal ones. Despite activists' claim for a community-wide orientation of their organi-zations, interviews revealed that this orientation is actually practiced in only a few cases. In fact, many of the organizations were established on a tribal basis, aimed specifically at attracting resources and thus improving the wellbeing of their tribal or subtribal group members. Another major difficulty is the almost complete dependence of the organizations on external funding to supplement the meager membership fees. A few receive partial funding from governmental offices, but in most cases activists have to resort to the more difficult avenue of fund-raising from domestic and even international private and semipublic sources.

The stated areas of action of the organizations conform in general to the above-described issues with which Bedouin society has been con-cerned. Some of the organizations are active in several areas, and hence there is a certain degree of overlap between them. The most intensive area of stated action is the social arena, conforming to the above observa-tion that social resources have in recent years become the leading issue of protest. Within this field, formal education is of major concern, and lob-bying and action are directed at the following fields: establishment and operation of pre-kindergarten classes, establishment of new schools, con-ducting achievement tests, preparation of high-school students for matri-culation examinations, access to stipends for high-school and higher edu-cation, establishment of special education facilities, provision of enrich-ment classes in modern technology and computers, fostering talented school-children, teaching Bedouin heritage and folklore, teaching staff accreditation, organization of parent associations, establishment of school libraries, provision of school equipment and infrastructure, and provision of self-organized bussing from remote locations in the periphery.

From among the other stated areas of social activities of the organiza-tions, improvement of the general wellbeing of individuals is of particu-lar importance. This includes establishment of day-care centers for chil-dren and elders, sports centers, summer camps, prevention of drug abuse, rehabilitation of ex-convicts, instruction in proper community ac-tion, and charity and religious activities. Related to these are a few orga-nizations that are concerned with Bedouin history and heritage, and their stated aims are research and documentation of historical and current events and preservation of Bedouin historical sites. Some of the organiza-tions act alone or jointly with other areas in promoting health services—namely establishment of new clinics, especially in the periphery, operat-

ing an independent mobile unit, and recruiting young women to participate in nursing and paramedical courses.

Of special interest within Bedouin society are those organizations that
are concerned with women. This area of concern originates in the activities of Jewish organizations which were approached by the few highly
educated Bedouin women for their help in convincing Bedouin male
leadership of the urgent need for action among Bedouin women. This
resulted in the recent establishment of a few women-oriented Bedouin
voluntary organizations. These are concerned primarily with provision of
basic literacy for adult women and higher education for young women,
exploring avenues for women's employment including special courses in
elementary vocations such as sewing and operation of home bazaars,
instruction for mothers in child-care, home economics, proper nutrition,
primary health care, and medical problems associated with endogamy,
instruction in problems of adolescence and sexual maturity, social activities for adolescent girls, establishment and operation of women's clubs,
trips, camps and so forth. These activities, however, still face strong
objection from males, hence they are still very minor and sporadic.

Direct economic activities conducted by the organizations are very
few. Some attempts have taken place to launch ethnic tourism projects,
incorporating agropastoral activities, and some initiatives have been
taken in vocational training for males as carpenters and locksmiths. Other
areas of concern of the various organizations are related to the broader
issues of relationships of the Bedouin with the state. They refer primarily
to legal aspects of land, property (primarily domicile) and water rights in
the periphery, recognition of settlements or at least provision of services
and physical infrastructure to them, lobbying for adoption of new concepts of Bedouin settlements by the state, dealing with occasional problems associated with the granting of Israeli citizenship to the few Bedouin
groups for whom the problem has not yet been resolved, and civil rights
in general.

The above list encompasses many crucial areas of contemporary
Bedouin affairs. However, its length, as well as the large number of organizations should not mislead us. Interviews with activists and information from the Organizations Registrar reveal that many organizations are
virtually inactive and, in other cases, activity is very minor. Indeed, relatively few organizations, primarily the Association for Bedouin Rights
and some others which have been successful in fund raising, have
brought benefit to the Bedouin. In general, however, these activities and
their impact are still minor, local and sporadic.

Perhaps it is somewhat premature to expect these voluntary organizations to have a major impact, particularly in a society which has only
recently emerged from a framework of premodern, less-developed and

tribally oriented identity towards an early modern, developing, and civil-oriented identity. The significance of the voluntary organizations at this juncture lies, however, in their very existence rather than in their success. They constitute an early manifestation of Friedmann's principle of empowerment within the context of a development process (Friedmann 1992). The activities of these organizations—in conjunction with public protest action—can empower Bedouin society to shape their society space and landscape within the centrifugal-centripetal tension arena.

Bedouin Centrifugal Manifestations

The evolution of protest and the emergence of voluntary organizations are the social and organizational forms of Bedouin centrifugal response to the centripetal force of the state. This response, however, has primarily taken other forms. Almost every issue of tension between the Bedouin and the state has generated Bedouin centrifugal response in either spatial or functional forms. While some of these responses were associated with protest or were supported by the voluntary organizations, many others were unrelated to these manifestations, at times even predating them. All these spatial and functional centrifugal manifestations are inter-related, as they are part of the same hierarchy of issues discussed above.

In the context of land ownership, the above mentioned case of evacuation of Bedouin from the site of the military airbase in Tel-Malchata is illustrative of their capability to apply a functional centrifugal force. Under the land law—it will be recalled—*mawat* lands are classified as state property. This definition justified evacuation of the Bedouin from that area deep within the periphery, an act which they resisted forcefully. The authorities realized that the land dispute would entail lengthy and non-constructive court deliberations that could both impede the project and deepen the already wide rift between the state and the Bedouin (Marx 1981b; 1981c). A new legal approach was initiated which resulted in the enactment of a special Land Procurement Law in 1980 in which—for the first time—the government acknowledged the need to compensate the Bedouin for expropriated lands. Furthermore—due primarily to Bedouin protest—the initial area in dispute contracted from 30,000 ha. to only 6,500 ha.

The importance of the new law reaches far beyond its immediate consequences for the local Bedouin. As shown by Abu-Rabia, A. (1994b), drafters of the law intended to extend it to land in other disputed areas in the Negev. The fact that the state has began to recognize Bedouin as land claimers is therefore significant in itself. But beyond it, this recognition now relates to the two different land-claiming groups within the Bedouin population as described in the first section above. This does not imply that all Bedouin land disputes (about 6,000 claims for a total of about 700,000 dunams) have been solved or are approaching solution. But the significance of the Tel-Malchata evacuation case is that it became a landmark in the gradual process of settlement of Bedouin land ownership issues either by allowing them formal ownership and residence on the land they claimed, or by evacuating them in return for compensation. This achievement stemmed primarily from their resistance to the centripetal tendency of the state to subject all Bedouin to the land law that regards *mawat* lands as state property.

Related closely to the issue of land ownership are Bedouin centrifugal manifestations concerning the settlement and urbanization schemes. It has been indicated several times above that about half of the Bedouin population are still living in the periphery, a major spatial centrifugal manifestation. It reflects not only the still unresolved land dispute but also the past and present deep dissatisfaction of the Bedouin with the nature, internal plans, size, and number of towns offered by the state. From their outset in the mid-1960s, the very idea of semiurban towns has received scant Bedouin support, as evinced by the failure of the initial development stages of Tel-Sheva. Together with the land ownership problem, this is attributed to lack of an economic base in towns as a substitute for agropastoral ventures, but primarily to inappropriate socioterritorial internal planning. As shown in Chapter 4, the idea was gradually accepted in certain Bedouin circles only when the pressures they had exerted led to appropriation of land for private ownership within towns and the adoption by government planners of more appropriate internal socioterritorial planning. This was achieved primarily by division of towns into separate tribal neighborhoods.

Yet, even after relocation into towns, the attempt of the state to enhance the centripetal tendency by maximizing centralization of service provision met with considerable Bedouin opposition. Interviews with municipal officials (Keidar and Meir 1995) revealed that there have been many cases in which the authorities were forced to yield to Bedouin demands over the specific location and number of public service and infrastructural facilities. These facilities included schools, clinics, mosques, sport centers, public clubs, industrial parks, roads, and so forth. The demands originated in intertribal and intratribal conflicts over unsettled land ownership problems, old rivalries, or sheer competition over public resources. Consequently, facilities were located in certain neighborhoods to the exclusion of others, or in neutral public areas, and at times their number was doubled and even tripled compared to initial planning.

Even in terms of the economic base of these towns, various government offices have recently recognized the need for alleviating the severe unemployment problems there. Thus, in 1995 the Ministry of Agriculture provided financial support for establishment of a greenhouse park in Rahat aimed at exporting flowers. In a similar vein, an industrial park was built there in the same year with partial support from the Ministry of Industry and Commerce. The same ministry has also initiated a project for guidance and support for smallscale economic entrepreneurship among the Bedouin. These recent ventures do not as yet constitute a solution to unemployment as they will provide only several hundred local jobs at best. However, their centrifugal significance is that the state has never before given such support for economic entrepreneurship in Bedouin towns, since in the past it anticipated that the Bedouin would be drawn centripetally into employment foci elsewhere in the Negev.

These ventures signify a gradual change in the state attitude toward Bedouin towns in terms of social and economic planning. However, persistent Bedouin centrifugal pressure has had an impact also on the number of towns established by the government. We recall that the initial policy during the early 1960s called for only three large towns into which all Bedouin were supposed to relocate. The various land ownership and social problems described above forced the government to relax this policy and add more towns to the semiurbanization scheme—their number eventually totaling seven, each with a smaller population. This change in policy may in part be attributed to the high Bedouin natural increase rate, itself a significant centrifugal effect. The main explanation is rooted, however, in the ethnic-tribal element of their centrifugal tendency. The case of negotiations with the Bedouin over evacuation of the Tel-Malchata area (Fenster 1995) may again serve to illustrate this point. Although the overall plan before the Tel-Malchata case called for seven towns, the state was not hasty to implement it. In the initial stages of negotiation, the establishment of only one new town (Ksifa) was on the agenda for absorbing certain groups of evacuees, whereas the rest of them were supposed to relocate into an existing town (Tel-Sheva). A group of Bedouin, however, managed to apply pressure that resulted in an official decision to establish one of the other originally planned towns (Aroer) earlier than scheduled. This outcome of the negotiations— whereby a relatively small group managed to achieve a change in policy—inspired subsequent pressures from other groups during the 1980s and a further relaxation of policy. The final result is that by the early 1990s all seven towns had been established. The state has thus retreated from its initial objective of minimal distribution of physical infrastructure and social services as a means to achieve maximum efficiency.

Furthermore, negotiations with the Bedouin in Tel-Malchata involved also their participation in the process of planning the evacuation and resettlement. This process itself contained ethnic centrifugal elements. As shown by Fenster (1995), the Bedouin appeared initially as one united front, led by the real Bedouin groups who refused to enter into any kind of negotiation. State representatives, however, were well aware of the ethnic division of Bedouin society into real Bedouin and fellahi Bedouin and sought amongst the latter any group willing to enter into negotiations. Very soon, a group of the fellahi Bedouin of this area were able to transform their lower-class status into a strong leverage. They exploited the double opportunity to wield strong bargaining power vis-à-vis the state and to improve their social position within Bedouin society. This is the same group which managed to impel the government to establish the additional town by taking advantage of the fact that the project deadline was approaching.

The issue of Bedouin towns represents one aspect of Bedouin centrifugality which has been manifested virtually since the initiation of the urbanization scheme. Within the wider settlement context, the recently emerging issue of unrecognized settlements represents still another centrifugal aspect. As shown above, dozens of such Bedouin settlements—devoid of infrastructure and services—exist in the northern Negev on a subtribal or *hamula* basis. In an attempt to realize land ownership, many of their inhabitants have been erecting illegal homes, and numerous demolition orders have been issued over the years by the courts. This illegal construction has grown to dimensions that recently required court orders for evacuation of several Bedouin groups. Some of these groups had adopted a protest initiative by returning to the territories from which they were evacuated during the 1950s and 1960s.

Recently, demands for the legalization of many of these unrecognized settlements have grown. In an attempt to contain the conflict with the Bedouin, the state has gradually began to yield to these demands, a policy which has resulted in more selective court orders, recent tacit recognition of one of these settlements (Abu-Rabia, A. 1995), and state readiness to consider recognizing several more. Plans are underway for establishing an additional four towns and seven agricultural villages. A further consequence of this process has also been recent official willingness to reconsider the nature of Bedouin settlements in remoter areas within the periphery. In particular, the idea of shepherd villages in the Negev Highlands, where pastoralism can take advantage of local conditions without competing with other land uses (Kressel 1988) has recently been put on the agenda of government offices (Algor 1994).

Allocation of resources has been another arena of Bedouin centrifugality. As far as economic resources are concerned, the state has maneuvered throughout the years to reduce the Bedouin agropastoral economy. Yet, livestock economy—a means of overcoming economic uncertainty during cultural transition—has survived these attempts. It has been viable not only in the periphery but, as shown by Ben-David (1988), even within towns. In recognition of this persistence and of the fact that agropastoralism still constitutes the major source of income for a considerable number of Bedouin in the periphery, the Ministry of Agriculture has taken several initiatives to channel this economy into more productive lines. Annual grazing permits have been granted selectively in more humid areas such as the Judea mountains, serving also some forestry management interests of various government agencies. Another initiative was the establishment of a livestock demonstration farm north of Beer-Sheva in the early 1980s (Perevolotsky and Landau 1989), aimed at improvement of Bedouin livestock economy. The idea of shepherd villages—now on the agenda of the Ministry of Housing and Construction, although not pursued yet—may prove very useful from both Bedouin and state perspectives. Even the Drought Line policy, denying compensation for Bedouin dry-farming drought damages, has recently been put on the agenda of the Ministry of Agriculture.

While these initiatives reflect growing centrifugally oriented good will on the part of the government, conflictive centrifugal elements still prevail in allocation of agropastoral resources. Many cases of illegal use of these resources by the Bedouin have been recorded over the years, often in connection with the land ownership dispute. In particular, primarily in land ownership disputed areas, many Bedouin have been involved in what has become known as "political" planting of olive groves and orchards and in ploughing and sowing, in order to maintain their rights and express protest against the state (Kressel et al. 1991). Of particular interest is the case of water allocation in the periphery. Hadar et al. (1995) describe in detail the method of water provision by the state to these settlements and the various stratagems some of the Bedouin have developed to bypass this method in order to increase the amount of water available and even to transform state water into a profitable source of income by selling it illegally to their neighbors. By thus illegally increasing water supplies to their agropastoral economy they support their centrifugal survival in the periphery.

In response to this reality, in 1995 the Ministry of Agriculture began to revise its water supply policy for the unrecognized settlements. For the first time, the Bedouin in the periphery will be integrated into the national water supply network. Some of these settlements are now in the process of becoming organized into local Water Associations, similarly to many other rural settlements in Israel. The Bedouin associations will purchase domestic and irrigation water from the national supplier, distribute it to the clients and maintain the local infrastructure (Abu-Siam 1995). Given that water supply to the peripheral Bedouin settlements has been one of the major and bitter issues of conflict, this last initiative is also a major Bedouin centrifugal manifestation.

The persistence of Bedouin settlements in the periphery is also related to centrifugal effects on allocation of social resources. The government, in fact, has been compelled to respond to various Bedouin demands for improvements in provision of public services and to gradually relax its policy of exclusive urban development of services. Until the late 1970s, when most Bedouin were still living in hamlets and tribal encampments, the more the government improved maintenance of temporary schools the stronger the Bedouin demand for new schools. Many tribes managed thus to win separate schools for their territories. The growth of Bedouin towns and the subsequent establishment of municipal departments of education there have left the peripheral unrecognized settlements without an organizational framework for provision of educational services. Consequently, the Ministry of Education established a separate Authority for Bedouin Education in 1981, aimed specifically at providing this public service in the periphery. This in itself is a major manifestation of centrifugality.

Upon its establishment, the Authority took over supervision of the eighteen schools in these areas, all elementary schools of a temporary nature. Their number has declined since then to ten due to migration to towns. Due to the slowing migration rates in recent years, the number of these schools has remained stable. On the other hand—in line with its policy—the government has refrained from establishing new schools. Due to population increase, however, it has been compelled since the early 1980s to replace the temporary wooden shack structures by prefabricated modular ones and to add classrooms and teaching staff in considerable numbers. Bedouin insistence on separate tribal schools had also led to more centrifugally oriented allocation of schooling resources. Melitz (1995) provides a typical example of a sheikh in one of the unrecognized settlements who refused to send girls to a high school in one of the neighboring Bedouin towns. He insisted on opening a special class for them in the tribal elementary school even at the cost of lower educational standards. The Ministry—which till then insisted on a policy of restricting high-schools to towns—eventually succumbed and ordered the Authority to open higher-division classes in this school despite its provisional nature.

While these examples attest to spatial centrifugality in provision of educational services, particularly to the periphery, this tendency has been manifested also functionally with regard to the broader Bedouin community. In recent years awareness of the need to train Bedouin teachers to inculcate Bedouin traditional culture and heritage has grown among officials (Melitz 1995). Some schools have already began to incorporate this subject in their curricula. In another area, the Ministry of Education initiated a campaign in 1994 for the promotion of educational achievement in socioeconomically deprived segments of the Israeli population (Ministry of Education 1994). This project, known as the Thirty Settlements' Project, is not the first in the Ministry's history. Yet, for the first time a Bedouin town (Tel-Sheva) has been included in such a national project. While it is too early to assess its success and long-range impact, the allocation of funds via the local municipality for the purpose of improving Bedouin teaching and school management standards represents a functional centrifugal response by the state in social resource distribution.

In the health services field, several indications of the manifestation of Bedouin centrifugal tendency have been mentioned in the previous chapter. These refer primarily to expansion of services in the peripheral settlements in recent years in recognition, once again, of their persistence. Thus, from a spatial perspective, not only has the Ministry of Health established two new preventive-care mobile units but one of the Bedouin voluntary organizations has been receiving partial subsidy from the Ministry for operating two additional units on a private basis. In light of the high natural increase and infant mortality rates in the periphery, the Ministry has lately approved special funding for six mother-and-child clinics there. The various state-supported sick funds have also established several new clinics in peripheral unrecognized settlements where the state previously refused to grant any kind of formal support, and approval of funds for more clinics is under consideration. To these may be added four recently established private clinics operated by the above mentioned voluntary organization, with partial state funding. From a functional perspective, the paramedical course for Bedouin women (see previous chapter) is aimed primarily at overcoming the shortage of medical personnel in these areas.

Even in less socially critical areas, recent Bedouin centrifugality is clearly manifested. Until the late 1980s the Bedouin did not receive police services directly, and were dependent upon police stations in Jewish towns. Although in many respects the Bedouin still prefer the traditional internal conflict resolution methods, there are areas in which police involvement is required by them. Consequently, a police station was established in 1992 at a central junction in the heart of the Bedouin previous *sayig*. To mention an even more prosaic service, the Bedouin in the periphery and even in some of the new towns did not enjoy mail delivery services and resorted to major cities, particularly Beer-Sheva, for this service. In 1995 the Postal Authority started a delivery service to special distribution centers near Bedouin towns and major unrecognized settlements, from which tribal mailmen make further delivery.

The final area of manifestation of Bedouin centrifugality relates to distribution of political power resources. This also has taken several forms. First, the constant desire of the state to control the Bedouin population via co-optation of sheikhs and tribes has had a boomerang effect. Until 1972 there were only eleven officially recognized tribes and sheikhs. For various internal and external reasons, real Bedouin and fellahi Bedouin groups in towns and in the periphery have been demanding state recognition as independent official tribes, despite the decline in the strength of tribal organization and in the status of sheikhs. In some cases these groups took advantage of special circumstances—as in the Tel-Malchata affair (Fenster 1995)—while in others they exploited their good connections with government officials, and the general political-electoral scene in Israel. This resulted in a centrifugal effect of a more than fourfold increase of the number of official tribes and sheikhs to forty eight in 1995 (with several more under consideration). Although the nomination of sheikhs and the institution of tribes means relatively little in terms of external benefits, its significance lies in diffusion of some internal political power and dignity to groups that previously had no access to it.

This process is closely related to the issue of the official post of the Prime Minister's Advisor on Bedouin Affairs. This powerful function—fulfilled by Jewish officials—persisted after the abolition of the military administration. In 1987, for the first time a Bedouin was nominated for this job. While carrying a centrifugal element, this nomination notwithstanding entailed considerable unrest within the Bedouin community both for reasons of general internal competition for power and because of the fellahi origin of the individual appointee. While previously advisors gained the cooperation of the various tribal sheikhs and other local leaders, the latter were now reluctant to cooperate, demanding direct contact with the government. Consequently this official post was abolished altogether in 1991 (Abu-Ajaj 1995).

These processes of centrifugal empowerment of the Bedouin community are also manifested in its process of municipalization. The latter involves two subprocesses. The first relates to the transfer of municipal power from the state to the Bedouin in terms of self-management. Two decades were to lapse from the introduction of the urbanization program and several appeals submitted by the Bedouin to the Supreme Court, before municipal elections were held in the first two Bedouin towns of Rahat and Tel-Sheva. Following these elections, local government in these towns was transferred from nominated Jewish officials to elected Bedouin politicians. The municipal status of Rahat was even upgraded in 1995 from a local council to a city, making it eligible for preferred and expanded allocation of resources according to state regulations.

The second subprocess relates to a recent Bedouin campaign to dismantle one of the regional councils (Masos), which incorporates the towns of Ksifa, Aroer and Segev-Shalom, established in the early and mid-1980s. This council, headed by a Jewish official, was superimposed in 1988 upon these towns in order to provide them with local government and public services. Various problems have arisen in the functioning of this municipality due primarily to the heterogeneous socioethnic composition of its population and various spatioeconomic constraints (Keidar and Meir 1995). Consequently, representatives of some tribes appealed to the Supreme Court in 1994 for dismantling of the regional council into three separate local councils. The appeal was initially denied, due to opposition of the Ministry of the Interior. In 1995, however, a special committee established by the Ministry recommended a positive response to Bedouin demands. The municipalization of these towns is currently underway, but the problematic process of the first type described above is again on the agenda here. Nevertheless, similarly to centrifugal relaxation of various other kinds, this process of centrifugal political empowerment may also affect the regional council of Shoket (incorporating Laqiah and Khoura), but primarily will have an impact on future recognition of unrecognized Bedouin settlements in the periphery, especially given the growth in the number of official tribes.

Conclusions

Several direct and indirect factors may explain the gradual devitalization of the centripetal force of the state. First, the response to Bedouin demands has been part of a more open policy towards the Israeli Arabs that began around the mid-1980s and gained momentum in the 1990s. This openness is a reflection of a more favorable and tolerant public atmosphere toward equality and integration of the Arab community in Israel. A recently established joint Jewish-Arab voluntary organization has even began to conduct annual evaluations of government policy toward the Arabs and its implementation (Har Even 1994). This public atmosphere is an outcome of the peace-making process that commenced with the Peace Treaty with Egypt in 1978. This treaty paved the road to the treaty with Jordan in 1994 and the present ongoing process with the Palestinians, with whom the Negev Bedouin have many family connections.

The second explanation is rooted in the internal political game in Israel. As far as the Negev Bedouin are concerned, all political parties in Israel have discovered the present and future growing electoral power of the Bedouin population, resulting from its high natural increase rate.

Their present electoral power, for example, is equivalent to about one seat in the Knesset. This process began in the late 1970s when a Bedouin sheikh became a member of the Knesset after being nominated by one of the largest Jewish parties. It continued in the 1992 general elections with another elected Bedouin Knesset member representing a small Arab party. This process has resulted in a gradual increase of Bedouin ability to lobby and apply pressure on the government and politicians, contributing to easing the centripetal pressure.

The final explanation lies in the role played by research on Bedouin society. Until about the late 1970s the government did not have sufficient knowledge at its disposal, nor did it sponsor any independent research that would produce tools for studying and evaluating its policy toward the Bedouin and its implementation. The few studies at that time—primarily of an independent nature—concentrated on the culture and history of traditional pastoral nomadic Bedouin society. However, by providing a base line, this important research laid the foundations for a subsequent growth of studies that shed light on processes of change among the Bedouin, on associated issues and problems and, consequently, on policy-oriented questions. Numerous annual and one-time symposia and public forums on Bedouin affairs have taken place in the recent two decades, with Bedouin researchers gradually taking part. Some of this research was even sponsored by various government offices, but most of it has been independent. Academics have also become directly and indirectly involved and influential in government circles in dissemination of research findings, lobbying, mediation, evaluation, consultancy and policy-making with regard to the Bedouin community.

In the past decade the accumulation of this research has resulted in gradual realization by the government of the problematic nature of its previous centripetal policies towards the Bedouin. Yet, while the various government ministries are presently attempting to ease this tendency, the role played by the local bureaucracy in the Negev still has some negative impact on its pursuance. This bureaucracy has been dealing with the Bedouin for many years and is perhaps slow to absorb the changing state tendency. As argued by Kressel (1994), it is largely responsible for the inability of the state to implement a more reflexive policy at a rapider pace. Perhaps most representative of this problem is the still unresolved issue of granting full Israeli citizenship to some small Bedouin groups, an issue left over from the geopolitical events in the Negev during the late 1940s and early 1950s.

This chapter argued that the tension between the Bedouin and the State of Israel carries both unique and universal elements. The unique element is anchored in the Israeli-Arab—and more specifically the Israeli-Palestinian—conflict as the Negev Bedouin are gradually becoming recognized as Israeli Palestinians. The more prominent universal element, however, derives from the persistence of centrifugality among pastoral nomads even after they sedentarize and settle. On the basis of the evidence provided above, it is suggested that spatial and functional centrifugality is an overriding cultural institutionalized alternative for the Bedouin. Jakubowska similarly refers to it as a strategy of marginalism and isolationism which is part of the pastoral nomadic ethos (Jakubowska 1992). Its manifestation produces a landscape of conflict between the Bedouin and the state in the northern Negev. This landscape serves as an arena for the cultural interplay between the centripetal and centrifugal forces.

In this process of space production, the centripetal force emphasizes maximum spatial and functional centralization and convergence of people and their activities while the centrifugal force seeks maximum decentralization and divergence. It is possible to outline historically the dynamics of this macro cultural-political process among the Bedouin. Until 1948, under the Ottoman Empire and the British Mandate, centrifugality was manifested by the Bedouin in their Negev territories within a pastoral nomadic context with little interruption. It was constrained only by internal forces, that is intertribal or intergroup relationships. Under the State of Israel, for the first time in modern history, it became constrained by an external force. Bedouin freedom to sustain this culturally institutionalized alternative was thus greatly reduced by centripetality applied by the state. Therefore, for about a quarter of a century, from the late 1940s to about the mid-1970s, it was mostly kept by them in reserve. They began to reactivate it gradually—now within a rural settled context— only when military administrative pressures were physically and psychologically relieved toward the late 1960s, and it has reached its recent culmination within a semiurban context.

It transpires from the above analysis that neither the state nor the Bedouin were able to fully manifest their respective tendencies. The dialectics of the tension between the centripetal and centrifugal forces have therefore inevitably yielded some equilibrium. The spatial and functional frameworks of this equilibrium were indeed determined by the centripetal force of the state. Yet, Jakubowska's (1992) conclusion notwithstanding, to a considerable extent the Bedouin have been able to outpower this force, especially in the recent two decades. They expanded somewhat the margins of these frameworks but, more significantly, they managed to introduce a centrifugal content into them.

By compelling the state to comply more favorably with this tendency, the Bedouin have proved capable also of self-empowerment. The manifestation of this process is, however, also capable of alleviating another kind of tension. This is the tension between the more traditional pastoral nomadic and recently also Arab-Islamic ethnic identity and the growing modern civil identity. Paradoxically thus, by reinforcing their ethnicity, centrifugality can contribute to enhanced integration of this society, hitherto regarded by the government and the public as a separate "Bedouin sector," into the modern Jewish state and its cultural systems.

9

As Nomadism Ends

This book has been concerned with a series of successive processes that have swept the Negev Bedouin society in the past century and a half. These processes occurred under three different political regimes, each progressively carrying the Bedouin closer to the present cultural point where only the remnant of pastoral nomadism is left. They have been carried away from a tribal-traditional, Third World-oriented pastoral nomadic mode of production towards a sedentary and Western-oriented, semiurban labor-market setting. With time, the once chiefly pastoral nomadic Bedouin society became stretched along a nomadism-sedentarism-urbanism continuum which has contracted once again in recent decades, this time closer to the urban edge of this continuum. This society was also severed from its previous exclusive Middle Eastern Islamic-cultural environment, and became a relatively isolated cultural enclave within a modern Jewish cultural environment. While in early phases, these changes were voluntary, the later and most crucial ones developed under considerable coercion. This has been indeed a highly dense web of economic, social, and political processes. To the best of our knowledge, in modern times no other pastoral nomadic society in Africa, the Middle East, and Asia has crossed as many wide cultural frontier lines during a relatively short span as did the Negev Bedouin in Israel.

In light of these developments it is understandable why the accumulation of individual and communal stress within Bedouin society has found an outlet in considerable protest. The stress and protest are epitomized most sharply by two recent minor events that, to our mind, are representative of macro processes. The first event concerns public debate over a recent well publicized solo theater performance by a Jewish dramatist and actress. She played a young Bedouin woman who describes her personal dilemmas relating to women's social status and wellbeing during a period of cultural transformation. Among other things, she presented on stage an incident concerning one of the most discreet, intimate and sensitive Bedouin customs. This is the issue of female circumcision, which is apparently still common among some circles in this society. The actress naturally viewed this issue from a modern Western and feminist cultural perspective. Bedouin reactions to this issue included denial and dismissal of the custom as marginal and irrelevant, and—most important—protest against what they perceived as crude intervention in their internal cultural affairs through public exposure. Their dilemma over this specific issue is clearly symptomatic of their wider dilemmas, namely the articulation between the traditional pastoral nomadic ethnic cultural code and the modern civil one. The tension generated by this specific dilemma reflects, therefore, the general tension with the diametrically different surrounding culture, particularly the political environment represented by the state and the government.

The second event concerns a Bedouin girl high-school graduate who enrolled in 1989 in an Israeli university despite strong opposition from her expanded family. Brought up in a fellahi family in one of the older Bedouin towns, she had never experienced the traditional pastoral nomadic life style. Her father had long before become engaged in business, considered himself modern and was proud of allowing his daughter to acquire higher education. She thus became one of the handful of Negev Bedouin women students. In her freshman year she was escorted to campus by either her father or one of her elder brothers. However, as time went on her father gained confidence, and allowed her to attend classes unescorted. She dressed in modern style, and was quite friendly with and accepted by her Jewish classmates despite initial communication barriers. She managed to do well academically and after graduating in 1992, applied successfully for graduate studies at the same university and received a scholarship.

However, she never showed up for graduate school and disappeared without trace. The detailed background to her disappearance was later revealed by her family to her designated academic tutor. It turned out that her expanded family had stipulated a condition for approval of her undergraduate education. The condition was that—upon completing her degree—she would return home to marry her first cousin (the son of her father's elder brother) to whom she had been promised long before according to traditional Bedouin mating custom. However, since her designated husband had virtually no education, she refused to marry him. Rumors—never substantiated—had it that she fell in love with a fellow Bedouin student at university. It was revealed by other sources that—fearing for her life—she ran away and apparently managed to leave Israel. Her father consulted all possible contacts, including the state authorities and searched for her everywhere, even overseas, but she has never been traced.

This apparently minor, personal event was widely communicated within Bedouin society. It caused considerable turmoil because the father was not able to fulfill the mating agreement with his elder brother, thereby considerably damaging his honor and that of the entire expanded family. In Bedouin eyes this constituted a severe violation of a Bedouin custom which was a traditional and crucial cornerstone in internal pastoral nomadic social order. Such a violation could entail severe social sanctions against the father and his entire nuclear family. Yet—beyond this important social aspect—the significance of this event for the present discussion lies elsewhere. In lengthy conversations with Bedouin during fieldwork, many asserted categorically that the direct responsibility for this particular event and—by implication—for many other recent social evils within Bedouin society, lay in modern schooling and education for Bedouin girls. Many household heads even declared that, following this event, they considered discontinuing high-school education for their daughters, arguing that elementary education is sufficient for the proper functioning of Bedouin wives and mothers. Others—taking a less radical position—did not deny the importance of education but insisted on the need to tighten family supervision on girls' schooling.

The significance of these two events is twofold. First, they concern the status of Bedouin women, young and adult alike. In several respects status of women may be considered a test issue for the social development of Bedouin society. It reflects the ability of this society to promote further those elements of modern fertility behavior that have already emerged in recent decades. It indicates further the potential impact of mothers on the wellbeing of their children in terms of physical health and personal development through education. And it has a bearing on the economic development of the nuclear household in terms of generation of additional income by women within an economically constrained semiurban and labor-market context. As shown in the discussion of those Bedouin voluntary organizations which aim at improving the wellbeing of women, Bedouin society is as yet virtually unprepared for the complete accommodation of modern ideas concerning status of women into their traditional sociocultural patriarchal code. From a sociocultural perspective, there is perhaps some justification for their desire to decide on and pursue this accommodation internally—subject to state laws—at their own desirable pace with minimal external intervention. The provision of internal and independent choice between old and new institutionalized alternatives from the range between "complete" change and "complete" stability may also be beneficial for Israeli society and the state from the wider perspective of pluralistic integration of this society into the modern Westernized environment.

Yet, the wider significance of the events cited above lies in the key process that was postulated in Chapter 2 as ushering in the shift away from pastoral nomadism. This process entails the ideological departure of members of the pastoral nomadic Bedouin society away from tribalism towards individualism. True, it is somewhat difficult to determine the cause and effect relationships within this complex process of sociospatial change. Yet, throughout this book we have shown how—during the process of sedentarization and semiurbanization—independence from social bonds that committed individuals to the traditional social organization has gradually developed. This has taken place through an adoption of a newer, more personal, complex, and varied value system concerning the role and wellbeing of individuals within this society and the wider cultural environment.

The process of individualization began during the nineteenth century with the gradual shift away from pastoral to agropastoral and, later on, to labor-market engagements. It led to a shift in the interrelationships between social and spatial definitions towards a spatial definition of social relations. This process of territorialization has trickled down from the tribal to the extended and nuclear family levels. Its major manifestation has been the privatization of space and of physical land, pasture, and water resources. Due to the coercive loss of agropastoral opportunities, partial integration into the labor-market economy, and the introduction of modern schooling and education under the State of Israel, the process of individualization continued with several forms of "privatization" of family human resources. First, the changing value of children began to produce changes in fertility behavior. Second, the decline of the collective family fund through which the centrality of elders was manifested, and the narrowing of the public phase as regards women's spatial mobility, have generated changes in their social status. Two subprocesses have intervened here. These have been the changes in the traditional roles of children, elders, and women, and the loss of Bedouin society's traditional communal institutions and mechanisms that previously provided for the social and economic wellbeing of these individuals. Instead, the responsibility for individuals' well being has been externalized to state authorities through provision of public social services. In fact, throughout the book we have seen the gradual growth of externalization of economic and social resources as an outcome of the search for external alternatives. But this growth has compelled Bedouin society to become public service-dependent and, hence, open to manipulation by the government—a process that has been diametrically opposed to their traditional centrifugal political raison d'être. It introduced the political dimension into the process of change within this society, creating, in turn, a conflict with the state.

This brief summary of processes highlights the relationships between the micro-process of individualization within Bedouin society—as part of its development towards modernization—and its rather macro manifestation of centrifugality. The centripetal attempt by the state to converge Bedouin society spatially and functionally into certain locations and activities reflects in fact an endeavor towards their convergence around the universal Western model of the modernization process. This was supposed to become the prime tool for maneuvering the previously pastoral nomadic Bedouin society as rapidly as possible into integration within Israeli society and thus for controlling them. Yet, from a traditional pastoral nomadic Bedouin perspective this process—leading to changes in roles and status of individuals and social institutions—jeopardized their personal and communal cultural identity. It is suggested, thus, that their spatial and functional centrifugal reaction was adopted as a defense mechanism against this menace. While in several cases in modern history centrifugality of settled nomads was manifested by nomadization, this institutionalized alternative is no longer available to the Negev Bedouin. Instead, the centrifugal alternative has been manifested within a settled context that is also modern Western-oriented.

These two institutionalized alternatives have been articulated through the cultural interplay within the centripetal-centrifugal arena. Given the unique circumstances, the Bedouin could not altogether ignore the process which the state desired them to undergo. They have been attempting to bypass it by resorting to their natural centrifugal tendency, but this could not be achieved completely. On the other hand, neither could the state—in implementing its centripetal approach—take full advantage of the various modernity traits that have been penetrating Bedouin society. The cultural "compromise" that has eventually been reached lies therefore between the two edges of the spatial and functional centripetal-centrifugal continuum at a point where the polarized tradition and modernity are mediated.

It appears that this juncture is most suitable for returning to the conceptual discussion of sociospatial change among sedentarizing pastoral nomads. The Israeli Negev Bedouin society has gone through this process within a highly unique context. Yet, every case study—however unique—carries some general relevance, in this particular case for pastoral nomadic societies elsewhere. For the Bedouin—as a non-Western society—ideal change from a nonmodern to a modern society has been but one among several possible paths available to them even within the constrained cultural-political context. There have been various degrees and diverse forms of penetration of Western influence and retention of prevalent traditional traits within this society. This indeed supports the current view in social science that sociospatial change in non-Western societies is flexible and involves a plethora of options.

Each of these possible options and actual forms of change taken by the Bedouin may carry a specific—not necessarily direct—microscale implication for other pastoral nomadic societies. There is, however, one macroscale implication that appears to be quite direct and most relevant. This is the centrifugal institutionalized alternative which, as suggested in this book, is an umbrella concept that covers the entire web of microscale subprocesses. It transpires that, because centrifugality of pastoral nomads is individually and communally so immanently inbuilt into their culture, it may also become the most persistent cultural element upon sedentarization. If we carry this notion to its extreme, spatial and functional centrifugality of pastoral nomads may be—under certain cultural-political circumstances—a condition for their cultural survival. Since the centrifugal response of the Negev Bedouin to state centripetal power has been successful under the constrained conditions of geopolitical conflict existing in Israel, it seems likely that pastoral nomads elsewhere are capable of it under less conflictual conditions vis-à-vis their own government.

Here lies the single most applied and most conclusive policy implication for governments involved with development of pastoral nomadic societies. Recent discussions of the issue of pastoral nomadism within the context of the development of the state suggest that—by definition—the latter requires the suppression of independent local political power of any kind and not only that of pastoral nomads. We submit that local political power need not necessarily be manifested independently. It can alternatively be manifested in cultural forms. Governments, therefore, should not ignore the centrifugal tendency of these peoples in its widest sense, because the centripetal-centrifugal tension and the cultural-political struggle involved are capable of undermining their policies seriously to the disadvantage of both sides. In contrast, recognition of this structurally unique cultural trait of pastoral nomads can be highly beneficial for many systems within the state, particularly in those countries with a considerable proportion of pastoralists. This implication is relevant when these pastoralists still practice a nomadic way of life. However, its relevance is most significant for them and for the wider social, economic, and political environment when they sedentarize and undergo processes of social and economic change as pastoral nomadism ends.

References

Abu-Ajaj, M. 1995. Personal Communication.

Abu-Ajaj, S. and Y. Ben-David. 1988. "Traditional Education Among the Negev Bedouin." *Notes on the Bedouin* 19: 1–14, (Hebrew).

Abu-Rabia, A. 1979. *Traditional vs. Modern Medicine among the Bedouin*. M.A. Thesis, Jerusalem: Department of Social Medicine, The Hebrew University (Hebrew).

_____. 1994a. "Cross-Cultural Bedouin Medicine." *Collegium Anthropologicum* 18: 215–218.

_____. 1994b. "The Bedouin Refugees of the Negev." *Refuge* 14: 15–17.

_____. 1994c. *The Negev Bedouin and Livestock Rearing—Social, Economic and Political Aspects*. Oxford: Berg.

_____. 1995. Personal Communication.

Abu-Saad, I. 1991. "The Role of Higher Education in Advancing the Bedouin Society." Paper presented at a symposium: *The Bedouin and Development of the Negev*. Ben-Gurion University of the Negev, Beer Sheva, June 11, 1991 (Hebrew).

_____. 1994. "The Negev Bedouin: Educational Profile of a Community in Transition." *Negev Center for Regional Development Newsletter* 1, 2: 3–7.

Abu-Siam, S. 1995. Personal Communication.

Abu-Zeid, A. M. 1959. "The Sedentarization of Nomads in the Western Desert of Egypt." *International Social Science Journal* 11: 550–8.

Adaw, E. 1986. *Education for the Pastoral Nomads of Northern Kenya: An Alternative Approach for Basic Education*. M.Ed. Dissertation, London: Institute of Education, University of London.

Al-A'assem, S. 1983. "Social Services to the Negev Bedouin—Provision and Shortage." *Notes on the Bedouin* 14: 72–81.

Al-A'finish, S. 1987. "Processes of Change and Continuity in a Kinship System and Family Ideology in Bedouin Society." *Sociologia Ruralis* 27: 323–340.

Al-Aref, A. 1937a. *The Bedouin Tribes in Beer-Sheva District*. Tel-Aviv: Bustenai (Hebrew).

_____. 1937b. *The History of Beer-Sheva and its Tribes*. Tel-Aviv: Shoshani (Hebrew).

Al-Huzayil, A. 1994. "The Neutralized Citizenship." *HaAretz*, August 12, 1994 (Hebrew).

Algor, A. 1994. "'National Handling' of Bedouin Settlements." *Mivnim* 140: 49–60 (Hebrew).

Altman, I. 1975. *The Environment and Social Behavior*. Monterey, Ca.: Brooks-Cole.

Amiran, D. H. K. 1963. "Nomads and Bedouin Population in the Census Returns of Mandatory Palestine." *Israel Exploration Journal* 13: 247–253.

Amiran, D. H. K., A. Shinar and Y. Ben-David. 1979. "Bedouin Settlements in the Beer-Sheva Basin," in A. Shmueli and Y. Gradus, eds., *The Land of the Negev*. Pp. 652–665. Jerusalem: Defense Ministry Press (Hebrew).

Amitai, Y. 1983. *Gvulot—A Pioneer Settlement in the Negev*. Eshkol: Eshkol Regional Council Archive (Hebrew).

_____. 1988. *Comradeship Between Nations—An Evaluation*. Tel-Aviv: Gomeh-Cherikover (Hebrew).

Anson, J. 1991. "Age Structure as a Measure of Need in Local Populations: An Analysis of Israeli Data." *Social Work Research and Abstracts* 27: 16–23.

Aronson, D. R. 1981. "Development for Nomadic Pastoralists: Who Benefits," in J. G. Galaty, D. R. Aronson, P. C. Salzman, and A. Chouinard, eds., *The Future of Pastoral Peoples*. Pp. 42–51. Ottawa: International Development Centre.

Artzieli, M. 1978. "1978–The Year that Severed our Ties with the Bedouin." *Notes on the Bedouin* 10: 48–61 (Hebrew).

Asad, T. 1970. *The Kababish Arabs: Power, Authority and Consent in a Nomadic Tribe*. London: C. Hurst.

Ashkenazi, T. 1957. *The Bedouin—Their Origin, Life and Customs*. Jerusalem: Reuben Mass (Hebrew).

Avni, G. 1991. "Employment Within the Bedouin Sector." Paper presented at a symposium: *The Bedouin and Development of the Negev*. Ben-Gurion University of the Negev, Beer-Sheva, June 11, 1991 (Hebrew).

Baddie, B. 1990. "Community, Individualism and Culture," in P. Birnbaum and J. Leca, eds., *Individualism: Theories and Methods*. Pp. 95–115. Oxford: Clarendon Press.

Baer, G. 1970. *The Arabs of the Middle East—Population and Society*. Tel-Aviv: HaKibbutz HaMeuchad (Hebrew).

Bahaddy, F.A. 1981. "Recent Changes in Bedouin Systems of Livestock Production in the Syrian Steppe." in J. C. Galaty, D. Aronson, P. C. Salzman and A. Chouinard, eds., *The Future of Pastoral Peoples*. Pp. 258–266. Ottawa: International Development Research Centre.

Bailey, C. 1971. "Bedouin Policy in Arab States." *Notes on the Bedouin* 2: 59–74 (Hebrew).

_____. 1980. "The Negev in the Nineteenth Century—Reconstructing History from Bedouin Oral Traditions." *Asian and African Studies* 14: 35–80.

Bar, A. 1985. Bedouin vs. Fellaheen in Rahat: Social Processes in Sedentarization. Unpublished paper, Beer-Sheva (Hebrew).

_____. 1989. *Physical Design of the Environment in Rahat—The Concept of the Bedouin vs. the Concept of the Planners*. M.A. Thesis, Beer-Sheva: Department of Geography, Ben-Gurion University of the Negev (Hebrew).

Bar-Zvi, S. 1971. "The First Settlers in Revivim and the Bedouin." *Notes on the Bedouin* 2: 49–67 (Hebrew).

_____. 1976. The First Days of Revivim. Unpublished paper, Revivim: Revivim Archive (Hebrew).

_____ . 1977. Negotiations Between the British Mandate and Bedouin Sheikhs Concerning British Evacuation of Palestine. Unpublished paper, Beer-Sheva: Tuviahu Archive (Hebrew).

_____ . 1991. *The Jurisdiction Among the Negev Bedouin*. Tel-Aviv: Ministry of Defense (Hebrew).

Bar-Zvi, S. and Y. Ben-David. 1978. "The Negev Bedouin in the 1930s and 1940s as a Semi-Nomadic Society." *Studies in the Geography of Israel* 10: 107–136 (Hebrew).

Barslevski, Y. 1946. *Knowing the Land—The Land of the Negev B*. Tel-Aviv: HaKibbutz HaMeuchad (Hebrew).

Barth, F. 1964. *Nomads of the South Persia: The Baseri Tribe of the Khamesh Confederacy*. London: Allen and Unwin.

Barzilai, R. 1992. "The Islamic Movement in Israel," in I. Pepe, ed., *Islam and Peace: Islamic Approaches to Peace in Contemporary Arab World*. Pp. 100–102. Peace Studies Series, No.1, Giv'at Haviva: Institute for Peace Research (Hebrew).

Be'er, S. and II. Factor. 1989. *Demographic Development of the Elderly Population in Israel, 1988–2000*. Jerusalem: Brookdale Institute of Gerontology and Man and Society Development in Israel (Hebrew).

Beck, L. 1978. "Women Among Qashqai Nomadic Pastoralists in Iran," in L. Beck and N. Keddie, eds., *Women in the Muslim World*. Pp. 351–373. Cambridge: Harvard University Press.

Becker, G. S. 1981. *A Treatise on the Family*. Cambridge, Mass.: Harvard University Press.

Behnke, R. H and I. Scoones. 1993. "Rethinking Range Ecology: Implications for Range Management in Africa," in R. H. Behnke, I. Scoones and C. Kerven, eds., *Range Ecology at Disequilibrium: New Models of Natural Variability and Pastoral Adaptation in African Savannas*. Pp. 1–30. London: Overseas Development Institute.

Ben-Arieh, Y. 1970. *The Rediscovery of the Holy Land in the Nineteenth Century*. Jerusalem: Carta Jerusalem and The Israel Exploration Society (Hebrew).

Ben-Assa, B. J. 1960. "Vital Statistics Concerning Tuberculosis Among Bedouin of Southern Israel." *Israel Medical Journal* 19: 69–73.

_____ . 1964. "Medical Observations on 2000 Bedouin Patients." *HaRefuah* 17: 451–453 (Hebrew).

_____ . 1974. "The Bedouin Patient." *HaRefuah* 27: 73–76 (Hebrew).

Ben-David, Y. 1978. *The Bedouin Tribes in Southern Sinai*. Jerusalem: Keshet Publishing (Hebrew)

_____ . 1982. Stages *in the Development of the Bedouin Spontaneous Settlement in the Negev*. Ph.D. Dissertation, Jerusalem: Department of Geography, The Hebrew University (Hebrew).

_____ . 1986. "The Bedouin in the Negev, 1900–1960." *Idan* (Yad Ben-Zvi) 6: 81–99 (Hebrew).

_____ . 1988. *Bedouin Agriculture in the Negev—Policy Proposals*. Jerusalem: The Jerusalem Institute for Israel Research (Hebrew).

_____ . 1989. "The Negev Bedouin: From Nomadism to Agriculture," in R. Kark, ed., *The Land that Became Israel: Studies in Historical Geography*. Pp. 181–195. Jerusalem: The Magness Press.

_____ . 1992. *Turnaround in Negev Bedouin Urbanization in the 1980's—The Case of Kuseifa*. Jerusalem: The Jerusalem Institute of Israel Research (Hebrew).

_____ . 1993. *Bedouin Settlement in the Negev—Policy and Practice, 1967–1992*. Jerusalem: Ministry of Housing and Jerusalem Institute for Israel Research (Hebrew).

_____ . 1994a. "Adaptation Through Crisis—Ph ıl and Social Perspectives of Urbanization among the Negev Bedouin," . ʹrossman and A. Meir, eds., *The Arabs in Israel: Geographical Dynamics*. 48–76. Jerusalem: Magness Press (Hebrew).

_____ . 1994b. *The Bedouin Educational System in the Negev: The Reality and the Need for Advancement*. Jerusalem: The Floersheimer Institute for Policy Studies (Hebrew).

_____ . 1995. "The Land Conflict Between the Negev Bedouin and the State— Historical, Legal and Actual Perspectives." *Karka* 40: 61–91 (Hebrew).

Ben-David, Y. and G. M. Kressel. 1995. "Bedouin Market—Cornerstone of Beer-Sheva." *Notes on the Bedouin* 25: 15–38.

Ben-David, Y. and E. Orion. 1990. Mode of Living and Survival Patterns of the Azazmeh Bedouin in the Negev Mountain (Late 19th and Early 20th Centuries). Unpublished paper, Sde Boker (Hebrew).

Ben-Dror, G. and A. Meir. 1995. Social Protest Among the Bedouin. Unpublished paper, Beer-Sheva: Department of Geography and Environmental Development, Ben-Gurion University of the Negev (Hebrew).

Ben-Gurion, D. 1954. The Negev is Still Waiting. Unpublished document, Tel-Aviv: The Labor Party Archive (Hebrew).

Berginer, M., J. Posner and E. Kahana. 1982. "Multiple Sclerosis in Israeli Bedouin." *Israel Journal of Medical Science* 18: 635–639.

Bergman, E. F. 1975. *Modern Political Geography*. Dubuque, Iowa: W. M. C. Brown.

Biruk, Y., D. Tedla and D. Dires. 1986. *Pastoralist Rehabilitation Feasibility Study. Part 1: Reconnaissance Study*, Addis Ababa: Relief and Rehabilitation Commission and F.A.O.

Boneh, D. 1983. *Facing Uncertainty: The Social Consequences of Forced Sedentarization Among the Jaraween Bedouin, Negev, Israel*. Ph.D. Dissertation, Waltham, Mass.: Brandeis University.

Bongaarts, J., O. Frank and R. Lesthaege. 1984. "The Proximate Determinants of Fertility in Sub-Saharan Africa." *Population and Development Review* 10: 511–537.

Boudon, R. 1990. "Individualism and Holism in the Social Sciences," in P. Birnbaum and J. Leca, eds., *Individualism: Theories and Methods*. Pp. 33–45. Oxford: Clarendon Press.

Bradburd, D. A. 1995. Re-thinking the Tribe and the State in Southwest Asia: The Implication of Recent Studies of the Nation State. Paper presented at the *Commission on Pastoral Peoples, Inter-Congress*, International Union of Anthropological and Ethnographical Sciences, Lucca/Florence, Italy.

Brainard, J. 1981. *Herders to Farmers: The Effects of Settlement on the Demography of the Turkana Population of Kenya*. Ph.D. Dissertation, Ann Arbor: Department of Anthropology, University of Michigan.

Bruggeman, H. 1994. *Pastoral Women and Livestock Management: Examples from Northern Uganda and Central Chad*. International Institute for Environment and Development, Dryland Networks Programme, Issue Paper No. 50, London.

Caldwell, J. C. 1975. *The Sahelian Drought and Its Demographic Implications*. Overseas Laison Committee, Washington D.C.: American Council on Education, Paper No. 8.

_____. 1982. *Theory of Fertility Decline*. New York: Academic Press.

Carmel, S., O. Anson and M. Levin. 1990, "Emergency Department Utilization by Two Sub-Cultures in the Same Geographical Region." *Social Science and Medicine* 31: 557–563.

Cashdan, E. 1983. "Territoriality among Human Foragers: Ecological Models and an Application to Four Bushmen Groups." *Current Anthropology* 24: 47–66.

Casimir, M. J. 1992. "The Dimensions of Territoriality: An Introduction," in M. J. Casimir and A. Rao, eds., *Mobility and Territoriality—Social and Spatial Boundaries among Foragers, Fishers, Pastoralists and Peripatetics*. Pp. 1–26. Oxford: Berg.

Castells, M. 1983. "Crisis Planning and the Quality of Life: Managing the New Historical Relationships Between Space and Society." *Environment and Planning, D: Society and Space* 1: 3–21.

Central Bureau of Statistics. 1993. *Statistical Abstract of Israel, 1992*. Jerusalem (Hebrew).

_____. 1994. *Statistical Abstract of Israel, 1993*. Jerusalem (Hebrew).

Chatty, D. 1972–3. "Pastoralism: Adaptation and Optimization." Folk 14–15: 27–38.

_____. 1980. "The Pastoral Family and the Truck," in P. C. Salzman, ed., *When Nomads Settle: Processes of Sedentarization as Adaptation and Response*. Pp. 80–93. New York: Praeger.

Chatty, D., M. Zaroug and A. Osman. 1991. *Pastoralism in Oman*. Rome: Food and Agriculture Organization of the United Nations.

Chetley, D. 1979. *The Baby Killer Scandal*. London: War on Want.

Clarke, J. I. 1959. "Studies of Semi-Nomadism in North Africa." *Economic Geography* 35: 95–108.

Clement, C. 1987. *Pre-Settlement Intrusion into the East Kimberly*. East Kimberly Working Paper No.24, Canberra City: East Kimberly Project.

Cole, D. 1981. "Bedouin and Social Change in Saudi Arabia," in J. G. Galaty and P. C. Salzman, eds., *Change and Development in Nomadic and Pastoral Societies*. Pp. 129–149. Leiden: E.J. Brill.

Cox, K. R. 1991. "Comment: Redefining Territory." *Political Geography Quarterly* 10: 5–7.

Cronan, W. 1983. *Changes in the Land; Indians, Colonists and the Ecology of New England*. New York: Hill and Wang.

Cross, A. R. and W. D. Kalsbeck. 1983. "The Challenge of Surveying Nomads on the Move." *Intercom* Jan./Feb.: 11–12, Washington, D.C.: Population Reference Bureau, Inc.

Cunnison, I. 1966. *The Baggara Arabs: Power and Lineage in a Sudanese Nomad Tribe*. Oxford: Oxford University Press.

Dahl, G. 1987. "Women in Pastoral Production: Some Theoretical Notes on Roles and Resources." *Ethnos* 52, I–II: 246–279.

———. 1991a. "Pastoral Strategies After Drought," in F.A.O., ed., *Report of a Sub-Regional Seminar on the Dynamics of Pastoral Land and Resource Tenure in the Horn of Africa.* Pp. 15–31. Rome: Food and Agricultural Organization of the United Nations.

———. 1991b. "The Beja of Sudan and the Famine of 1984–1986." *Ambio* 20: 191–198.

Danin, A. 1977. *An Unconditional Zionist.* Jerusalem: Kidum (Hebrew).

Danin, Ch. 1988. "On Land Acquisition in the Land of Israel," in E. Schiller, ed., *The Book of Vilnai, B.* Pp. 258–261. Jerusalem: Ariel (Hebrew).

Davies, J. 1963. "The Theory of Change and Response in Demographic History." *Population Index* 29: 345–366.

Davies, S. 1977. *People of the Mediterranean: An Essay in Comparative Social Anthropology.* London: Routledge and Kegan Paul.

Dayan, M. 1976. *Milestones.* Tel-Aviv: Yediot Acharonot (Hebrew).

de Bruijn, M. 1995. "A Pastoral Women Economy in Crisis: The Fulbe in Central Mali." Paper presented at the *Commission on Pastoral Peoples, Inter-Congress, International Union of Anthropological and Ethnographical Sciences,* Lucca/Florence, Italy.

Denga, D. I. 1983. "The Effect of Mobile Group Councelling on Nomadic Fulanis' Attitudes Toward Education." *Journal of Negro Education* 52: 267–273.

Deutsch, K. 1981. "On Nationalism, World Regions and the Nature of the West," in P. Torsvik, ed., *Mobilization, Center Periphery Structures and Nation Building.* Pp. 51–93. Bergen: Universitetsforlaget.

Dinero, S. 1995. *Human Settlement in Post-Nomadic Bedouin Society: An Assessment of Social and Economic Transformation in Segev Shalom, Israel.* Ph.D. Dissertation, New Brunswick: Rutgers-The State University of New Jersey.

Douglas, M. 1966. "Population Control in Primitive Groups." *British Journal of Sociology* 17: 263–273.

Dyson-Hudson, R. and N. Dyson-Hudson. 1980. "Nomadic Pastoralism."*Annual Review of Anthropology* 9: 15–61.

Dyson-Hudson, R. and E. A. Smith. 1978. "Human Territoriality: An Ecological Reassessment." *American Anthropologist* 80: 21–41.

Easterlin, R. A. 1978. "The Economics and Sociology of Fertility," in C. Tilly, ed., *Historical Studies of Changing Fertility.* Pp. 57–123. Princeton, N.J.: Princeton University Press.

Edgerton, R.B. 1971. *The Individual in Cultural Adaptation: A Study of Four East African Peoples.* Berkeley: University of California Press.

Edney, J. J. 1976. "Human Territories: Comment on Functional Properties." *Environment and Behavior* 8: 31–47.

Efrat, A. 1982. *Neighbors in the Negev Gates.* Jerusalem: Cana (Hebrew).

———. 1992 *Pratte from the Saddlebag.* Jerusalem: Ministry of Defense (Hebrew).

Efrat, E. 1981. "Patterns of Frontier Settlement in Israel." *Studies in the Geography of Israel* 11: 87–99 (Hebrew).

EFSHAR. 1992. *Care for the Retarded in the Bedouin Community.* Jerusalem: Association for Development of Welfare Services (Hebrew).

Eisenstadt, S. N. 1973. *Tradition, Change and Modernity.* New York: Wiley.

El-Samani, M. O. 1989. *A Study on Rehabilitation Alternatives for Pastoral Population in Sudan.* Department of Geography, University of Khartoum, Khartoum.

Entrikin, J. N. 1991. "The Characterization of Place." Wallace W. Atwood Lecture Series No. 5: Clark University Press, Worcester.

Etzioni-Halevy, E. 1981. *Social Change: The Advent and Maturation of Modern Society.* London: Routledge and Kegan Paul.

Ezeomah, C. 1979. "The Constraints on Cattle Fulani Education and the Role of the Educational Planner." *South Australian Journal of Education Research* 1: 43–51.

_____. 1985. "Land Tenure Constraints Associated with some Experience to Bring Formal Education to Nomadic Fulani in Nigeria." *Pastoral Development Network* Paper No. 20d. Overseas Development Institute, London.

F.A.O. 1991. *Workshop on Pastoral Communities in the Near East: Traditional Systems in Evolution.* Rome: Food and Agricultural Organization of the United Nations.

Fabietti, U. 1986a. "Control and Alienation of Territory Among the Bedouin of Saudi Arabia." *Nomadic Peoples* 20: 33–40.

_____. 1986b. "The Control of Resources among the Bedouin of Arabia: The Role of the Domestic Group." Paper presented at the *12th International Congress of Anthropological and Ethnological Sciences,* Zagreb.

_____. 1991. "Control of Resources and Social Cohesion: The Role of the Bedouin Domestic Group." *Nomadic Peoples* 28: 18–27.

Falah, G. 1983. "The Development of the 'Planned Bedouin Settlement' in Israel, 1964–1982: Evaluation and Characteristics." *Geoforum* 14: 311–323.

_____. 1985. "Planned Bedouin Settlement in Israel: The Reply." *Geoforum* 16: 441–451.

Fenster, T. 1991. *Participation in the Settlement Planning Process: The Case of the Bedouin in the Israeli Negev.* Doctoral Dissertation, London School of Economics, London.

_____. 1993. Ethnicity versus Citizenship in Frontier Development—The Challenge of the Negev, Israel. Proceedings of the International Conference on *Regional Development—The Challenge of the Frontier,* The Negev Center for Regional Development, Ben-Gurion University of the Negev.

_____. 1995. "Participation as a Political Process in Enforced Resettlement Projects: The Bedouin in Israel." *Geography Research Forum* 15: 33–48.

Finkelstein, I. and A. Perevolotski. 1990. "Processes of Sedentarization and Nomadization in the History of Sinai and the Negev." *BASOR* 279: 67–88.

Forman, M. R., G. L. Hundt, D. Towne, B. Graubard, B. Sullivan, H. Berendes, B. Sarov and L. Naggan. 1990. "The Forty Days Rest Period and Infant Feeding Practices among Negev Bedouin Arab Women in Israel." *Medical Anthropology* 12: 207–216.

Frank, R.W. 1981. "Mode of Production and Population Patterns: Policy Implications for West African Development." *International Journal of Health Services* 11:361–387.

Frantz, C. 1975. *Pastoral Societies, Stratification and National Integration in Africa.* Research Paper No. 30, Uppsala: The Scandinavian Institute of African Studies.

———. 1981. "Settlement and Migration among Pastoral Fulbe in Nigeria and Cameroun," in P. C. Salzman, ed., *Contemporary Nomadic and Pastoral Peoples: Africa and Latin America.* Pp. 57–94. Williamsburg, Va.: Studies in Third World Societies.

Frenkel-Horner, D. 1982. "Planning for Bedouins: The Case of Tel Sheva." *Third World Planning Review* 4: 159–176.

Friedmann, J. 1992. *Empowerment: The Politics of Alternative Development.* Oxford: Blackwell Publishers.

Frisch, R. E. 1975. "Critical Weights, a Critical Body Composition, Menarche and the Maintenance of Menstrual Cycles," in F. E. Johnston, G. E. Lasker, and S. Elizabeth, eds., *Biosocial Interrelations in Population Adaptation.* Pp. 319–352. The Hague: Mouton.

Gal-Pe'er, I. 1979. "Beer-Sheva and the Bedouin," in Y. Gradus and E. Stern, eds., *The Book of Beer-Sheva.* Pp. 269–298. Jerusalem: Keter (Hebrew).

———. 1985. "Jewish Presence in Beer-Sheva Before Statehood." *Idan* (Yad Ben-Zvi) 6: 30–48 (Hebrew).

Galaty, J. G. 1981. "Introduction," in J. G. Galaty, and P. C. Salzman, eds., *Change and Development in Nomadic and Pastoral Societies.* Pp. 4– 26. Leiden: E.J. Brill.

Galaty, J. G., D. Aronson, P. C. Salzman, and A. Chouinard, eds. 1981. *The Future of Pastoral Peoples.* Ottawa: International Development Research Centre.

Galaty, J. G. and P. C. Salzman, eds. 1981. *Change and Development in Nomadic and Pastoral Societies.* Leiden: E.J. Brill.

Ganon, M. 1975. "The Nomads of Niger," in J. Caldwell, ed., *Population Growth and Socio-Economic Change in West Africa.* Pp. 694–700. New York: Columbia University Press.

Gavri, Y. 1985 *In Blood and Sweat.* Tel-Aviv: Am Oved (Hebrew).

Gesler, W. M. 1984. *Health Care in Developing Countries.* Resource Publications in Geography 1984/1, Washington D.C.: Association of American Geographers.

Geva, Y. 1994. Personal Communication (Hebrew, courtesy of Menuha Gilboa).

Gidron, B. 1979. "Organizing the Work of Community Workers in Social Welfare Systems." *Society and Welfare (Chevra veRevacha)* 2: 178–186 (Hebrew).

Gilles, J. L. and J. Gefu. 1990. "Nomads, Ranchers, and the State: The Sociocultural Aspects of Pastoralism," in J. G. Galaty, and D. L. Johnson, eds., *The World of Pastoralism: Herding Systems in Comparative Perspective.* Pp. 119–144. New York: The Guilford Press.

Ginat, Y. 1987. *Blood Disputes Among the Bedouins and Rural Arabs in Israel: Revenge, Mediation, Outcasting and Family Honor.* Pittsburgh: Pittsburgh University Press.

Golant, S. M. 1984. "The Geographic Literature on Aging and Old Age: An Introduction." *Urban Geography* 5: 263–272.

Gold, J. R. 1982. "Territoriality and Human Spatial Behavior." *Progress in Human Geography* 6: 44–67.

Goldschmidt, W. 1980. "Career Reorientation and Institutional Adaptation in the Process of Natural Sedentarization," in P. C. Salzman, ed.,*When Nomads Settle:*

Processes of Sedentarization as Adaptation and Response. Pp. 48–61. New York: Praeger.

Golley, F. B. 1993. "Environmental Attitudes in North America," in R. J. Berry, ed., *Environmental Dilemmas—Ethics and Decisions.* Pp. 20–32. London: Chapman and Hall.

Gorham, A. B. 1978. "The Provision of Education in Pastoral Areas." *Pastoral Development Network Paper* No. 6b. London: Overseas Development Institute.

_____. 1980. "Education and Social Change in a Pastoral Society, Government Initiatives and Local Responses to Primary School Provision in Kenya, Maasailand." *Studies in Comparative and International Education,* Stockholm: University of Stockholm.

Graham-Brown, S. 1980. *Palestinians and Their Society 1880–1946.* London: Quartet Books.

Granott, A. 1952. *The Land System in Palestine.* London: Eyre and Spottishwood.

Grossman, D. 1992. *Rural Process-Pattern Relationships: Nomadization, Sedentarization, and Settlement Fixation.* New York: Praeger.

_____. 1994a. *Expansion and Desertion: The Arab Village and its Offshots in Ottoman Palestine.* Jerusalem: Yad Ben-Zvi (Hebrew).

_____. 1994b. "The Fellaheen and the Bedouin on the Desert Margin: The System of Relationship and Survival Strategies," in D. Grossman, and A. Meir, eds.,*The Arabs in Israel: Geographical Dynamics.* Pp. 21–47. Jerusalem: Magness Press (Hebrew).

Hadar, Y., H. Bruins, and A. Meir. 1995. Water Among the Bedouin: Sources and Usage. Unpublished paper, Beer-Sheva: Department of Geography and Environmental Development, Ben-Gurion University of the Negev (Hebrew).

Harbeson, J. W. 1991. "Post-Drought Adjustments Among Horn of Africa Pastoralists: Policy and Institution-Building Dimensions," in F.A.O., ed., *Report of a Sub-Regional Seminar on the Dynamics of Pastoral Lands and Resource Tenure in the Horn of Africa, Mogadishu, 1990.* Pp. 32–41. Rome: Food and Agriculture Organization of the United Nations.

HarEven, A., ed. 1994. *Annual Progress Report—Equality and Integration.* Jerusalem: Sikkui, The Association for Advancement of Equal Opportunity (Hebrew).

Hartshorne, R. 1950. "The Functional Approach in Political Geography." *Annals, Association of American Geographers* 40: 95–130.

Hashi, A. M., and M. S. Muhamud. 1991. "Pastoral Resource Use Systems of Somalia," in F.A.O., ed., *Report of a Sub-Regional Seminar on the Dynamics of Pastoral Lands and Resource Tenure in the Horn of Africa, Mogadishu, 1990.* Pp. 48–54. Rome: Food and Agriculture Organization of the United Nations.

Havakuk, Y. 1986. *From Goat Hair to Stone: Transition in Bedouin Dwellings.* Jerusalem: Ministry of Defense (Hebrew).

Henin, R. A. 1968. "Fertility Differentials in the Sudan (with Reference to the Nomadic and Settled Populations)." *Population Studies* 22: 145–164.

Heron, P. 1983. "Education of Nomads." *Nomadic Peoples* 13: 61–68.

Hobbs, J. 1989. *Bedouin Life in the Egyptian Wilderness.* Austin: University of Texas Press.

Horowitz, D., and M. Lisack. 1977. *From "Yishuv" to State—The Jewish Political Community During the British Mandate.* Tel-Aviv: Am Oved (Hebrew).

Howell, N. 1980. "Demographic Behavior of Hunter Gatherers: Evidence for Density-Dependence Population Control," in T. K. Burch, ed., *Demographic Behavior: Interdisciplinary Perspectives of Decision Making.* Pp. 185–200. Boulder, Co.: Westview Press.

Humphrey, C. 1978. "Pastoral Nomadism in Mongolia: The Role of Herdsmen's Cooperatives in the National Economy." *Development and Change* 9: 133–160.

Hundt, J. 1976. "Patterns of Conflict among Bedouin Women." *Notes on the Bedouin* 7: 19–29 (Hebrew).

Ibrahim, S. E., and D. P. Cole. 1978. "Saudi Arabian Bedouin: An Assessment of Their Needs." *Cairo Papers in Social Sciences* Vol. 1, Monograph 5, Cairo: The American University.

I.L.O. 1967. *Report on the International Study Tour and Seminar on the Sedentarisation of Nomadic Populations in the Soviet Socialist Republics of Kazakhstan and Kirghizia.* Geneva: International Labour Organization.

Imperato, P. J. 1975. "Problems in Providing Health Services to Desert Nomads in West Africa." *Tropical Doctor* 5: 116–123.

Inkeles, A. 1973. "Making Men Modern," in A. Etzioni, and E. Etzioni-Halevi, eds., *Social Change.* Pp. 342–361. New York: Basic Books.

Inkeles, A., and D. H. Smith. 1974. *Becoming Modern: Individual Change in Six Developing Countries.* Cambridge, Mass.: Harvard University Press.

Irons, W. 1975. *The Yomut Turkmen: A Study of Social Organization Among Central Asian Turkic Speaking Populations.* Paper No. 58, Museum of Anthropology, University of Michigan, Ann Arbor.

Jakubowska, L. A. 1984. "The Bedouin Family in Rahat: Perspectives on Social Change." *Notes on the Bedouin* 15: 1E–24E.

Jakubowska, L.A., 1992. "Resisting "Ethnicity": The Israeli State and Bedouin Identity," in C. Nordstrm and J. Martin, eds., *The Paths to Domination, Resistance, and Terror.* Pp. 85–105. Berkeley: University of California Press.

Johnson, D. L. 1969. *The Nature of Nomadism.* Chicago: The University of Chicago Press.

_____ . 1993. "Nomadism and Desertification in Africa and the Middle East." *Geojournal* 31: 51–66.

Jowkar, F. and M. M. Horowitz. 1991. *Gender Relations of Pastoral and Agro-pastoral Production: A Bibliography with Annotations.* Institute for Development Anthropology, Working Paper No. 79, Binghamton.

_____ . 1992. *Pastoral Women and Change in Africa, the Middle East and Central Asia.* Institute for Development Anthropology, Working Paper No. 91, Binghamton.

Kaplan, A., Y. Amit, A. Shmueli, P. Treitel, and A. Mor. 1979. *A Master Plan for Settling the Bedouin in the Negev.* Tel-Aviv (Hebrew).

Kark, R. 1974.*The History of Pioneer Settlement in the Negev.* Tel-Aviv: HaKibbutz HaMeuchad (Hebrew).

Kazaz, N. 1972. "Problems in Settling the Bedouin." *Notes on the Bedouin* 2: 68–75 (Hebrew).

Keidar, M. and A. Meir. 1995. The Regional Council of Masos. Unpublished paper, Beer-Sheva: Department of Geography and Environmental Development, Ben-Gurion University of the Negev (Hebrew).

Keidar, R. and A. Meir. 1995. Locational Conflicts Over Public Facilities Among the Bedouin. Unpublished paper, Beer-Sheva: Department of Geography and Environmental Development, Ben-Gurion University of the Negev (Hebrew).

Kellerman, A. 1993a. "Settlement Frontiers Revisited: The Case of Israel and the West Bank." *Tijdschrift voor Economische en Sociale Geographie* 84: 27–39.

_____. 1993b. *Society and Settlement—Jewish Land of Israel in the Twentieth Century.* Albany: State University of New York Press.

_____. 1994. "The Conceptualization of Time and Space in Geographical Social Theory." *Geography Research Forum* 14: 1–12.

Keren, R. 1987. Hazerim in the War of Independence. Unpublished paper, Hazerim: Hazerim Archive (Hebrew).

Keren, Z. n.d., A Desert Oasis: The Story of a Member of Hazerim. Unpublished paper, Hazerim: Hazerim Archive (Hebrew).

Kimmerling, B., 1982, Settlers without Frontier, *The Jerusalem Quarterly* 24: 114–128.

King, K. 1972. "Development and Education in the Narok District of Kenya: The Pastoral Maasai and Their Neighbors." *African Affairs* 71: 385–407.

Knaani, A. 1981. *Rouchama—The First Jewish Settlement in the Negev.* Jerusalem: Yad Ben-Zvi (Hebrew).

Knodel, J., N. Chayovan, and S. Siriboon. 1992. "The Impact of Fertility Decline on Familial Support for the Elderly: An Illustration from Thailand." *Population and Development Review* 18: 79–103.

Kressel, G. M. 1976. *Individuality Against Tribality: The Dynamics of a Bedouin Community in a Process of Urbanization.* Tel-Aviv: HaKibbutz HaMeuchad (Hebrew).

_____. 1982. *Blood Feuds Among Urban Bedouin: An Anthropological Study.* Jerusalem: Magness Press (Hebrew).

_____. 1988. "A proposal for Bedouin Shepherd Villages." *Svivot* (Environments) 27: 182–185 (Hebrew).

_____. 1991. "Continuity and Endurance of Patrilineage in Towns." *Middle Eastern Studies* 27: 79–93.

_____. 1992a. *Descent Through Males: An Anthropological Investigation into the Patterns Underlying Social Hierarchy, Kinship, and Marriage among Former Bedouin in the Ramla-Lod Area (Israel).* Weisbaden: Otto Harrassowitz.

_____. 1992b. "Shame and Gender." *Anthropological Quarterly* 65: 34–46.

_____. 1993. "Nomadic Pastoralists, Agriculturalists and the State: Self-Sufficiency and Dependence in the Middle-East." *Journal of Rural Cooperation* 21: 33–49.

_____. 1994. "Difficulties in Instituting Reflexible Government Policy for the Bedouin." *Notes on the Bedouin* 25: 73–77 (Hebrew).

Kressel, G., J. Ben-David, and H. Abu-Rabia. 1991. "Changes in Land Usage by the Negev Bedouin since the Mid-19th Century." *Nomadic Peoples* 28: 28–55.

La Bianca, O. S. 1990. *Sedentarization and Nomadization.* Berrien Springs, MI: Andrews University Press.

Lancaster, W. and F. Lancaster. 1986. "The Concept of Territory among the Rwala Bedouin." *Nomadic Peoples* 20: 41–47.

_____ . 1990. "Desert Devices: The Pastoral System of the Rwala Bedu," in J. G. Galaty, and D. L. Johnson, eds., *The World of Pastoralism: Herding Systems in Comparative Perspective*. Pp. 177–194. New York: The Guilford Press.

_____ . 1992. "Tribe, Community and the Concept of Access to Resources: Territorial Behaviour in South East Ja'alan," in M. J. Casimir, and A. Rao, eds., *Mobility and Territoriality-Social and Spatial Boundaries among Foragers, Fishers, Pastoralists and Peripatetics*. Pp. 343–364. Oxford: Berg.

Layish, A. 1981. "The Status of Islam Among the Bedouin of the Judean Desert." *Cathedra* 20: 81–96 (Hebrew).

_____ . 1984. "The Islamization of the Bedouin Family in the Judean Desert, as Reflected in the Sijill of the Shar'ia Court," in E. Marx, and A. Shmueli, eds., *The Changing Bedouin*. Pp. 39–59. New Brunswick, N.J.: Transaction Books.

_____ . 1991. "The *Fatwa* as an Instrument of Islamization of Tribal Society in Process of Sedentarization." *HaMizrach HeChadash (The New East)* 33: 120–132 (Hebrew).

Legesse, A. 1973. *Gadda: Three Approaches to the Study of African Society*. New York: The Free Press.

Lerman, R. and A. Lerman. 1987. "Planning and Establishment of Aroer." *Mivnim* 62: 44–45 (Hebrew).

Levi, A. J. 1969. *Essays in Jurisprudence*. Jerusalem: The Magness Press (Hebrew).

Levi, S. 1987. *The Bedouins in the Sinai Desert—A Pattern of Desert Society*. Tel-Aviv: Schoken (Hebrew).

Lewando-Hundt, J. 1979. "Tel-Sheva—A Planned Bedouin Village," in A. Shmueli and Y. Gradus, eds. *The Land of the Negev*. Pp. 662–672. Jerusalem: Defense Ministry Press (Hebrew).

_____ . 1980. "Patterns of Utilization of Health Services Among the Bedouin." *Notes on the Bedouin* 11: 26–35 (Hebrew).

_____ . 1984. "The Exercise of Power by Bedouin Women in the Negev," in E. Marx, and A. Shmueli, eds., *The Changing Bedouin*. Pp. 83–124. New Brunswick, N.J.: Transaction Books.

Lewis, N. N. 1987. *Nomads and Settlers in Syria and Jordan, 1800–1980*. Cambridge: Cambridge University Press.

Ley, D. 1983. *A Social Geography of the City*. New York: Harper and Row.

Livingstone, I. 1985. *Pastoralism: An Overview of Practice, Process, and Policy*. Rome: Food and Agriculture Organization of the United Nations.

Lukes, S. 1973. *Individualism*. Oxford: Basil Blackwell.

Lustick, A. 1985. *Arabs in a Jewish State*. Haifa: Mifras (Hebrew).

Mace, R. 1989. "Gambling with Goats: Variability in Herd Growth among Restocked Pastoralists in Kenya." *Pastoral Development Network*, Paper No.28a, London: Overseas Development Institute.

Maddrell, P. 1990. *The Bedouin of the Negev*. London: Minority Rights Group, No. 81.

Marx, E. 1967. *Bedouin of the Negev*. Manchester: Manchester University Press.

_____ . 1973. "The Organization of Nomadic Groups in the Middle East," in Milson, M., ed., *Society and Political Structure in the Arab World*. Pp. 305–336. New York: Humanities Press.

_____ . 1974. *The Bedouin Society in the Negev*. Tel-Aviv: Reshafim (Hebrew).

_____ . 1978. "The Ecology and Politics of Nomadic Pastoralists in the Middle East," in E. Weissleder, ed., *The Nomadic Alternative*. Pp. 41–47. The Hague: Mouton.

_____ . 1980. "Wage Labor and Tribal Economy of the Bedouin in South Sinai," in P. C. Salzman, ed., *When Nomads Settle: Processes of Sedentarization as Adaptation and Response*. Pp. 111–123. New York: Praeger.

_____ . 1981a. "Changes in the Way of Life of Nomads," in L. Berkofsky, D. Faiman, and J. Gale, eds., *Settling the Desert*. Pp. 173–90. London: Gordon and Breach.

_____ . 1981b. "Resettlement of the Bedouin from Malhata Region." *Notes on the Bedouin* 12: 36–44 (Hebrew).

_____ . 1981c. "The Anthropologist as Mediator," in J. G. Galaty, D. Aronson, P. C. Salzman, and A. Chouinard, eds., *The Future of Pastoral Peoples*. Pp. 119–126. Ottawa: International Development Research Centre.

_____ . 1984. "Changing Employment Patterns of Bedouin in South Sinai," in E. Marx, and A. Shmueli, eds., *The Changing Bedouin*. Pp. 1–16. New Brunswick, N.J.: Transaction Books.

_____ . 1986. "Relationships Among Couples within the Bedouin Society in the Negev," *Israel—People and Land, HaAretz Museum Yearbook*, 2–3: 177–192 (Hebrew).

Meade M., J. Florin, and W. Gesler. 1988. *Medical Geography*. New York: Guilford Press.

Meir, A. 1983. "Diffusion of Modernization among Bedouins of the Israeli Negev Desert." *Ekistics* 50: 451–459.

_____ . 1984. "Demographic Transition among the Negev Bedouin in Israel and its Planning Implications." *Socio-Economic Planning Sciences* 18: 399–409.

_____ . 1985. "Delivering Essential Public Services to Arid Zone Nomads," in Y. Gradus, ed., *Desert Development: Man and Technology in Sparselands*. Pp. 132–149. Dordrecht: Reidel.

_____ . 1986a. "Demographic Transition Theory: A Neglected Aspect of the Nomadism-Sedentarism Continuum." *Transactions, Institute of British Geographers*, NS. 11: 199–211.

_____ . 1986b. "Pastoral Nomads and the Dialectics of Development and Modernization: Delivering Public Educational Services to the Israeli Negev Bedouin." *Environment and Planning D: Society and Space*. 4: 85–95.

_____ . 1987a. "Comparative Vital Statistics Along the Pastoral Nomadism-Sedentarism Continuum." *Human Ecology* 15: 91–107.

_____ . 1987b. "Nomads, Development and Health: Delivering Public Health Services to the Bedouin of Israel." *Geografiska Annaler* 69B: 115–126.

_____ . 1988. "Nomads and the State: The Spatial Dynamics of Centrifugal and Centripetal Forces among the Israeli Negev Bedouin." *Political Geography Quarterly* 7: 251–270.

_____ . 1990. "Provision of Public Services to the Post-Nomadic Bedouin Society in Israel." *The Service Industries Journal* 10: 768–785.

_____ . 1992. "Territoriality among the Negev Bedouin in Transition from Nomadism to Semi-urbanism." Paper presented at the Symposium on: *Tribal and Peasant Pastoralism-The Dialectics of Cohesion and Fragmentation*, Commission on Nomadic Peoples of the International Union of Anthropological and Ethnographical Sciences, Pavia, Italy.

_____ . 1995. "Territoriality among the Negev Bedouin in Transition from Nomadism to Sedentarism," in P. C. Salzman, and U. Fabietti, eds., *Tribal and Peasant Pastoralism—The Dialectics of Cohesion and Fragmentation.* Pp. 187–207. Pavia, Italy: IBIS.

Meir, A. and D. Barnea. 1985. *Development of the Negev Bedouin Educational System.* Department of Geography, Beer-Sheva: Ben-Gurion University of the Negev (Hebrew).

Meir, A. and Y. Ben-David. 1989. *Demographic Fertility Behavior among the Negev Bedouin.* Research Report, Jerusalem: Israeli Academy of Sciences (Hebrew).

_____ . 1990. *Changes in the Status of Bedouin Elders and its Public Implications.* Research Report, Israeli National Council for Research and Development, Ministry of Science and Technology (Hebrew).

_____ . 1991a. "A Methodology of Analyzing Fertility Transition among Sedentarizing Pastoral Nomads." *Kieler Geographische Schriften* 78: 17–27.

_____ . 1991b. "Socio-Economic Development and the Dynamics of Child Mortality Among the Negev Bedouin." *Tijdschrift voor Economische en Sociale Geografie* 82: 139–147.

_____ . 1992. "A Latent Surplus—Changing Value of Sedentarizing and Semi-Urbanizing Nomadic Bedouin Children in Israel." *Urban Anthropology* 21: 137–152.

_____ . 1993. "Welfare Support for Israeli Negev Bedouin Elders: Adaptation During Spatio-Ecological Transformation." *The Gerontologist* 33: 308–314.

_____ . 1994. "Demographic Processes among the Urbanizing Negev Bedouin," in D. Grossman, and A. Meir, eds., *The Arabs in Israel: Geographical Dynamics.* Pp. 77–95. Jerusalem: Magness Press (Hebrew).

_____ . 1995. "From Latent Surplus to Changing Ideals: Fertility Behavior of the Israeli Bedouin along the Nomadism-Urbanism Continuum." *Journal of Comparative Family Studies* 26: 389–408.

Meir, A., H. Tsoar, and O. Khawaldi. 1992. *The Impact of Changes in Bedouin Land-use on the Physical Environment in the Israeli-Egyptian Border Zone since the 1940's.* Research Report, Lahav: Joe Alon Center (Hebrew).

Meir, A., and Z. Zivan. forthcoming. "Socio-cultural Encounters in the Frontier: Jewish Settlers and Bedouin Nomads in the Negev," in O. Yiftachel, and A. Meir, eds., *Ethnic Frontiers in Israel.* Boulder. Co., Westview Press.

Meitiv, B. 1958. *They Who Sow in the Desert.* Merchavia: Sifriyat Poalim (Hebrew).

_____ . 1969. *Under the Shade of Tze'elim.* Tel-Aviv: Cherikover (Hebrew).

_____ . 1977. "The Relationships of Kibbutz Nirim and the Bedouin, 1946–1948." *Notes on the Bedouin* 8: 23–29 (Hebrew).

_____ . 1986. *The Story of the Border.* Jerusalem: Ministry of Defense (Hebrew).

Melitz, A. 1995. *Changes in the Bedouin Educational System.* Beer-Sheva: Ministry of Education (Hebrew).

Milshtein, U. 1985. *The History of the Paratroopers, A.* Tel-Aviv: Shalgi (Hebrew).

Ministry of Education, 1994. *There Are Other Ways: Israeli Government Believes in Education.* Jerusalem (Hebrew).

_____ . 1995. *Changes in the Bedouin Educational System.* Beer-Sheva: Ministry of Education, The Southern District (Hebrew).

Mirga, A. 1992. "Roma Territorial Behaviour and State Policy: The Case of the Socialist Countries of East Europe," in M. J. Casimir, and A. Rao, eds., *Mobility and Territoriality-Social and Spatial Boundaries among Foragers, Fishers, Pastoralists and Peripatetics.* Pp. 259–278. Oxford: Berg.

Mor, A. 1971. "The Negev Bedouin—A General Account," in Office of Prime Minister, Adviser for Arab Minority Affairs, *The Bedouin.* Pp.1–27. Jerusalem: Prime Minister's Office (Hebrew).

Morris, B. 1987. *The Birth of the Palestine Refugee Problem, 1947–1949.* Cambridge: Cambridge University Press.

_____ . 1993. *The Israeli Border Wars 1949–1956.* Oxford: Clarendon Press.

Muhsam, H. V. 1950. "Fertility and Reproduction of the Bedouins." *Population Studies* 4: 354–363.

_____ . 1956a. "Enumerating the Bedouin of Palestine."*Scripta Hierosolymitana* 3: 263 279.

_____ . 1956b. "Fertility of Polygamous Marriages." *Population Studies* 10: 3–16.

_____ . 1966. *The Beduin of the Negev: Eight Demographic Studies.* Jerusalem: Academic Press.

Nag, M. 1975. "Marriage and Kinship in Relation to Human Fertility," in M. Nag, ed., *Population and Social Organization.* Pp. 25–38. The Hague: Mouton.

Naggan, L. 1984. Bedouin Demographic and Health Services Utilization Data, Paper presented in a Symposium: *Health Services to the Bedouin,* Ben-Gurion University of the Negev, Beer-Sheva (Hebrew).

Naor, N. 1986. "A Concerto to the Pipeline No. 1—The First Pipeline to the Negev, 1947." *Idan* (Yad Ben-Zvi) 6: 74–80 (Hebrew).

Natur, A. 1991. "*Shari'a* and Custom in the Negev Bedouin Family as Reflected in the Decisions of the *Shari'a* Court in Beer-Sheva." *HaMizrach HeChadash (The New East)* 33: 94–112 (Hebrew).

Negev Center for Regional Development. 1993. *Statistical Yearbook of the Negev,* 1. Beer-Sheva: Ben-Gurion University of the Negev (Hebrew).

Nelson, C. 1973. "Women and Power in Nomadic Societies in the Middle East," in C. Nelson, ed., *The Desert and the Sown: Nomads in the Wider Society.* Pp.43–60. Berkeley, University of California, Institute of International Studies.

Nestel, P. S. 1985. *Nutrition of Maasai Women and Children in Relation to Subsistence Food Production.* Ph.D. Thesis, London: Nutrition Department, Queen Elisabeth College, University of London.

Nimrod, Y. 1994. The Department of Liaison in the Political Department of the Jewish Agency. Paper presented at a symposium: *Jewish-Arab Relationships during the British Mandate,* The Hebrew University, The Truman Institute, Jerusalem.

Nkinyangi, J. A. 1981. "Education for Nomadic Pastoralists: Development Planning by Trial and Error," in J. C. Galaty, D. Aronson, P. C. Salzman, and A. Chouinard, eds., *The Future of Pastoral Peoples.* Pp. 183–197. Ottawa: International Development Research Centre.

Nortman, D. 1977. "Changing Contraceptive Patterns: A Global Perspective." *Population Bulletin* 32: 1–37.

O.D.I. 1976a. "Human Pastoral Populations." *Pastoral Development Network* 2c. London: Overseas Development Institute.

_____ . 1976b. "Size and Importance of Pastoral Populations." *Pastoral Development Network* 1c. London: Overseas Development Institute.

Omran, A. R. 1971. "The Epidemiological Transition: A Theory of the Epidemiology of Population Change." *Milbank Memorial Fund Quarterly* 49: 509–538.

_____ . 1977. "Epidemiological Transition in the United States: The Health Factor in Population Change." *Population Bulletin* 32: 3–42.

Omran, A. R., and F. Roudi. 1993. "The Middle East Population Puzzle." *Population Bulletin* 48: 2–40.

Oron, M., 1987, An Outline Plan for Tel-Sheva, *Mivnim*, 62, 39–43 (Hebrew).

Oxby, C. 1989. "The Involvement of Pastoral and Agro-pastoral Women in Livestock Programmes." *Oxfam Newspeak* 9, Oxford.

Parsons, T. 1951. *The Social System*. Chicago: The Free Press.

_____ . 1966. *Societies: Evolutionary and Comparative Perspectives*. Englewood Cliffs, N.J.: Prentice-Hall.

Paydarfar, A. A., 1974. "Social Change in a Southern Province of Iran: A Comparative Analysis of Social, Cultural and Demographic Characteristics of the Tribal Rural and Urban Populations of Fars Ostan." *Comparative Urban Studies Monographs* 1, University of Northern Carolina, Institute for Research in Social Sciences.

Peres, Y., and I. Brosh. 1991. "The Impact of Social and Economic Factors on the Size of Israeli Jewish Families." *Journal of Comparative Family Studies* 22: 367–378.

Perevolotsky, A. 1987. "Territoriality and Resource Sharing among the Bedouin of Southern Sinai: A Socio-Ecological Interpretation." *Journal of Arid Environments* 13: 153–161.

_____ . 1991. "A Rehabilitation of the Black Goat." *HaSadeh* 71: 619–622 (Hebrew).

Perevolotsky, A., and Y. Landau. 1989. *Improvement and Development of Bedouin Livestock in the Northern Negev—Bedouin Demonstration Farm, Professional Report 1982–1988*. Beit Dagan: Agricultural Research Administration and Ministry of Agriculture (Hebrew).

Petit, J. 1962. "The Attitude of the Population and the Problem of Education in the Sahara," in UNESCO, ed., *The Problems of Arid Zones*. Pp. 459–470. Arid Zone Research 18, Paris: UNESCO.

Ponsi, F. T. 1988. Sex and Birth Order Selective Underenrolment in the Primary Schools of Kenya's Arid and Semi-Arid Districts and the 'Kepyiong' Phenomenon, Working Paper, No. 462, Nairobi: Institute of Development Studies, University of Nairobi.

Porat, C. 1985. *The Strategic, Political, and Economic Status of the Negev as Viewed by the British Government and the British Mandate*. Master Thesis, Beer-Sheva: Department of History, Ben-Gurion University of the Negev (Hebrew).

_____ . 1992. "Plans and Implementation of Agricultural Experiments in the Observation Posts in the Negev and the Impact of Desert Conditions and Bedouin Agriculture Upon Them, 1943–1946." *Ofakim BaGeografia* 33–34: 29–42 (Hebrew).

Porat, H. 1991. "Policy of Land Acquisition and Settlement in the Negev at the Eve of the War of Independence." *Cathedra* 62: 123–154 (Hebrew).

Porat, Y. and Y. Shavit, eds. 1982. *The History of Palestine—The Mandate and the National Home (1917–1947)*. Jerusalem: Keter (Hebrew).

Porteous, D. 1977. *Environment and Behavior*. Reading, Mass.: Addison-Wesley.

Pounds, N. J. G. 1972. *Political Geography*. New York: McGraw Hill.

P.R.B. 1989. World Population Data Sheet-1989. Washington, D.C.: Population Reference Bureau, Inc.

Prochansky, H., N. Ittleson, and L. Rivlin, eds. 1970. *Environmental Psychology: Man and His Physical Setting*. New York: Holt, Rinehart and Winston.

Rafiq, A. 1985. Accessibility to Health Services Among the Negev Bedouin. Unpublished paper, Beer-Sheva: Department of Geography, Ben-Gurion University of the Negev (Hebrew).

Randall, S. C. 1984. *A Comparative Demographic Study of Three Sahelian Populations: Marriage and Child Care as Intermediate Determinants of Fertility and Mortality*. Ph.D. Thesis, London: London School of Hygiene and Tropical Medicine, University of London.

Randall, S., and M. Winter. 1986. "The Reluctant Spouse and the Illegitimate Slave: Marriage, Household Formation and Demographic Behaviour among Malian Tamesheq from the Niger Delta and the Gourma." *Pastoral Development Network*, Paper 21c, London: Overseas Development Institute,.

Rapoport, A. 1972. "Some Perspectives on Human Use and Organization of Space." *Australian Association of Social Anthropologists* 5: 27–37.

———. 1978. "Nomadism as a Man-Environment System." *Environment and Behavior* 10: 214–247.

Reifenberg, A. A. 1950. *The Battle of the Desert and the Sown*. Jerusalem: Bialik Institute (Hebrew).

Relph, E. 1976. *Place and Placelessness*. London: Pion.

Rimalt, A. 1991. "Patterns of Utilization of Services and Employment of Bedouin Women Exposed to Processes of Development: The Case of Salama." *Notes on the Bedouin* 22: 52–58 (Hebrew).

Robinson, W. C., and S. E. Harbeson. 1980. "Toward a Unified Theory of Fertility," in T. K. Burch, ed., *Demographic Behavior: Interdisciplinary Perspectives on Decision Making*. Pp. 201–235. Boulder, Co.: Westview Press.

Roboff, F. V. 1977. "Moving Target-Health Status of Nomadic Peoples." *Economic Geography* 33: 421–428.

Rosen, S. A. 1987. "Byzantine Nomadism in the Negev: Results from the Emergency Study." *Journal of Field Archaeology* 14: 29–41.

Roth, E. A. 1985. "A Note on the Demographic Concomitants of Sedentism." *American Anthropologist* 87: 380–382.

Roth, E. A., and A. K. Ray. 1985. "Demographic Patterns of Sedentary and Nomadic Juang of Orissa." *Human Biology* 57: 319–325.

Rowles, G. D. 1978. *Prisoners of Space? Exploring the Geographical Experience of Older People*. Boulder, CO.: Westview Press.

———. 1986. "The Geography of Aging and the Aged: Toward an Integrated Perspective." *Progress in Human Geography* 10: 511–540.

Rudzitis, G. 1984. "Geographical Research and Gerontology: A Review." *The Gerontologist* 24: 536–542.

Sack, R. D. 1983. "Human Territoriality: A Theory." *Annals, Association of American Geographers* 73: 55–74.

_____. 1986. *Human Territoriality: Its Theory and History*. Cambridge: Cambridge University Press.

Salzman, P. C. 1980. *When Nomads Settle: Processes of Sedentarization as Adaptation and Response*. New York: Praeger.

_____. 1980. "Processes of Sedentarization as Adaptation and Response," in P. C. Salzman, ed., *When Nomads Settle: Processes of Sedentarization as Adaptation and Response*. Pp. 1–20. New York: Praeger.

_____. 1995. Reliable Uncertainties in the Economy of Baluch Nomads. Paper presented at the *Commission on Pastoral Peoples, Inter-Congress*, International Union of Anthropological and Ethnographical Sciences, Lucca/Florence, Italy.

Samantar, M. S. 1991. "Study on Drought-Induced Migration and its Impact on Land Tenure and Production in the Inter-Riverine Region of Somalia," in F.A.O., ed, *Report of a Sub-Regional Seminar on the Dynamics of Pastoral Land and Resource Tenure in the Horn of Africa*. Pp. 42–47. Rome: Food and Agricultural Organization of the United Nations.

Sandford, S. 1977. "Pastoralism and Development in Iran." *Pastoral Development Network Paper* 3c, London: Overseas Development Institute.

_____. 1983. *Management of Pastoral Development in the Third World*. New York: John Wiley.

Schnit, D. 1988. *The Law, the Individual, and Social Services: The Legal Basis for Social Work in Israel*. Jerusalem: The Magness Press (Hebrew).

Schreibman, Y. 1984. Some Thoughts on Planning Health Services to the Bedouin, Paper presented in a Symposium: *Health Services to the Bedouin*, Ben-Gurion University of the Negev, Beer-Sheva (Hebrew).

Schultz, T.W. 1973. "The Value of Children: An Economic Perspective." *Journal of Political Economy* 81: S2–S13.

_____. 1974. "Fertility and Economic Values," in T. W. Schultz, ed., *Economics and the Family*. Pp. 3–24. Chicago: The University of Chicago Press.

Scoones, I., ed. 1994. *Living with Uncertainty: New Directions in Pastoral Development in Africa*. London: Intermediate Technologies Publications.

Seers, D. 1977. "The New Meaning of Development." *International Development Review* 3: 2–7.

Seif, Ch., and A. Meir. 1995. Development from Below Among the Bedouin: Voluntary Associations. Unpublished paper, Beer-Sheva: Department of Geography and Environmental Development, Ben-Gurion University of the Negev (Hebrew).

Selwyn, T. 1995. "Landscapes of Liberation and Imprisonment: Towards an Anthropology of the Israeli Landscape," in E. Hirsch, and M. O'Hanlon, eds., *The Anthropology of Landscape: Perspectives on Place and Space*. Pp. 114–134. Oxford: Clarendon Press.

Shafir, G. 1989. *Land, Labor, and the Origins of the Israeli-Arab Conflict, 1882–1914*. Cambridge: Cambridge University Press.

Shoshani, D. 1954. "On the Role of the Mukhtar." *Nitzotzot Lahav* 9–10 (Hebrew).

Sifuma, D. 1984. "Indigenous Education in Nomadic Communities: A Survey of the Samburu, Rendille, Gabra, and Boran of North Kenya." *Presence Africaine* 131: 66–88.

Sindiga, I. 1987. "Fertility Control and Population Growth Among the Maasai." *Human Ecology* 15: 53–66.

Smelser, N. J. 1973. "Toward a Theory of Modernization." in A. Etzioni, and E. Etzioni-Halevi, eds., *Social Change*. Pp. 268–284. New York: Basic Books.

Smith, E. A. 1988. "Risk and Uncertainty in the "Original Affluent Society": Evolutionary Ecology of Resource-Sharing and Land Tenure," in T. Ingold, D. Riches, and J. Woodburn, eds., *Hunters and Gatherers* 1. Pp. 222–251. Oxford: Berg.

Soen, D. and A. Shmuel. 1985. "The Bedouin in Israel—Political Organization and Behavior in a Tribal Sedentary Population." *Sociologicus* 35: 142–165.

Soffer, A. and Y. Bargal. 1985. "Planned Bedouin Settlement in Israel—A Critique." *Geoforum* 16: 423–451.

Sommer, R. and F. D. Becker. 1979. "Territorial Defence and the Good Neighbor." *Journal of Personality and Social Psychology* 11: 85–92.

Spencer, P. 1972. *Nomads in Alliance: Symbiosis and Growth Among the Rendille and Samburu of Kenya*. London: Oxford University Press.

Spicer, E. H. 1961. "Types of Contact and Processes of Change," in E. H. Spicer, ed., *Perspectives on American Indian Cultural Change*. Pp. 517–544. Chicago: The University of Chicago Press.

State of Israel. 1974. *Bedouin of the Negev*. Jerusalem: Prime Minister's Office (Hebrew).

Stea, D. 1965. "Space, Territory and Human Movements." *Landscape* 15: 13–26.

––––––. 1994. Rethinking Territoriality. Unpublished paper, Hamilton, New Zealand: University of Waikato.

Stea, D. and B. Wisner. 1984. "Introduction to "The Fourth World: A Geography of Indigenous Struggle." *Antipode* 16: 3–12.

Sreering Committee for the Negev Frontier. 1991. *The Negev Frontier: Summary and Recommendations*. Jerusalem: Ministry of the Treasury (Hebrew).

Stewart, F. H. 1986. *Bedouin Boundaries in Central Sinai and the Southern Negev: A Document from the Ahaywat Tribe*. Wiesbaden: Otto Harrasowitz.

––––––. 1987. "Tribal Law in the Arab World: A Review of the Literature." *International Journal of Middle Eastern Studies* 19: 473–490.

––––––. 1991. "The Individual and the Group in Sinai Bedouin Law." *HaMizrach HeChadash (The New East)* 33: 4–23 (Hebrew).

Stone, J. C., ed. 1991. *Pastoral Economics in Africa and Long Term Responses to Drought*. Aberdeen: Aberdeen University African Studies Group.

Swidler, N. 1972. "Some Demographic Factors Regulating the Formation of Flocks and Camps Among the Brahui of Baluchistan," in N. Irons, and N. Dyson-Hudson, eds., *Perspectives on Nomadism*. Pp. 69–75. Leiden: Brill.

Swift, J. 1977a. "In Defense of Nomads." *Mazingira* 2: 26–30.

––––––. 1977b. "Sahelian Pastoralists: Underdevelopment, Desertification and Famine." *Annual Review of Anthropology* 6: 457–478.

––––––. 1984. *Pastoral Development in Central Niger: Report of the Niger Range and Livestock Project*. Niamey: Ministere du Developpement Rurale and USAID.

_____ . 1988. *Major Issues in Pastoral Development, with Special Emphasis on Selected African Countries*. Rome: Food and Agricultural Organization of the United Nations.

Swift, J., C. Toulmin, and S. Chatting. 1990. *Providing Services for Nomadic People: A Review of the Literature and Annotated Bibliography*. UNICEF Staff Working Paper 8. New York: UNICEF.

Tabbarah, R. B. 1971. "Toward a Theory of Demographic Development, *Economic Development and Cultural Change*." 19: 257–276.

_____ . 1976. "Population Education as a Component of Development Policy." *Studies in Family Planning* 7: 197–201.

Tal, S. 1993. "From Nomadism to Mobility: Mobility as a Measure and Condition to Changes in Bedouin Women's Life." *Notes on the Bedouin* 24: 55–68 (Hebrew).

_____ . 1995a. "Regression to Modernity—The Negev Bedouin Woman in Processes of Urbanization," in S. Tal, ed., *The Negev Bedouin Women in an Era of Change*. Pp. 11–20. Lahav: Joe Alon Center (Hebrew).

_____ . 1995b. "Trends of Change and Innovation in Bedouin Women's Dress," in S. Tal, ed., *The Negev Bedouin Women in an Era of Change*. Pp. 31–56. Lahav· Joe Alon Center (Hebrew).

Tan, J. P. and M. Haines. 1984. *Schooling and Demand for Children*. World Bank Staff Working Papers 7, Population and Development Series 22, Washington, D.C.: The World Bank.

Tapper, R. 1979. "The Organization of Nomadic Communities in Pastoral Societies in the Middle East," in Equip Ecologie et Anthropologie des Societe Pastorales, ed., *Pastoral Production and Society*. Pp. 43–65. London: Cambridge University Press.

Taylor, P. J. 1985. *Political Geography: World Economy, Nation State and Locality*. London: Longman.

Toennies, F. 1957. *Community and Society: Gemeinschaft and Gesellschaft*. C. P. Loomis, transl. and ed., East Lansing: Michigan State University Press.

Tsoar, H. 1995. "Desertification in Northern Sinai in the Eighteenth Century." *Climatic Change* 29: 429–438.

U. N. 1984. *Women's Component in Pastoral Community Assistance and Development: A Study of the Needs and Problems of the Harasiis, Oman. Project Findings and Recommendations*. Report TCD/OMA-80–WO1/1, New York: United Nations.

Vago, S. 1980. *Social Change*. New York: Holt, Rinehart and Winston.

Varlet, H. and J. Massoumiam. 1975. "Education for Tribal Populations in Iran." *Prospects* 5: 275–281.

Wallach, Y. 1985. *Karta Atlas of the History of the State of Israel, The first Decade, 1948–1960*. Jerusalem: Israel (Hebrew).

Wargo, J. 1988. "Property Theory of Land Use Behavior." *Society and Natural Resources* 1:189–203.

Warnes, A. M. 1990. "Geographical Questions in Gerontology: Needed Directions for Research."*Progress in Human Geography* 14: 25–56.

Weeks, J. R. 1988. "The Demography of Islamic Nations." *Population Bulletin* 43: 1–55.

Weitz, Y. 1960. *My Path to Settling the Country*. Jerusalem: Nir (Hebrew).

———. 1965. *My Diary, 3–4*. Ramat-Gan: Massada (Hebrew).

Willis, R. J. 1980. "The Old Age Security Hypothesis and Population Growth," in T. K. Burch, ed., *Demographic Behavior: Interdisciplinary Perspectives on Decision Making*. Pp. 43–70. Boulder, Co.: Westview Press.

Wilson, G. 1991. "Models of Ageing and Their Relation to Policy Formation and Service Provision." *Policy and Politics* 19: 37–47.

Wishart, D. 1976. "Cultures in Cooperation and Conflict: Indians in the Fur Trade on the Northern Great Plains." *Journal of Historical Geography* 2: 311–328.

Wolfe, M., and H. Laufer. 1974. The Concept of Privacy in Childhood and Adolescence. Paper presented at the *Environmental Design Research Association (EDRA)*, Milwaukee.

Woods, R. 1982. *Theoretical Population Geography*. London: Longman.

Yaari, M. 1943. On the Day of Settling the Land. Unpublished document, Tel-Aviv: Labor Movement Archive (Hebrew).

Yagupsky, P., B. Sarov, I. Sarov, A. Keysary, and R. Goldwasser. 1990. "The Prevalence of IgG Antibodies to Spotted-Fever Group Rickettsiae among Urban and Rural Dwelling Children in Southern Israel." *Scandinavian Journal of Infectious Diseases* 22: 19–23.

Yiftachel, O. 1995. The Arab Minority and the Israeli State: Collective Protest and the Emergence of Ethnic Regionalism. Paper presented at the International Conference: *The New Politics of Ethnicity, Self-Determination and the Crisis of Modernity*, Tel-Aviv University, Tel-Aviv.

Zilber, Y. 1961. Prevailing Diseases Among the Bedouin. Unpublished paper, Beer-Sheva: Beer-Sheva Hospital.

Zivan, Z. 1990. *Jewish-Bedouin Frontier Relationships and their Impact on Shaping Kibbutz Settlement Patterns in the Negev, 1940s–1950s*. A Master Thesis, Beer Sheva: Department of Geography, Ben-Gurion University of the Negev.

Zohar, A., ed. 1982. *Data Book on Implementing Nevatim Airbase Program*. Tel-Aviv: Tahal (Hebrew).

Index

About the Book and Author

As pastoral nomads become settled, they face social, spatial, and ecological change in the shift from herding to farming, toward integration into the market economy. This book analyzes the socio-spatial changes that follow the end of nomadism, especially in the unique case of the Bedouin of the Negev.

The culture of the Negev Bedouin stands in sharp contrast to that of the westernized Israeli Jews. The Bedouin live as an Arab Muslim minority within a Jewish state whose people have until very recently been in political conflict with their Arab neighbors. Such a cultural and political gap generates conflicting forces that can drive change in unpredictable directions.

Focusing on the structural consequences of the shift to sedentarization, the author explores the related socio-spatial issues of the encounter with the modern, westernized world within a settlement frontier context: The adaptation of territorial behavior; the adoption of western demographic patterns; changes in the social status of individuals; integration into a system of social services; and the spatial conflict between state governments and pastoral nomads.

Avinoam Meir teaches in the Department of Geography and Environmental Development at Ben-Gurion University of the Negev, Beer-Sheva, Israel.